Managing Cities in Developing Countries

Managing Cities in Developing Countries

The Theory and Practice of Urban Management

Meine Pieter van Dijk

Professor of Urban Management in Emerging Economies, Erasmus University Rotterdam, Professor of Water services management, UNESCO-IHE, Delft, Affiliate Professor of Urban Management at the Institute of Social Studies, The Hague

Edward Elgar
Cheltenham, UK • Northhampton, MA, USA

© Meine Pieter van Dijk 2006

Published in Chinese by Renmin University Press 2006

All rights reserved. No part of this publication may be reproduced, stored in a retrieval system or transmitted in any form or by any means, electronic, mechanical or photocopying, recording, or otherwise without the prior permission of the publisher.

Published by
Edward Elgar Publishing Limited
Glensanda House
Montpellier Parade
Cheltenham
Glos GL50 1UA
UK

Edward Elgar Publishing, Inc.
136 West Street
Suite 202
Northampton
Massachusetts 01060
USA

A catalogue record for this book
is available from the British Library

ISBN-13: 978 1 84542 880 8 (cased)
ISBN-10: 1 84542 880 3 (cased)

Printed and bound in Great Britain by MPG Books Ltd, Bodmin, Cornwall

Contents

List of Figures	*vii*
List of Tables	*viii*
List of Boxes	*x*
Abbreviations	*xiii*
Foreword	*xvii*
Preface	*xix*

PART I OLD ISSUES AND NEW OPPORTUNITIES IN URBAN MANAGEMENT

1.	Introduction	3
2.	New Opportunities for Urban Managers	15

PART II THE NEED FOR THEORETICAL UNDERPINNING AND A DEFINITION OF URBAN MANAGEMENT

3.	A Theoretical Framework for Urban Management	31
4.	What is Urban Management?	50
5.	Methods and Tools for Urban Management	59

PART III EXAMPLES OF URBAN MANAGEMENT

6.	Improving Urban Service Delivery: Water Sector Reform in Ethiopia and its Impact in Addis Ababa	75
7.	Urban Environmental Management in Cities in The Netherlands	97
8.	Financing Options for Urban Infrastructure in India	109
9.	The Use of Information Technology in Urban Management	123

PART IV CHINESE CASES IN URBAN MANAGEMENT

10.	Urban Employment Promotion, the importance of Micro and Small Enterprises	137
11.	Urban Management in Nanjing and the Role of the IT Sector	156
12.	Competition Based on Successful Urban Management: Pearl River Delta Versus the Yangtze River Delta	174

PART V NEW CHALLENGES AND EMERGING THEMES IN URBAN MANAGEMENT

13.   Conclusions   191

References   199
Index   209

Figures

1.1	Different approaches to urban management	7
1.2	Elements of good governance	11
3.1	Framework for analyzing the relationship between an organization and its environment	45
3.2	The degree of effective autonomy of a local government or utility	46
6.1	Different forms of private sector involvement in the water and sanitation sector	77
6.2	Conceptual overview of accountability between utility and its environment	79
11.1	Example of an integrated instead of a sectoral approach to urban management: the housing supply system	161
11.2	Example of integrated urban infrastructure	162
11.3	Map of Nanjing IT clusters	165
12.1	Map of Yangtze River Delta	175
12.2	Map of Guangdong Province and Pearl River Delta	177
12.3	Map of Pearl River Delta	180

Tables

1.1	Time necessary to grow from 1 to 8 million inhabitants	5
1.2	Keys to urban success according to The State-of-the-Cities report	9
1.3	WBI and approach to urban management in this book compared	12
2.1	Challenges and opportunities for urban managers	16
3.1	Mandatory sectors for the local governments in Indonesia	35
3.2	Statutory and discretionary functions of local government in Thailand	36
3.3	Competitiveness, productivity and comparative advantage	40
3.4	Factors influencing competitiveness of the urban economy	42
3.5	Indicators of competitiveness measurable at different levels	42
3.6	Geographical level and most concerned disciplines	43
4.1	Theories, methods and tools for urban management	57
5.1	Methods and tools for urban management used in subsequent chapters	59
5.2	Methods and tools for urban management	60
5.3	Overview of management theories and skills	63
5.4	Key elements of organizing capacity	68
6.1	NPM principles and corresponding NPM instruments	78
6.2	Functions of the board and the managing directors	81
6.3	Matrix of reform actions at the utility level	88
8.1	Instruments for infrastructure finance	110
8.2	Example of a Bond Bank: the Bank of Dutch Municipalities	115
8.3	Failed private sector participation efforts in Bangalore	118
10.1	Examples of urban informal sector activities in Chinese cities	147
11.1	Different urban social issues/dominant sectoral approach in China	160
11.2	Different urban infrastructural issues/dominant sectoral	

	approach	160
11.3	Public-private cooperation for IT cluster development in Nanjing	168
12.1	The Pearl River Delta versus the Yangtze River Delta	176

Boxes

1.1	A further 700 million people in Indian cities	6
1.2	Urban management, an Indian example	8
1.3	Lack of urban managers in Cambodia and Laos	13
2.1	Rural urban linkages in Africa, strategic options for Kaya	25
3.1	Devolved functions to local government (India)	33
3.2	Indonesia, a history of decentralization?	37
3.3	Decentralization and urban management in India	38
3.4	Decentralization requires more local revenues	39
3.5	Dynamics of an African urban cluster	41
3.6	Mumbai versus Gujarat and Hyderabad versus Bangalore	44
4.1	Urban management in two mega Indian cities	51
4.2	Ahmedabad: from an industrial to a service economy	52
4.3	Dynamics of research into the urban economy in India	53
4.4	Critique on the traditional urban master plan approach	54
4.5	Infrastructure financing corporations: another actor	55
5.1	Action planning as a tool for urban management	64
5.2	City marketing: required information and choices to make	65
5.3	Different terms related to research	70
7.1	Environmental problems as urban management problems	98
7.2	Principles of the NEPP	100
7.3	Source-oriented measures in the NEPP	101
7.4	Recommendations how to deal with urban environmental problems	102
8.1	Reforms at the municipal level to qualify for financial support	111
9.1	Applications of information technology in urban management	126
9.2	Access to the town hall in Dakar through internet, a UNESCO supported project	131
9.3	Recommended use of computers in Mysore, India	132

10.1	Proto-capitalism as defined by Frank (1990)	144
11.1	Support for IT sector in the national press	167
13.1	Global cities according to Sassen	192

Abbreviations

AAWSA Addis Ababa Water and Sewerage Authority
ADB Asian Development Bank
AMC Ahmedabad Municipal Corporation
APUSP Andhra Pradesh Urban Services for the Poor
AUDA Ahmedabad Urban Development Authority
BDA Bangalore Development Authority
BIS Basle Bank of International Settlements
BNG Bank of the Dutch Municipalities
BOD Board of Directors
BOO Build Operate and Own
BOT Build Operate and Transfer
BUPP Bangalore Urban Poverty Program
BWSSB Bangalore Water Supply and Sewerage Board
CBA Cost benefit analysis
CBO Community Based Organizations
CCF City Challenge Fund
CD Compact Disc
DCA Development Credit Authority
DFBO Design, Finance, Build and Operate
DFID Directorate For International Development
DL Distance Learning
DVD Digital Video Disc
ECAP Expenditure Priorities Improvement Plans
ECSC Ethiopian Civil Service College

EUR Erasmus University in Rotterdam
EURICUR European Institute for Comparative Urban Research
FDI Foreign Direct Investment
FIE Foreign Investment Enterprises
FIRE Financial Institutions Reform and Expansion Project
GDP Gross Domestic Product
GIDB Gujarat Infrastructure Development Board
GIS Geographical Information Systems
HRD Human Resources Development
HUDCO Housing and Urban Development Corporation
ICAI Institute of Chartered Accountants of India
ICT Information and Communication Technology
IHE Institute for Infrastructural, Hydrological and Environmental Engineering
IHS Institute of Housing and Urban Development Studies
ILO International Labor Organization
IMF International Monetary Fund
IS Information Systems
IT Information Technology
IUIDP Integrated Urban Infrastructure Development Program
KUIDFC Karnataka Urban Infrastructure Development Finance Corporation
MAPP Municipal Action Plan for Poverty eradication
MC Municipal Corporations
MDG Millennium Development Goals
MNC Multinational Corporations
MSM Maastricht School of Management
NEPP National Environmental Policy Plan
NGO Non-Governmental Organizations
NMP National Environmental Policy Plan (NEPP)
NPM New public management
OCF Other contractual forms

OECD Organization for Economic Cooperation and Development
OFI Other Forms of Investment
O&M Operation and Maintenance
PDCOR Project Development Corporation of Rajasthan
PPP Public Private Partnerships
PPcP Private Public Community Partnerships
PRD Pearl River Delta
PRISMA Project Industrial Successes with Waste Management
PSI Private sector involvement
RIAP Revenue Improvement Action Plans
RIVM Institute for Public health and the Environment
RLDS Regional and Local Development Studies
RMB Renminbi, Chinese currency, also called Yuan
RMT Research Methods and Techniques
ROSCA Rotating Saving and Credit Associations
ROT Rehabilitation Operate Transfer
RPD National Physical Planning Agency in the Netherlands
R&D Research and Development
SAR Special Administrative Region
SDO Subsidi Daerah Otonomi
SEZ Special Economic Zones
SLFI State Level Financial Institutions
SOE State Owned Enterprises
S&T Science and Technology
SRA Slum Redevelopment Authority
STP Sewage Treatment Plants
SWOT Strength-Weakness Opportunity Threats
TCS Tata Consultancy Services
TVE Township and Village Enterprises
UDA Urban Development Authority
UDD Urban Development Department

UFW Unaccounted For Water
UIS Urban Information Systems
ULB Urban Local Bodies
UMC Urban Management Center
UMP Urban Management Program
UNCED United Nations Conference on the Environment and Development
UNCHS United Nations Center for Human Settlements (UN Habitat)
UNDP United Nations Development Program
UNESCO United Nations Education and Science Organization
UNFPA United Nations Fund for Population Activities
US/USA United States of America
US$ US Dollar
USAID United States Agency for International Development
VAT Value Added Tax
WBI World Bank Development Institute
WSJE Wall Street Journal of Europe
WSP Water and Sanitation Program
WTO World Trade Organization
YRD Yangtze River Delta

Foreword

To manage a city is to attempt to manage something spontaneous. Cities emerge, grow and evolve as a result of vast numbers of individual decisions about where to live, work, locate a firm, source suppliers, recreate, get educated and so on. Each of these decision interact with many others directly and indirectly in complex networks of exchange and co-operation. The chaos theory idea of the butterfly effect – the moving wings of an insect leading to a hurricane in another part of the world – may be applied to cities. One more crime incident or traffic accident tips a balance that triggers a household relocation or a policy change that reshapes a city's future. One more car on a crowded road, or one more report about congestion, triggers new investment, road pricing or tighter regulation that changes a city's fortunes. One more family moving into a neighborhood tipping some delicate balance of co-existence and triggering an unstoppable wave of social-spatial segregation .

It is interconnections that make a city attractive, endowing it with agglomeration and scale economies. Interconnections also mean that externalities are ubiquitous and dense in cities. Everything is connected to everything else in an economy. A bus driver giving a tiny fraction of his passengers' fares to a street vendor for a bag of fruit helps employ the workers in a plastic bag factory, the trucker who conveyed the fruit to town and workers in the chemical factory that provided pesticides to the fruit farmer. Each individual in a city exchanges his or her particular bit of knowledge and skill in exchange for something valued, usually money, used to purchase products and services provided by the specialist knowledge and skill of other individuals.

The indestructible drive to survive and to better oneself and ones family creates social and individual wealth as entrepreneurs and governments provide the opportunities for skill creation and exchange that lead to organized production and consumption. In well functioning competitive markets, prices provide the signals about costs and benefits that help co-ordinate the individual economic projects of autonomous households and firms. Governments, communities, religious groups and other collective action agencies have to organize this co-ordination where resources, goods and services are subject to collective consumption and difficult to price.

Entrepreneurs may discover how to organize collective action, assigning property rights to groups of co-consumers and pricing services normally delivered by municipalities. Informal voluntary sector entrepreneurs tend to become more organized and more professional over time and the boundary between voluntary and commercial sectors blurs. The boundary between government and market, as different mechanisms for organizing economic co-operation, is rapidly evolving at present. Traditional understanding of the role of the public sector is being challenged by experimentation. Cities are at the vanguard of this social experimentation. Nowhere is this more apparent than in contemporary urban China. Every municipal, district and street office administration in China seems to be an entrepreneur – investing in projects in and out of their jurisdictions. Street offices are having to discover what the role of a neighborhood tier of public government is in the modern era and are doing so in parallel to a rapidly growing market in private entrepreneur-delivered urban management services.

In the developed world, partnership institutions are emerging to tackle problems of social housing supply, neighborhood deprivation and infrastructure renewal - often mute recognition that old models of public governance have not worked. Institutions have always been more fluid in the developing world – many of the West's established organizations in finance and education for example, started life in the 19th century as informal institutions (for example multi-national insurance or mortgage firms that started as informal savings schemes). Cities in transitional and developing economies are full of innovation and creativity. This is sometimes driven by an open and risk-taking government, sometimes by political initiative and sometimes by a vibrant entrepreneurial sector – including for profit and not-for-profit entrepreneurs - that presents governments with challenges and with new models of partnership working.

In this context, a book that takes a detailed and reflective look at the theory and practice of urban management in developing countries is of great value. Urban managers face two kinds of handicap in updating their knowledge: some are locked into city and professional networks that give them far more information than they can usefully process. Others find themselves isolated from wider experiences, good practice stories and critical evaluation.

Decentralization and delimitation of responsibility go hand in hand. They are not always harmonized, however. Administrative decentralization without clear allocation of responsibility and reward and rights to residual benefits and costs, does not make for good governance in public, private or partnership organizations. Managing Cities in Developing Countries provides general guidelines and tactical tips for better aligning function and form in urban governance. Its message is to be real – about institutional capacity, institutional structure, finance, the objectives and means of various types of urban management intervention. Urban managers need to be increasingly smart. Smart about the way limited resources are deployed; smart about strategies for delivering services that cannot possibly be provided on the basis of taxation revenue; sharp PPP negotiators at the table with private sector counterparts; clever at packaging up grant proposals; ingenious in creating, interpreting and implementing vision. This book's thinking tools will help urban managers develop these qualities.

Chris Webster, Professor of Urban Planning, Cardiff University

Preface

Urban management is a relatively new topic, which has gained importance with increased urbanization and a wave of decentralization programs in the 1980s and 1990s. I have taught the master course of Urban management in developing and Eastern Europe at the Erasmus University in Rotterdam the Netherlands, since its beginning in 1992. I came originally as an expert on the economic dynamics of cities in developing countries because of my Ph.D. on the urban informal sector (micro and small enterprises) in West Africa. In Chapter 10 I will argue that micro and small enterprises can also contribute to the competitiveness of urban centers in other developing countries.

In due course I started to stress the relations between the most important urban issues. This has led to a definition of urban management emphasizing the importance of an integrated approach to solving complex and interrelated issues. The question: private or public supply of certain services is now in the center of attention. Financial aspects of urban management are part of the priorities of most cities and I am particularly interested in using relatively new instruments to finance urban infrastructure in emerging economies (Chapter 8).

An effort is made to provide a definition of and a perspective on urban management. The use of theories is emphasized, just like the use of analytical methods and practical tools to achieve the desired objectives of urban development (Chapter 5). Cities will be put in their regional context and I will emphasize the important interactions between cities and their hinterland. Participants in our master course in Rotterdam, coming mainly from developing countries and Eastern Europe, are very much interested in the experiences with urban development in Western Europe and emerging economies. Examples are given in Part III (the Netherlands and India) and in Part IV (with three examples of urban management in China).

In the book I develop the following four key ideas:

1. Decentralization offers opportunities to the urban manager, who can learn from experiences elsewhere in the world.
2. Urban management requires good governance, which implies vision and leadership. These elements can be written up in a city development strategy and are implemented by elected mayors or nominated urban commissioners

who know to inspire their colleagues and citizens.
3. An urban manager does not go for the sectoral approach, but focuses on issues brought up by the stakeholders.
4. Stakeholders participation leads to an integrated analysis of urban problems and where possible to integrated solutions. Stakeholders also indicate what they can contribute, including private finance, contributions in kind and efforts to recover the cost.

There are a number of other ideas in the book, elaborated in different chapters, for example:

1. Use can be made of theoretical frameworks: the theory of economic competition and the new public management theory (Chapter 3). The NPM is applied to the drinking water sector in Ethiopia in Chapter 6 and the theory about urban competitiveness is used in the Chinese case studies in Chapters 11 and 12.
2. Urban managers have to deal with environmental issues (Chapter 7). Ecological cities could be used for an approach to urban management focusing on long term urban sustainability.
3. The urban manager makes use of information technology (Chapter 9).
4. The urban manager can also focus on creating urban employment in the formal sector like for example in the information technology and software sector (Chapter 11).
5. That the urban manager put the city in its regional context (Chapter 12).

All this means in the first place that urban management is not just a question of physical planning, providing housing or making a master plan. Second, we are not just looking for technical solutions, but for an integrated approach with the stakeholders where in particular private parties can make contributions to the solutions (inhabitants, NGOs/CBOs and financial institutions). Finally, this approach can be illustrated by presenting issues, which normally are considered sectoral (for example drinking water, sanitation in Chapter 6 and the environment in Chapter 7).

The emphasis in this book is on the economic and financial aspects of urban management and on the importance of involving different stakeholders. With a stakeholder approach it is important that the choice of the issues that should be the priority for the urban manager depends on the stakeholders. Governance issues will also receive a lot of attention, just like the role of modern information technology for the economy of cities and for the improvement of urban management. The book ends with Part V, with a retrospective and review of some emerging new themes in urban management.

I wish to thank the following at Erasmus University Leo van den Berg and Willem van Winden; at IHS Jan Fransen; and at UNESCO-IHE Kala Vairavamoorthy and Marco Schouten; but most of all Maaike Galle for comments and suggested improvements.

Meine Pieter van Dijk, Aerdenhout 30 May 2006

PART ONE

Old issues and new opportunities in urban management

1. Introduction

1. URBAN MANAGEMENT IN A COMPETITIVE WORLD

UN Habitat, previously called the United Nations Center for Human Settlements, publishes an annual report on cities. In 2004 this report, called The State of the World's Cities, indicated that in 2030 60 percent of the world population will live in cities, with rural people moving to the existing big cities, and the small centers in the rural areas becoming new small cities (UNCHS, 2004). Urban is defined by the UN as counting at least 5000 inhabitants. The threshold is not so important, but the issues that arise with the densification process are typical problems for urban managers. UN Secretary General Kofi Anan calls the problems of cities most pervasive because of the persistence of the following problems: 'growing poverty, deepening inequality and polarization, widespread corruption at the local level, high rates of urban crime and violence and deteriorating living conditions'.

It is difficult to stop the growth of cities, but it is good to realize the interdependency between poverty, inequality and polarization. In China rapid growth of the population of cities may be the result of fast development of their economies. However, it should be apprehended that it is not rapid economic development that explains the vast growth of urban agglomerations in South Asia of cities such as New Delhi (India), Dhaka (Bangladesh), Karachi (Pakistan), Kolkata and Mumbai (India). According to the UN Habitat report the poverty in the rural areas is the most important reason for people to move to these cities. The same mechanism seems to work in most African and Latin American cities.

The form and image of a city are mainly decided by the inhabitants, rather than by officials or urban managers.[1] I will argue in this book that the role of inhabitants and other actors is very important indeed. Urban management in developing countries is often limited to administering urban developments and to indicating where the roads will be located, or to checking building permits and insisting on respect for minimum building standards. Often local authorities cannot do much more given the legal framework and the local traditions. Many slum inhabitants are happy with the situation, because they can then build their own house and continue to develop their (informal) economic activities in the neighborhood. However, if a large number of these spontaneous initiatives have taken place without a vision and coordination, an urban management issue has been created. The problem of a poor infrastructure and the environmental and health problems of the neighborhood need to be solved, even if the solutions proposed by the urban manager conflict with the solutions put in place by the inhabitants themselves. Urban management will prove to be even more complicated because of decentralization. In the framework of decentralization urban managers are not only dealing with social issues (such as urban poverty and inequality), but also responsible for the economic development of their city and for the environmental impact of the development process.

The world in which urban managers function is changing fast and the challenges to be met by local officials shift accordingly. The body of knowledge and experience of how to deal with different urban issues is growing rapidly (UNCHS, 2004). Constantly, new responses are tried and evaluated. Theoretical developments and practical experiences both contribute to a better insight in urban development and the options governments have to influence it. Globalization is a process affecting cities and at the same time cities have become the major actors in the globalization process. They compete with each other on a global scale.

Cities are faced for example with an ever-increasing demand for services and infrastructure to improve the quality of life of its citizens and to enable economic development. Over the last 10 years new mechanisms and insights have developed on the role of urban government and the private sector in urban service delivery. Developments in the regulatory framework and in (international) financial markets have opened up opportunities to mobilize more private capital for urban development. The conclusion so far is that private capital is needed more and is indeed coming more and more from the private sector, but this also requires a different kind of project. In fact this requires a different approach to urban projects. These projects now have to convince financial people that it is worth putting their money into them. This requires identification of the possible risks (Lindfield, 1998) and the identification of the cost and benefits of these projects, as will be discussed below. First briefly the background of increased urbanization and the need to respond through improved urban management will be explained. Reacting appropriately is possible in the framework of decentralization, which is the trend in most developing countries.

2. URBANIZATION REQUIRES URBAN MANAGEMENT

The challenge for urban management is to focus on the most important urban issues and develop a strategy concerning the future development of the city. The question is who determines what these issues are? Urban management also has become more complicated because it has become more and more a multi-actor event. Inhabitants, entrepreneurs, organizations of inhabitants or entrepreneurs, environmental activists and project developers (or organizations of these actors) all want to play a role. To be able to deal with this situation the urban manager needs clear responsibilities. This leads to the theme of decentralization, which provides new opportunities for local actors to take initiatives. The conditions for successful decentralization will be discussed in Chapter 3. First I shall briefly describe the major issues for cities in emerging economies, before presenting the new opportunities in Chapter 2.

Table 1.1 Time necessary to grow from 1 to 8 million inhabitants

City	Number of years
London	130
Bangkok	45
Dhaka	37
Seoul	25

Source: UNCHS (2004).

The world population doubled between 1960 and 2000 to reach 6 billion inhabitants, of which almost half already lived in cities in 1995 (45%) (UNFPA, 1998). In one generation there will be another 2 billion people living on the earth and already the number of cities with more than 1 million inhabitants has increased from about 10 in 1900 to about 440 cities in 2000. In 1960 there were three cities with more than 10 million inhabitants and all three were located in the Northern Hemisphere. Now there are 25, of which 18 are in developing countries. The time necessary for cities to grow from 1 to 8 million inhabitants has gradually been reduced from 130 years in the case of London, the capital of the United Kingdom, to 25 years in the case of Seoul, the capital of Korea (see Table 1.1).

I have calculated that under certain assumptions in India there will be a further 700 million people living in cities in a period of two generations (50 years) because of a combination of population growth and increased urbanization (Box 1.1)!

More examples could be given of the consequences of rapid population growth and urbanization. Cheema (1993) mentions that two approaches are possible in the case of rapid urbanization: "to reduce the population pressure [or] to improve urban management". I focus on the second approach in this book.

What are the most important issues? In a democracy local government elections bring politicians to power who campaign that they can effectively deal with certain issues in the city.

> BOX 1.1 A FURTHER 700 MILLION PEOPLE IN INDIAN CITIES
>
> At present many people in developing countries still live in the rural areas. However, ever more people migrate towards the cities. This has enormous consequences in a country like India, where about 1 billion people are living. Until recently the population grew at 3 percent per year. Population growth, among other factors because of better health care, has decreased to 2 percent (1990–98). It takes until 2050 before the share of the population in the reproductive age is smaller. According to the Population Fund of the United Nations, population growth will decrease to zero only in 2050 (UNFPA, 1998). Hence the absolute population growth will continue for some time. The expectation is that the population in India will stabilize at 1.5 billion in 2050. At the moment there are already some 300 million people in India who are living in cities, or about 30 percent. In Latin America about 75 percent of the population lives in the cities. The 75 percent figure is also possible in India in 50 years, especially if the present reasonable economic growth (about 6 percent per year) continues. That could mean in a land like India a further 700 million people living in the cities in 50 years time!

In other political systems nominated officials determine the most important issues. However, for you and me it is not difficult to identify urban issues when we jog in a Third World city on an irregular sidewalk or step into water where we do not expect it, or see poor people and dilapidated neighborhoods. It is more important to identify in a systematic way what are the most important issues and how they can be tackled in an integrated way. Different methods and tools are available and will be summarized in Chapter 5. Action and strategic planning techniques can be used and may result in a different list of priorities (Davidson, 1999). Action planning helps to focus on a relevant issue and suggests actions to deal with such an issue. It is defined more elaborately in Box 5.2 below. Strategic planning helps to focus on priorities and translates a strategic vision about the future into a strategic plan for an environment in which the actions of one player depend on and affect the actions of other players (see Mintzberg, 1994).

Local government's role is serving the people, looking at all interests of the population. The local authorities traditionally are supposed to plan and coordinate activities in the city. They supply services such as water and transportation, deal with municipal finance and regulate the behavior of the major actors and urban markets. However, the essence seems to be missing in this definition of urban management, namely that the local authorities should focus on the major issues identified by the population and pay attention to the most important problem: the further development of the urban economy. Urban managers can help to create a dynamic urban economy, which can help to tackle a number of social problems. Jane Jacobs (1970) already pointed to the importance of a good economic basis for the development of cities. It creates jobs for the people and financial means for the urban manager. The issue should be phrased as how can a city compete at the global level? Although the urban population may not immediately understand this, it is the task of the politicians to explain the influence of this competitive environment and the need to develop a strategy to deal with it.

3. URBAN MANAGEMENT: A SHORT DEFINITION

So what is urban management? There are many definitions of, different approaches to and different theories about urban management. This proliferation of ideas makes it such an interesting topic. In Figure 1.1 I distinguish two approaches from the outset of this book. One approach stems from a spatial planning tradition and one takes a more economic and management approach to urban management. The first group of urban managers believe: urban development also requires some planning. The World Bank (2000) summarizes this view as 'successful urban development also requires strategic city wide or regional planning to guide trunk investments and identify the most appropriate locations for jobs, residences, and transportation'.

The second approach advises the urban manager, wanting to make his or her city more competitive in the global economy, that there is nothing as practical as using sound economics and management theories. Different theoretical approaches are then still possible, as theories focus on different aspects of the urban economy.[2] However, the emphasis is on managing the development process (putting a plan in practice) and not on the planning processes itself.

1. Spatial planning approach		2. A more economic and management approach	
1.1 Based on geography	1.2 Based on physical planning theories	2.1 Stressing urban competitiveness	2.2 Stressing the New public management approach

Figure 1.1 Different approaches to urban management

Urban management can be defined as 'the effort to co-ordinate and integrate public as well as private actions to tackle the major problems the inhabitants of cities are facing and to make a more competitive, equitable and sustainable city' (van Dijk, 2000). Urban management is multi-sector and multi-actor (Cheema, 1993) and should be concerned about the economic basis of the city, about the environment, participation of and equality among its citizens (Devas and Radkodi, 1993). However, the world is dynamic and hence the urban manager will face new challenges all the time (Chapter 2).

Given this definition, how should the Indian government react to rapid urbanization? Probably not by investing more in the big cities. Already over 10 million inhabitants live in Bombay, and cities like Calcutta, Madras and New Delhi will soon reach the same figure. These State capitals are presently relatively better off than other cities in India, because the State government is stationed in these cities. The challenge is to try to direct growth to smaller cities. An example of urban management focusing on these smaller cities is given in Box 1.2.

BOX 1.2 URBAN MANAGEMENT, AN INDIAN EXAMPLE

The British development cooperation (DFID) has recently decided to contribute to an urban management program in the Indian State Andhra Pradesh. The program intends to reach the urban poor by improving their environmental infrastructure. This seems to be possible if the program is properly implemented. The program will invest € 100 million in 32 cities with more than 100 000 inhabitants during the next five year, leaving out the capital Hyderabad, which counts several million inhabitants. The money can be used by these secondary cities for water supply, drainage (including protection from floods) and sewerage, roads, waste collection and street lighting. In Andhra Pradesh with 60 million people this would mean some 5.5 million people would be reached.

This initiative is only the beginning of a different approach to urban development. India wants to stimulate the private sector to invest in infrastructure. This will mean that poor people will probably have to pay more for their water and electricity. However, currently they do not get it, or for only a few hours per day. If cities want to be centers of economic development they need this infrastructure. Hence American electricity companies have built power plants in Bombay and shortly French water corporations help to supply drinking water to Chinese cities, like they are doing already in Argentina (Lindfield, 1998).

Fortunately, the attitude of many international organizations and donors has become more positive with respect to urban areas in the 1990s. In the past most attention went to rural development. However, some of the bigger donors (such as the United States and the United Kingdom) and international development banks (in particular the Asian Development Bank and the World Bank) are willing to invest on a large scale in cities in emerging economies. The World Bank, the United Nations Development Program (UNDP) and the Netherlands Ministry of Foreign Affairs finance for example the Urban Management Program (UMP), which started in the 1980s (McAuslan, 1997). Urbanization is a one-way process and cities are a source of economic growth.[3] Maybe part of the growth of very big cities can be directed to secondary cities, which seems to be the case in India for example (Box 1.2).

A more positive view on urban development is gaining force and also decentralization offers urban managers more opportunities to create the conditions for growth, as will be explained in Chapter 3. Comparative research as undertaken by my colleagues of the Department of Regional, Port and Transport economics at Erasmus University, has shed more light on the factors which contribute the dynamics of cities.[4] Key factors contributing to the success of urban development according to The State-of-the-Cities report are summarized in Table 1.2.

Table 1.2 Keys to urban success according to The State-of-the-Cities report

Strategic factors	Social factors
National safety strategies	Human development strategies
Regional alliances	Reform of education and training
Strategic economic vision	Accommodating diversity
Innovative partnerships	Rebuilding the sense of community

Note: Based on Widner (1992), my classification.

In this book the theoretical framework for urban management is on the one hand the new public management theory (Kettl, 2000) and on the other hand the theory of competition (Chapter 3). Cities compete with each other and urban managers should know their competitors and the theories behind the competition. Therefore Urban Management Courses are also competing with each other, as we will show in the next section.

4. A COMPARISON BETWEEN WORLD BANK DEVELOPMENT INSTITUTE AND THIS BOOK

Urban management is a relatively new field of specialization. At Erasmus University Rotterdam (EUR) the Netherlands, a joint master course on Urban Management in Developing Countries and Eastern Europe started in 1992, making this the first master course in urban management. Similar degrees could be obtained for example in Australia, in Germany, in the UK, or from the World Bank Development Institute (WBI, see Freire and Stren, 2001). The master course at Erasmus University started with the creation of the Urban Management Center (UMC), a joint venture between the Institute for Housing and Urban

Development Studies (IHS) and Erasmus University. The demand for this course is substantial.

The World Bank is a development bank providing loans to developing countries. It has been very active in the urban sector since the beginning of the 1970s.[5] In the beginning the emphasis was on providing urban infrastructure. Gradually the Bank moved to housing (starting with sites and services and slum improvement projects) and to housing finance (creating the conditions for sustainable municipal credit markets and markets for housing finance). Only in 1980s did urban management become important, but in the way urban management is presented the focus of the World Bank on generating bankable projects for investment purposes was still there. The World Bank wants the urban management process to result in projects it can finance imposing its conditions to it.

The World Bank considers good urban management important. In fact the WBI organizes an Urban and City Management course. The World Bank even defines the key issues urban managers have to deal with: governance and municipal finance; competitiveness of cities and enhanced capacity to attract private sector investment and promote employment; capacity to deliver public services in an efficient manner, including environmental managerial capacity. As explained in more detail below, an integrated approach to urban management would deal with all these issues in relation to each other. If certain issues are related to each other, the proposed solutions should also deal with the problems in an integrated way. It would be up to the urban manager to coordinate between the team doing the integrated problem analysis and those responsible for the implementation of the proposed integrated solution.

According to the World Bank urban management wants to achieve sustainable urban development. This is defined in terms of promoting the welfare of citizens. According to Freire and Stren (2001: xx) cities must be sustainable in four respects: they must be 'livable' (a decent quality of life); well managed; well governed; and financially sustainable, which means bankable for the World Bank. It should be noted that good management and good governance are distinguished. The first refers to the officials executing the policies (delivering the services and enforcing of regulations), while governance in the case of local government refers to more. UNCHS (1999) states that: 'Good urban governance involves participatory decision making'. It refers to 'the complex set of values, norms, processes and institutions by which cities are managed'. UNCHS and the World Bank, the leading organizations in the field of urban development, like in this book, stress the importance of good governance.[6]

My definition of good governance, which will be discussed also in Chapter 3, is depicted in Figure 1.2. The emphasis in Figure 1.2 is on the norms and values of the urban manager, on participation of the urban population and on controlling what is going on. In a decentralized transparent system such managers are accountable for what they are doing and the results of their interventions can be monitored.

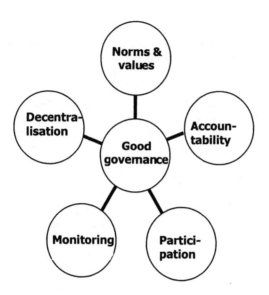

Figure 1.2 Elements of good governance

Table 1.3 provides a comparison between the urban management courses provided by Erasmus University and the WBI on five dimensions (based on the WBI brochure 'Flagship course on urban and city management').

As common elements in the WBI and Erasmus University courses first I should mention the attention for metropolitan issues.[7] This is reflected in the chapters of the book of Freire and Stren (2001: Chapter 1), which accompanies the World Bank course. Second, both courses stress the importance of city strategy development and governance issues (Chapter 2, ibid), of municipal and sub-national financial management (Chapter 3, ibid), of financial management (Chapter 4, ibid), of private sector involvement (Chapter 5, ibid), of land and real estate markets (Chapter 6, ibid), of urban poverty (Chapter 7, ibid), of the urban environment (Chapter 8, ibid)) and of transportation and metropolitan growth (Chapter 9, ibid). It must be noted that this reflects very much the sectoral approach to urban management also present in the older textbooks on urban economics (for example, Richardson, 1976). We will argue in favor of a more integrated approach to urban management.

Table 1.3 WBI and approach to urban management in this book compared

Characteristic urban management course	World Bank Development Institute	At Erasmus University
Approach	Planning approach, emphasis on successful examples (best practices)	Economic theory and lessons from practical experiences, successful and unsuccessful
Ideology	Markets should work, less attention for the role of institutions	Competition, but markets need an appropriate institutional context; stakeholders are important
New topics	Urban violence, integrating gender in urban development and the emphasis on the environment and sustainability	The role of IT in urban development, services for the poor, training in social science research methods and techniques, the importance of housing
Focus	Big cities in isolation	Cities within a regional and national economic context
Emphasis	Third World in particular cities in Asia and Latin America	Africa, West and Eastern European cities and Indonesia

Box 1.3 gives a feeling of the need for urban management in the cases of Cambodia and Laos. Decentralization requires that people at lower levels of government can handle the responsibilities they acquired. In many countries these people need to be trained and the IHS-EUR Master course Urban Management provides an opportunity.

> **BOX 1.3 LACK OF URBAN MANAGERS IN CAMBODIA AND LAOS**
>
> After a difficult political period (the Pol Pot period and a coup d'etat in 1995), the 1997 elections provided more stability in Cambodia. The trials of the heads of the Red Khmer have started. They were responsible for killing between one and two million Cambodians.
>
> The representative of the EU on the spot noticed that Cambodia needs a period of centralization before seriously starting with decentralization. In Cambodia and also in neighboring Laos there are no elected local politicians at the moment, nor skilled officials who could implement modern urban management approaches to the problems of their cities.
>
> Also the idea of cooperation of local government with the private commercial sector and the non-governmental organizations (NGO) is not yet accepted after a long period of communism and absolutism. In Laos there is hardly a private sector to cooperate with. Decentralization requires trained people at the lower level and a role for all stakeholders.

Table 1.3 shows that in this book you can expect more emphasis on the economic and financial aspects of urban management and on the importance of involving different stakeholders. Governance issues will receive a lot of emphasis, just like the importance of information technology for urban economies and the reform of urban management. As European researchers we may believe less that markets will solve all issues, but rather point to the role of institutions. In particular new opportunities provided through decentralization and the development of information technologies for urban management, involving all major actors need to be explored (Chapter 2, this book). Finally we like to put cities in their regional context and emphasize the important interactions between cities and their hinterland.

5. CONCLUSION

The number of big cities is increasing in the world and hence urban managers face the challenge to make these cities economically competitive and pleasant to live in. Fortunately most central governments have given more freedom to cities to run their own business and many international donors and donor organizations are willing to support these efforts. Also the private sector, commercial and non-governmental organizations (or NGO sector), is willing to help to make cities better places to live. All this requires well trained urban managers to take up the challenges.

Urban management starts with a good look around you. Try to find out how things are working in your city and in other cities and use the available research material to better understand the dynamics of the city (for example van den Berg et al., 1993 and Bramezza, 1996). There are enough challenges to make the work of urban managers interesting; these challenges will be discussed in the next chapter.

In Part II of the book we discuss the need for a theoretical underpinning of the work of urban managers. We will show how decentralization would help to make things better in cities. Second, we will use a theory on how public organizations can be made to function better (the new public management or NPM) and theories about the factors explaining the competitiveness of cities. My adagio for an urban manager remains: there is nothing so practical as a good theory! Hence Chapter 3 will provide an overview of relevant theoretical frameworks for urban managers and Chapter 4 uses these insights for a more elaborate definition of urban management, while Chapter 5 summarizes some methods and techniques for urban management.

Our emphasis in Part III is on some successful and less successful examples of good urban management in Europe, India and Africa, while in Part IV some specific experiences with urban management in China are discussed. Some emerging themes are identified in Part V.

NOTES

1. Devas and Radkodi (1993) also note that: 'the form of cities is determined largely by the decisions of individuals and organizations rather than by governments'.
2. Colleagues in the Capacity Group Regional Port and Transport Economics of Erasmus University in Rotterdam, have made important contributions to urban theory formation: van den Berg et al. (1993) and van den Berg and van Winden (2000).
3. This point of view is defended by Jacobs (1970), Devas and Radkodi (1993), World Bank (2000) and Cheema (1993).
4. For example van den Berg (1987) and van den Berg and van Winden (2000). The research has shed light on the factors which contribute to the dynamics of cities and have helped to identify the key points for the success of urban development.
5. For the views of the Bank on urban service delivery, see World Bank (2004).
6. Wallis and Dollery (2001) give a good summary of the debate on government failure and the appropriateness of the New Zealand model for public sector reform (based on the new public management theory) in developing countries.
7. A metropolis is a large city region, which implies governance, economic and infrastructure problems, which need to be dealt with in a coordinated way (van den Berg et al., 1993).

2. New Opportunities for Urban Managers

1. INTRODUCTION

In this chapter we deal with the main challenges for urban managers and indicate how the managers would deal with these problems. These challenges can be turned into opportunities to improve things in our cities (see Table 2.1). Nine major challenges for urban management can be identified. In different chapters in van Dijk et al. (2002) these challenges are also discussed, based on case studies to which references will be made throughout this book. In this chapter we provide an overview of these issues and indicate that they also mean an opportunity for urban managers to improve their city.

2. AN OVERVIEW OF THE CHALLENGES

2.1 Changing Role of Government and Different Levels of Government

In many developing countries, after a period of structural adjustment in the 1990s and under influence of the World Bank and other donors, the role of the government and different levels of government is changing. From being a major provider, governments now are to be facilitators, act as an enabler or a partner in different partnerships. Examples are given in van Dijk et al. (2002). They concern in particular the role of different stakeholders in urban management.[1] The role of public-private partnerships in urban development in Belarus and Indonesia are analyzed for example by Baharoglu and Lepelaars (2002) and Suselo and van der Hoff (2002) respectively.

2.2 New Legal Frameworks Come into Existence Through Decentralization

Decentralization offers new opportunities to involve different stakeholders. Often newly created institutions, or special authorities deal with urban problems. Often local governments are created or revitalized. Desai (2002) analyzes the experience with the creation of a new authority for slum development in Mumbai, an experience that has been studied earlier by de Wit (1992) in the case of Bangalore, both Indian State capitals.

Table 2.1 Challenges and opportunities for urban managers

Challenges	Opportunity
1. A different role for governments	Go from direct providing to regulating, stimulating and enabling developments
2. New legal frameworks allowing decentralization	Decentralization offers opportunities to involve local governments and newly developed institutions
3. New technologies have become available	May allow leapfrogging and using improved communication technologies
4. New institutions appear on the urban scene	Civil society becomes part of the dynamic society and the challenge is to involve NGOs
5. New priorities are formulated and require attention	Importance of poverty eradication and of formulating economic and social policies
6. The importance of cultural diversity is recognized	Using diversity as an asset for urban development
7. Capacity building for urban management is considered important	Training people for a new integrated approach to urban issues
8. The relation between the city and its hinterland can be fruitful	Maximize the positive interactions between the urban and the rural areas
9. Big differences between European cities and cities in developing countries	We can learn from the experiences elsewhere!

2.3 New Information and Communication Technologies Become Available

The way people communicate with authorities, and the way officials and inhabitants can be trained and organized are very different because of internet and distant learning centers. This may allow leapfrogging and will certainly make communication easier between the population and the municipal authorities. The topic will be dealt with in Chapter 9 below on urban management and the use of information theory. The chapter deals with urban information systems and their use for urban management purposes.

2.4 New Institutions Appear

New institutions play a role in urban development. Examples are the community based and non-governmental organizations (CBOs and NGOs), or civil society. Civil society becomes part of the dynamic society and the challenge is to involve them in urban development.

2.5 New Priorities are Formulated

New priorities are emerging in urban management. Examples of this are issues like the importance of economic policies at the city level and the effects of urban development on the physical environment. Issues such as how to achieve local economic development, how to improve urban governance and how to achieve urban poverty reduction actions at the local government level. A number of examples (and references) of how to deal with these new priorities will be given in the following chapters.

2.6 The Importance of Cultural Diversity

It is one thing to be aware of the importance of cultural diversity, but for an urban manager the challenge is dealing with it as well. Cultural diversity should be seen as an asset, rather than a burden! Using diversity as an asset for urban development is the challenge formulated

2.7 The Importance of Capacity Building for Urban Management

The challenge of building capacity for urban management is faced on very different levels, ranging from self-help housing to setting up regulatory agencies in developing countries for utilities such as water and electricity supply companies. It requires training of urban mangers. This means training people for a new integrated approach to urban issues at different geographical levels: from major cities to rural towns.

2.8 The Relation Between the City and its Hinterland

The city and its hinterland are not separated, but very much related. The relations should be considered as beneficial and the interaction between both should be used to the maximum.

2.9 Do Cities in Europe and in Emerging Economies Face Similar Problems?

The question is whether we can compare European cities with cities in developing countries and whether we can learn from each other. The issues in European cities are often the same, however as far as the solutions chosen are concerned, they can be very different.

The following sections present each of these challenges as an opportunity for urban managers. However, we will often refer the reader to other literature as well, or to other chapters in this book. The leading idea is that if the environment for urban management has changed, the urban manager will also have to change his or her way of working.

3. OPPORTUNITY: CREATING A POSITIVE ENVIRONMENT

The role of government in cities is changing. From being the major delivery agent for urban services and infrastructure, local governments are now often assuming the role of facilitators of urban development; they act as an enabler or as a partner in different partnerships. The approach taken by national governments and the international donor community has also changed over the last three decades from providing housing for the urban poor, to focusing on urban management issues as defined by various stakeholders. The body of international experience and knowledge is more readily accessible to national and local officials for example through UN Habitat (UNCHS, 2004). These officials should pay special attention to experiences with urban poverty eradication, the formation of partnerships at the city level and to the need for more capacity building at the level of the municipality.

Correa de Olievera (2003) has carried out a systematical analysis of partnership-based instruments for urban policy in Brazil. These new institutions play an important role in Brazil. Her work shows how in some cases new institutional forms are 'discovered' locally. This is the case with the participatory budgeting method introduced by Brazilian local authorities. Voting on the municipal budget line has been introduced in a number of cities. For example the issue is to choose between: should local government spend more money for social purposes, or do we want them to create more employment? This approach is the result of strong municipal autonomy as well as dependence on democratic elections of the mayor and other members of local government. The citizens themselves are allowed to vote on the priorities in the municipal budget. They can choose between spending the money on social projects or on providing the necessary infrastructure, on increasing the budget for education and training, or spending more on sports facilities.

She shows how two urban management instruments are used in particular in Brazil by local government. The first instrument studied is the participatory municipal budgeting, which gives citizens the opportunity to co-decide what allocations are made in (certain parts of) the city budget. This instrument has been adopted 'spontaneously' by various municipalities in Brazil, and has forced local governments into highly transparent ways of operating. It is a good way of letting people participate. The second arrangement discussed is what she calls 'interlinked operations': the local authorities allow development rights to private sector parties, in return for their contribution to something that serves the community at large, say the construction of a roundabout in exchange for a piece of land. A salient detail is that these deals are made without much citizen control at all. This is justified by pointing at the win-win character of these deals.

Stimulating public-private partnerships (PPP) for urban development is becoming more and more important and is illustrated in Chapter 7 and 8 below. The costs and benefits of these PPP projects for different sectors and different actors within these sectors need to be analyzed. Such an analysis may show the drawbacks of such projects. Lindfield (1998) points to some negative effects of partnerships in a drinking water, a power generation and a ring road building project. The equity implications for society (who benefits from these projects) need to be made more explicit. Partnerships without transparency lack the basis for the trust that is necessary for cooperation between public and private parties.

Involving the population in different steps of a project and making them more responsible for the project is not always easy. Authorities in Ethiopia did not really involve participants in a housing project in the capital Addis Ababa. The case presented by Beeker (2002) shows that participation could be improved in the future. Based on his comparison of different approaches to improve access to urban land in Addis Ababa. Beeker concludes that the role of government should change towards becoming an enabler of the building process and that the inhabitants and traditional institutions should play a more important role in the decision making and building. He argues for example in favor of a regional agency for access to land in Addis Ababa. He shows how pressure to deal differently with low cost housing in different neighborhoods has been built up from below in this city by inhabitants, sometimes with and sometimes without the support of CBOs and NGOs. Here the urban managers can benefit from what the people directly concerned tell them.

However, not only local stakeholders have become more important, international organizations and bilateral donors also play an important role in urban development. There is clearly a changing perspective on how to achieve urban low-income housing for example. Originally the World Bank supported sites and services projects, then slum improvement became more important and in the 1980s the emphasis changed to improving urban management. There is a mutual influence of the policies of the donor community on the one hand and the developments at project level in developing countries, on the other hand. This can be concluded by looking at the World Bank's changes in urban policy and the development and implementation of different types of projects in the field (World Bank, 2004). The conclusion is that urban managers have to learn new roles. They should give more attention to processes of decision making, transparency of decisions and involvement of the principal stakeholders.

4. OPPORTUNITY: DECENTRALIZATION

Decentralization can be considered an institutional arrangement that brings about participation and local decision making. Legislation is very important in the case of decentralization. It prescribes a planning procedure and specifies the level where the responsibilities are put. Laws determine where industries can be located and which environmental norms apply.

New legal frameworks are developed for example through decentralization policies, which put more responsibilities at the local level or through the creation of special authorities to deal with specific urban problems. Dillinger and Fay (1999) give an overview of the experiences with decentralization and point out what it means for local government. Desai (2002) analyzes the experience with the creation of a new authority for slum development in Mumbai, after a visit of the then Prime Minister Rajiv Ghandi, which in the end became a failure.

The process of implementing an urban development project is often influenced by national political and economic circumstances in a particular country. Political statements may enhance the pressure put on the actors involved and contribute to the failure of an urban development project. Desai (2002) gives a good example of this. The Mumbai Slum Redevelopment Scheme, announced by the Indian government, turned out to be a highly political scheme. The coalition government in its election manifesto had promised it. The scheme intended to combine the forces of the public and the private sector. It became institutionalized through the Slum Redevelopment Authority (SRA), referred to as the single window. The 'free' housing promises made at an earlier stage of the scheme never materialized.

Desai (2002) shows that creating a new institution to deal with housing for the poor is not necessarily the solution, particularly not if the existing institutions do not want to be by-passed. She traces the changing institutional contexts within which the slum improvement program had to be implemented. The need for effective slum development is huge in India, but the improvement efforts in Mumbai have not had the effects envisaged. The poorly defined roles of different actors and institutions within a highly political environment and a very important and lucrative land market are the major components of this failure. This is also illustrated in Bangalore the capital of Karnataka state, where the Bangalore Urban Poverty Program (BUPP) was created outside the existing structures of the city to deal with poverty alleviation, but failed to have much impact (de Wit, 2002).

Suselo and van der Hoff (2002) also analyze an emerging institutional form for urban management in developing countries, by describing the institutionalization of the Integrated Urban Infrastructure Development Program (IUIDP) approach in Indonesia. They conclude that the key to success of this approach will be the development of a civil society, which will actually hold local governments accountable for their actions.

5. OPPORTUNITY: NEW TECHNOLOGIES AVAILABLE

New technologies and means of communication become available and change the functioning of cities and of urban management as will become clear in Chapter 9 (see also Sassen, 1991). Information and communication technologies have implications for the way people communicate with authorities. It also changes the way officials and residents can be trained and organized. In Chapter 9 we will show how different means of communication can be used in urban management. The use of computers and information systems can certainly help to improve urban management. It also allows for more participation in urban affairs by the inhabitants. New technologies can also give a boost to the local economy, see the example of Nanjing discussed in Chapter 11.

6. OPPORTUNITY: A ROLE FOR CIVIL SOCIETY

Wegelin et al. (1995) also concludes that the role of government is changing and that decentralization makes local government a new actor. Policies are often developed at the national level and need to be adapted and adopted, before being implemented at the local level. In this framework CBOs, NGOs, private sector development and PPPs become more important, because they cooperate with or are carried out jointly with local governments.

Van Dijk et al. (2002) aim to give international and local experts insight into efforts already undertaken to reform and to innovate the management of urban development. Their book provides a review of the newly emerging priorities and institutional forms. The reason for focusing on new institutional forms is that the authors feel that these are the basis for a dynamic development of these cities. Once a strategic vision has been developed of where the city should go these institutions should get a chance to make their contribution. Hence the importance of national, regional and local governments, acting as enablers for the initiatives of other actors and the importance of a strategic plan indicating where these actors want to go.

The role of institutions like NGOs and CBOs has become more important in urban development. An example of their approach to housing low-income people in Tirana (Albania) is given by Aliaj (2002). After the fall of the Berlin wall, immigrants flooded the Albanian capital from rural areas after four decades of restricted residential mobility. The government had to face the huge challenge presented by numerous squatter settlements with very low levels of services, while the country was still adjusting to the new reality of the post-communist period. Aliaj (2002) evaluates a number of different approaches to housing the poor, concluding that projects undertaken by NGOs and CBOs are more successful. He finds the latter score higher than the government-led housing projects on several criteria.

Another example of new institutions in the urban management area is given by Smets (2002). He analyzes the role of rotating saving and credit organizations (ROSCA) for housing finance in India. These are basically informal institutions, which have a different history in different countries, but can play a more important role in housing finance, if a more conducive environment for their development can be created.

7. OPPORTUNITY: NEW PRIORITIES ARE EMERGING

Many urban managers rightly feel responsible for the necessary economic policy reforms to improve the level of service delivery and to increase the competitiveness of their economy. However, municipal councils also have to deal with good governance issues, with urban environmental issues and with poverty.

De Wit (1996) analyzes the strengths and weaknesses of a new priority in Bangalore, the capital of the Indian state of Karnataka. Under donor pressure the priority of doing more for the poor was picked up and the Karnataka State government embarked on the Bangalore Urban Poverty Alleviation Program, a new institution. However, a newly created body cannot expect to compete successfully with all the existing organizations, who may feel threatened by this new program. In particular the success is limited if the project's role is temporary and if part of the funds (the local contribution) are not coming forward.

De Wit (1996) also points to a similar project in La Paz, Bolivia, where people involved in housing projects have learnt from the experiences in India and now do better. This is an interesting example of international cross-fertilization, where people from one country learn from what they see elsewhere and apply it to their own country.

8. OPPORTUNITY: CULTURAL DIVERSITY AS AN ASSET

Urban managers have become more aware of the importance of cultural diversity and how to deal with it. Two factors deserve special attention: accommodating diversity and rebuilding the sense of community. These factors explicitly refer to the importance of cultural factors.

Several authors give examples of the importance of cultural factors in urban development projects. For example Beeker (2002), in relation to housing problems in Addis Ababa; Desai (2002) when she discusses problems involving slum inhabitants in Mumbai; and De Wit (1996) in his analysis of the urban poverty alleviation program in Bangalore. The conclusion is that urban managers should take this diversity into consideration and deal with different groups differently. Rebuilding a sense of community is often a first step towards using different backgrounds successfully as assets in urban development. Cities with cultural diverse populations have the advantage of tapping the networks and resources of very different groups of people, who all in their own way can contribute to the development of their city. There is a good reason why dynamic cities such as New York and Shanghai are often called melting pots.

In the discussion about good governance, which was introduced by donors and donor organizations, there is often a cultural undertone as well. What is considered corruption in one country according to certain norms and values may be considered as providing incentives in another country. However, in several chapters in this book the need for good governance and more transparency is stressed to increase the chances of success of urban projects.

9. OPPORTUNITY: CAPACITY BUILDING FOR URBAN MANAGEMENT

The urban managers are confronted with many challenges, but are often ill-prepared. Capacity may be available at the national level, but is usually lacking very much at the local level, although more educational and training opportunities have become available for urban managers. New ideas for urban management are developed, tested and implemented, but they are not transferred to people in local governments in a systematic way.

Local and international experts, research and development institutes and donor agencies who develop new theories and recommendations for urban policies, need to find ways to get their ideas to cities in the Third World and Eastern Europe and capacity building is one way to do so. Baharoglu and Lepelaars (2002) give an example of the role of capacity building in urban development. They describe the introduction of community participation in urban planning in the former Soviet Republic Belarus. The concepts of community participation and action planning were new to Belarus, but were successfully introduced through cooperation with an international capacity building institute, in this case the Institute for Housing and Urban Development Studies (IHS). Action planning basically refers to ways of solving an urban problem in a limited time frame, in an innovative or non-routine way with the involvement of the stakeholders.

In Belarus, Baharoglu and Lepelaars (2002) focus on a technical assistance project carried out in a provincial town, Vitebsk. They start with a review of the efforts of the 1990s of moving urban planners towards a more participatory, performance-oriented approach. The 'action planning' approach was successfully introduced as a tool for urban management in Vitebsk in an environment devoid of any experience with participatory planning. Attention is paid both to factors that have made the approach a modest success locally, and the impediments to spreading it further.

The urban population should get an opportunity to participate in such action planning efforts or strategic planning exercises. Existing institutions are often not sufficiently coordinated. Institutional development is a long-term process, but institutions are necessary to direct the urban development process. In the end the interaction between actors and their institutions determines the final result. The city is typically the arena where such an interaction can be followed closely and can eventually be redirected for the better by all participants, who are living there and have a stake in its development. Institutional economics spends a lot of attention to the role institutions play in the development process. Institutions are based on values and norms and which are reflected in legislation and regulation (the rules on how the game is played). Subsequently the game is played in a certain way and that would be called the institutional form or institutional arrangement chosen.[2]

10. OPPORTUNITY: THE CITY AND ITS HINTERLAND

Cities always function in a certain region. This can be called the city's hinterland and the two are not separated, but very much related. Hence the relations between the city and its hinterland need to be taken into account (Box 2.1). What explains the dynamics of regions and what can be done to achieve a more equal distribution of the fruits of development within one country? What is the role of a city like Beijing in the regional productive system? Beijing clearly functions as a growth center, but how far does its impact reach and how much land is needed to feed the city and to absorb its pollution?

The challenge in the case of relations between a city and its hinterland is to maximize the positive interactions between the rural areas and the towns and vice versa. An example is given in Box 2.1 of how this could be achieved. Research has shown that regional economic systems with a clear role for their cities are a critical part of the development process.

BOX 2.1 RURAL URBAN LINKAGES IN AFRICA, STRATEGIC OPTIONS FOR KAYA

In the framework of decentralization, the issue of the relation between a city and its hinterland has become more important. Much depends on how the decentralization is given shape. Does it mean a transfer of power to cities (which seems to be the case in Indonesia) or to regions (or districts which is very much the case in Ghana and India).

Kaya is a medium-sized city in Burkina Faso, which in the framework of the decentralization process now has an elected mayor and a municipal council. It is the ninth city of Burkina Faso and it had in 1997 about 30 000 inhabitants. According to a prospective study of the Club du Sahel (which is part of the OECD) it could reach 106 000 inhabitants by 2020 (Snerch, 1994). The city is located 105 km north of the capital Ouagadougou, on the road to Dori. Kaya is the capital of the Sanmatenga Province and located in the Sahel. The road to Ouagadougou is tarred and the railroad connecting the two cities has been privatized and is mainly used for the transport of the metal manganese. Kaya is part of the telecommunication network of the country and has electricity. There is no real bus station in the city, but it does have a big central market (4 hectares). Although largely an agricultural city its potential for rural development is limited, given the low level of rainfall in the Sahel. I suggested developing a strategic plan what the role of Kaya could be in the future. Strategically, the major role of Kaya could be one of the following three functions:

1. A regional trade center for agricultural products bought from and industrial products sold to the rural population;
2. A link on an international transport axis (to Mali) with opportunities to add value to the products transported along this road; or
3. To become a distant suburb of the capital Ouagadougou, where it is convenient to live at relatively low cost (and hence lower wages), but which is well connected to the capital city.

11. OPPORTUNITY: SIMILAR PROBLEMS IN EUROPE

The previous discussion leads us to the question: do cities in Europe and emerging economies face similar problems? How different are cities in developing countries? I consider that they are facing a number of similar trends:[3] from a cry for more democracy to increased participation in the global economy and from the challenge to become more competitive to reacting to higher expectations of the people. Are the issues the same? I think they are not fundamentally different in developing or developed countries. Cohen et al. (1996) talks about convergence meaning that cities in the north and the south are facing similar problems more and more such as unemployment, environmental and drug problems.[4]

Cities have always learnt from experiences elsewhere. The water front development in Rotterdam, the Netherlands and Barcelona, Spain (Capel-Tatjer, 1999) was inspired by the American city of Baltimore. The local economy of Ahmedabad in India changed after the collapse of the textile industry, and similar developments have taken place in the Ruhr area of Germany. These regions have also restructured and managed to replace a number of heavy (polluting) industries by new technologically advanced and cleaner industries. These cities could have learned from each others experience.[5]

There may be no fundamental differences, but a difference of degree and the solutions may be different because each city tries to solve locally interrelated problems. Sometimes leapfrogging is possible in emerging economies, for example moving immediately to a cadastre based on aerial photography or satellite images and skipping the effort to measure every piece of land physically before going to a computerized system of land management.

Another example of leapfrogging is the introduction, by the EU in many Eastern European countries, of innovation diffusion centers for small enterprise development after the fall of the Berlin wall in 1989. Rather than trying to reform the financial sector first and then get the banks interested in providing credit to small enterprises the entrepreneurs were offered immediate access to new product ideas and process technology. Cultural factors may also influence the chosen solution for an urban problem. The fact that not enough money is available may finally force cities in emerging economies to opt for different approaches to the same problem.

The same issues may be important in a city in Europe and in an emerging economy but the causes and intensity of the problems studied may be differently. Also the approach may have been different in the past and the actual policy context differs. Unemployment may be a problem in Cairo and Rotterdam, but the origin and way of dealing with the problem is very different. In the same way poverty in Rotterdam is not easily comparable to the situation of a family living in a slum in Cairo. The question is whether urban management can be effective everywhere in the same way? I do not believe that. I agree with Rabinovitsch (1999) that we have to look for 'tailor-made' solutions, even when the issues are quite similar and we know how they have been tackled successfully elsewhere.

12. CONCLUSION

The urban manager dealing with these challenges needs to be well prepared. He or she should be able to work with the major stakeholders to find out what the real issues are and how the city and the stakeholders can contribute to the solution of these problems. The urban manager needs to understand that urban management can only be successful if there is support for it and if the necessary finance can be assured. It would help if the manager knows the theoretical literature. Theories summarize what we know already and provide the urban manager a platform to launch his or her interventions from.

NOTES

1. Stakeholders are those groups in society that have organized themselves to defend a particular interest. Slum dwellers, small enterprises, environmental organizations are stakeholders as opposed to shareholders, who are financially involved.
2. For an analysis of the role of institutions, see for example Best (1990), Bohle (1992), Burki and Perry (1998) and Chen (2000).
3. The urban problems in developing countries have changed because of democratization, decentralization and globalization processes (Sassen, 1991). All cities in emerging economies face globalization and the penetration of the information economy (Castells and Hall, 1994).
4. Cohen et al. (1996) has argued that there is a certain convergence as far as urban problems are concerned between developed and developing countries. A number of the issues here are indeed also major issues in Europe and North America.
5. This is the approach of the European Institute for Comparative Urban Research (Euricur) at Erasmus University Rotterdam. See for example van den Berg et al. (1993).

PART TWO

The need for theoretical underpinning and a definition of urban management

3. A Theoretical Framework for Urban Management

1. INTRODUCTION

Theories are about relations between phenomena and summarize past experiences and research. They help the urban manager to avoid errors others may have made because they did not have the theoretical knowledge needed.[1] In choosing a theoretical framework the urban manager can be eclectic because there are many different paradigms in urban economics.[2] They range from a neo-classical approach of subjects like the functioning of the land and house markets (Richardson, 1976) to an institutional approach to the financing of urban infrastructure (Lindfield, 1998). The theoretical approach chosen depends very much on the topic and the level of aggregation.[3]

For urban managers there are at least three bodies of important theory, which will be discussed in this chapter:

1. The theory of decentralization, which stems from public administration theory, see for example Rondinelli and Ruddle (1978).
2. The theory of competitiveness of cities, enterprises, regions, etc. This theory stems from economic theory with the work of Porter (1990) as an important source of inspiration.
3. The new public management theory, which has its roots in the more recent public administration theory, see for example Lynn (1996).

These theoretical frameworks will now be discussed in the following sections and will be used in the cases in parts III and IV. The first question to be treated is: does decentralization offer new opportunities to urban management in many countries? After discussing the advantages and disadvantages of decentralization we assume the urban manager has received enough responsibilities in the framework of the decentralization process to act.

The trend is that cities are increasingly becoming part of a global economy. Hence the consequence that they will have to be competitive will be discussed. At the global and the local level they have to compete with other cities. A good urban manager can help the city to remain competitive. Hence in Section 3 we will discuss a theory of urban competitiveness: which factors determine whether a city can compete? However, if the urban manager acts he or she has to know: what is a good urban manager going to do? Can we improve urban management by applying the principles of good governance? That is the next theoretical question we will consider. We opt for an integrated approach of urban issues based on a strategic plan, which spells out what needs to be done to make the city more competitive. To know what needs to be done good governance and the new public management theory will be discussed in Section 4. This is the third relevant theoretical framework. It provides an integrated approach to improving the efficiency of government organizations.

In Chapter 4 we will give a more elaborate definition of urban management and then discuss methods and tools the urban manager may use to reach his or her goals in Chapter 5.

2. DECENTRALIZATION CREATES SPACE FOR URBAN MANAGEMENT

Given a worldwide wave of decentralization efforts, discussing decentralization and what it means for urban managers is important. According to Lee and Gilbert (1999) in 63 of the 75 developing countries with more than 5 million inhabitants an active decentralization policy has been carried out. Decentralization is defined broadly as transferring functions and responsibilities to lower levels of government or as leaving tasks to the market (Helmsing, 2000). This process often creates the momentum for urban management. It creates the space necessary for formulating policy at lower levels of government. Box 3.1 shows what kinds of functions are devolved to local government in India.

The theory behind decentralization is that people will solve problems better at the local level, if they are allowed to do so. Hence central government has to delegate certain functions (for example Box 3.1) and responsibilities (as of now they have to do these things) to lower levels of government. Generally four main points are mentioned when discussing advantages of decentralized organizations over centralized organizations. The advantages attributed to 'decentralized' organizations include (Osborne and Gaebler, 1992):

1. Decentralized organizations are more flexible than centralized organizations: they can respond quickly to the changing needs of the customer.
2. Decentralized organizations are more effective than centralized organizations (see also Burki and Perry, 1998) – employees who work on the 'frontline' of the business are closest to the customers, the problems and the opportunities. They will know what actually happens on the ground. Often they will develop the best solutions because of their proximity to the problems and opportunities.

3. Decentralized organizations can stimulate innovation – often good and innovative ideas 'bubble up' from employees rather than being sent down by top-management.
4. Decentralized organizations can stimulate the moral of its employees – When an employee is entrusted with considerable decision making powers, it reflects a sign of respect and trust for the employee.

BOX 3.1 DEVOLVED FUNCTIONS TO LOCAL GOVERNMENT (INDIA)

1. Urban planning including town planning;
2. Regulation of land use and construction of buildings;
3. Planning for economic and social development;
4. Buildings, roads and bridges;
5. Water supply for domestic, industrial and commercial purposes;
6. Public health and sanitation, conservancy and solid waste management;
7. Fire services;
8. Urban forestry, protection of the environment and promotion of ecological aspects;
9. Safeguarding the interests of the weaker sections of the society, including the handicapped and the mentally retarded;
10. Slum improvement and up gradation;
11. Urban poverty alleviation;
12. Provision of urban amenities and facilities such as parks, gardens, playgrounds;
13. Promotion of cultural, educational aspects;
14. Burials and burial grounds, cremations, cremation grounds;
15. Cattle pounds, animal welfare;
16. Vital Statistics including registration of births and deaths;
17. Public amenities including street lighting, parking lots, bus stops and public conveniences;
18. Regulation of slaughterhouses and tanneries.

In order to establish to what extent functions and responsibilities have been decentralized within the organization, we will examine a number of decisions that are likely to be taken within local government.[4] To allow urban managers to deal with the major problems of their city an urban manager should know what these functions and responsibilities are and have the guts to implement the solutions. In my opinion, in the framework of decentralization, the following tasks and responsibilities should be put at his or her level at least (Van Dijk, 2000):

a. The formulation and implementation of economic policies at the urban level to stimulate economic activities;
b. The formulation and implementation of social policies to be able to deal with problems such as poverty and educational under performance;
c. The formulation and implementation of policies with respect to the urban environment; and finally
d. The formulation and implementation of policies to increase the revenues of the city are necessary, to allow the urban managers to take up the above mentioned responsibilities and implement the agreed solutions.

Having at least these responsibilities would make life a lot easier for an urban manager. Looking for successful cases of decentralization I concluded, after studying the decentralization process in India (van Dijk and Shivanand, 1999), Indonesia and Thailand (van Dijk, 2000), that it is sometimes too early to conclude. For example in the case of Indonesia the results were not yet clear.[5] In India decentralization, however, provides a lot of opportunities for urban managers, while urban management in Thailand has to work with very limited responsibilities. In fact the country is still governed in a highly centralized way.

The success of decentralization for urban management depends on a number of factors, which will now be discussed briefly. Much depends on the form that decentralization takes and in particular it depends on:

1. The historical background and the history of the decentralization process;
2. Which functions and responsibilities have been transferred?
3. To what level of government these responsibilities have been transferred?
4. Does implementing legislation follow?[6]
5. Are financial means available to make decentralization a success?

These five factors will now be discussed briefly. The history of the decentralization process in Indonesia is summarized in Box 3.2 and shows that it has been a long process, which resulted in a new law on regional governance being accepted by parliament at the end of 1999. The economic and political crisis of 1997 had fueled the decentralization debate. Typically one of the first statements of the then newly elected President Wahid was that he wanted to promote decentralization. The new law envisaged elections at the local level. From the urban management point of view the question was whether these elected councilors would have the opportunity to formulate their own economic and social development policies and whether they would have the means to finance them. Unfortunately the instruction as to how the new law will be implemented is not yet available, while the formula for the division of money is already contested before even being published.

The draft version of the law with respect to regional administration dates from 1998 and defines three types of regions: Provincial regions with a governor, District regions (a Kabupatan with a Regent or Bupati leading them) and 'the

Municipal region' with an elected mayor (the Wali Kota). Below the level of the regions there are sub-districts or Kecamatan. In the case of Surabaya there are for example more than ten.[7] The 'mandatory' sectors for the local governments in Indonesia are listed in Table 3.1.

Table 3.1 Mandatory sectors for the local governments in Indonesia

Typical 'ministries'	Social sectors
Public works	Manpower development
Land management	Education and culture
Agriculture	Cooperatives
Transportation	Health care
Trade and industry	Environmental management
Investment	

The second success factor for decentralization was: which responsibilities have been transferred? The long list of mandatory sectors for local government in Indonesia (Table 3.1) implies that really many responsibilities have been transferred. This makes Indonesia potentially very interesting for urban managers. However, the detailed instruction on how the system is going to work requires the harmonization of a large number of earlier laws concerning the responsibilities of local government. It took Indonesia more than a year to prepare this and the question now is how it will work out in practice.

In Thailand very few responsibilities have been transferred as can be seen in Table 3.2. Not enough for example to carry out economic, social or environmental policies at the city level, except for building some market places and providing some vocational training. Dillinger and Fay (1999) state that concerning the devolution of authority the central government is often 'more concerned with avoiding political instability than with encouraging greater openness'. The third critical success was to which level will tasks and responsibilities be transferred? The question regarding what would be the right level for certain tasks and responsibilities is raised in many countries and depends on the scale of the country, the type of problems and the experience in the past. The principle of subsidiarity used in the European Union suggests that responsibilities should be put at the level where the issues can still be handled in a satisfactory way. Typically, this is often the local government level for most urban problems.

The fourth factor is implementing the legislation (India), or detailed regulation (Indonesia), necessary to put national legislation to work. Does such detailed regulation provide space for local governments to function? In Indonesia local governments were eagerly awaiting the regulation on autonomy that is considered very important to start working at the local level (Jakarta Pos, 8 May 2000). In India implementing legislation is necessary at the state level and can be put in place by each state separately. That leads to big differences from one state to another. In some Indian states the mayor is the most important urban manager, in other states the nominated municipal councilor calls the shots. India is an emerging economy. It is a federal state where responsibilities with respect to urban affairs are divided between the national, the state and the local government level. A state is divided into a number of districts, which tend to have a rural focus, and are not that interested in the fate of the cities in their area.

Table 3.2 Statutory and discretionary functions of local government in Thailand

Statutory functions of local government	Discretionary functions of local government
Maintenance of law and order and the provision of:	Provision of:
- Public transport	- Market places, ports and ferry services
- Sanitary services	
- Fire engines	- Crematoriums
- Slaughterhouses	- Maintenance of parks, zoos and recreation areas as well as sports facilities
- Public health services	
- Welfare for mothers and children	
- Maintenance of public recreation space and facilities	- Vocational training
	- Promotion of citizen's occupation
- Primary education	- Improvement of slum dwellings
- Prevention and control of communicable diseases	- Maintaining government enterprises

Note: Functions specified by other legislation are: the Voice Advertisement Act of 1950, the Civil Registration Act of 1956, the National Order and Cleanliness Act of 1960, the Car Park Act of 1960, the City Planning Act of 1975, the Building Control Act of 1979 and the Civil Defense Act of 1979.

Only in the early 1990s when Rajiv Ghandi was Prime Minister was the idea of decentralization taken seriously in India. He came to the conclusion that a big country like India can only be governed when the responsibilities are put at the right level. For that reason the constitution was changed, see Box 3.3.

Finally, the financial means need to be available at lower levels of government to carry out the tasks assigned to them. It requires the authority to raise and increase taxes and often necessitates a reform of municipal finances to be able to pay for the activities which a city now has to undertake. It will be necessary to use to different 'user charges' and local taxes. Second local governments depend on intergovernmental income transfers and possible contributions of the private sector. Development projects can give a contribution to the successful implementation of decentralization policies, for example if they help cities to develop an action plan for poverty reduction and stimulate them to collect more local revenues (see Box 3.4).

BOX 3.2 INDONESIA, A HISTORY OF DECENTRALIZATION[8]

A new situation came into existence in Indonesia when the law on regional administration and a law regarding the fiscal ratio between the Central government and the regional governments was accepted by the Indonesian Parliament in 1999. The Indonesian government consists of 27 provincial governments and 298 local governments with 819 cities and towns. With the Decentralization Law of 1903 the Netherlands Indies government laid the foundation for urban administrations in a number of cities on Java. Further regulation of the urban areas was enacted with the Municipality Administration Ordinance of 1926. In 1948 the Dutch colonial government issued a Municipal Establishment Ordinance. Until recently the local government structure was based on the Local Government Law of 1974. The new law on local governments in Indonesia gives the districts and municipalities a much larger degree of autonomy.

The centralization versus decentralization debate in Indonesia not only has a long history it is also very closely linked to the issue of financial transfers. The system of Central government transfers consisted of subsidies called Subsidi Daerah Otonomi (SDO) and development grants (Instruksi Presiden or Inpres). Only some 10 percent of the SDO financed non-staff operational expenses. Hence the importance in the recent past of grants for development expenditures through various development grants. The so-called Inpres system has been very important for financing activities at lower levels of government. Inpres provided block grants subject to general guidelines from central government and specific grants for expenditures on specific services that are subject to more central government control in their use.[9] The question remains what will replace this financial redistribution system? That is a very political question, because it involves redistribution of national funds.

India is a big country. A key problem is that one finds political leadership at the national and state levels. However, there is not always a clear leader at the local government level, who could be responsible for the management of the city. In the bigger cities the nominated Municipal Commissioner, the head of the Municipal Corporation, is all-powerful, although often only in office for a few years (after four years they move to another place to avoid corruption). This period is too short to achieve much. The elected mayor often belongs to a minority or has to belong to the opposite sex and can change as often as every two years. For these reasons the elected officials never get the time to formulate and implement policies.

> BOX 3.3 DECENTRALIZATION AND URBAN MANAGEMENT IN INDIA
>
> The 73rd and 74th Constitutional amendments allow delegation of certain functions to a lower level of government. In practice many state governments have not bothered to put the so-called implementing legislation through the State level assemblies, or they do not implement these laws. Some politicians seem to be more interested in maintaining the present centralized system. They do not want to transfer power to the district or cities and also the implementation may differ considerably from one state to another.
>
> Most Indian cities face enormous economic and social problems but do not have the instruments to fight unemployment or to boost the local economy. The formulation and implementation of economic policies is a state function. Similarly health care and education are state functions. Recently Anil Sharma concluded that the actual decentralization process in India has only started recently and only after an initial learning curve through trial and error, it will embark on the firmer road to effective development (*India Today*, 6 February 2000).

On top of that, as mentioned, the Municipal Corporation usually only covers part of the city and is not interested in taking the responsibility for the other (poorer) parts of the city. There are few taxes that can be collected in those parts of the city while a lot of investment is required.

Decentralization also requires a good distribution of the tasks between the different government institutions and preferably some coordinating institution, for example a metropolitan authority in the case of large cities. In India and Indonesia a large number of cities are made up of several elected 'local governments' each focusing on the narrow area they represent. These 'local governments' have limited control over what happens in the rest of the city. They all tend to concentrate on their part of the city. Hence the relations between the different local governments that make up the metropolitan area are critical. Eventually an integrated policy needs to be developed for the whole city. For some issues concerning metropolitan governance in the Netherlands see Chapter 7 below.

The most important conclusion for a successful decentralization policy is that central government when preparing the plans for decentralization should adopt the perspective of the urban manager. What does an urban manager need to tackle as the most important issues in his or her city? Responsibilities in economic and financial matters seem to be very important. To judge the effects of decentralization cities can be ranked on the basis of indicators such as the growth of their revenues, their capacity to attract investments, etc. Mukundan (1998) suggests a number of indicators for this purpose.

> **BOX 3.4 DECENTRALIZATION REQUIRES MORE LOCAL REVENUES**
>
> In Andhra Pradesh the assessment of the financial capabilities of the municipalities by a team of consultants led to the following conclusions and recommendations:
>
> a. The current accounting system does not provide a sound basis for assessing their financial capabilities.
> b. Implied reform: Improve the current single accounting system.
> c. Revenue Improvement Action Plans (RIAPs) need to be prepared, indicating which revenues can be increased.
> d. Priorities Improvement Plans (ECAPs) need to be prepared, based on agreed priorities.
> e. Municipalities need to be helped to access other sources of finance.
> f. Implied reform: local governments need to develop their own expertise in evaluating, appraising and prioritizing their capital investment needs.
> g. Training to be provided for this purpose.
> h. Municipalities should create separate cost centers for project activities to record and accumulate items of receipts and payments.
> i. Municipalities should give more emphasis to cost recovery for services provided and introduce double accounting.
> j. They should enforce financial discipline in project preparation and execution and in repayment by monitoring reforms and progress.
> k. There is a need to improve the budgeting system.
> l. Municipalities should prepare an adequate loan administration.
> m. They should register and value all municipal assets with a view to eventually use them as guarantees or assured cash flows.

Source: Andhra Pradesh Urban Services for the Poor, or APUSP (1998).

3. A THEORY OF URBAN COMPETITIVENESS

Porter (1990) introduced competitiveness as a yardstick for the performance of enterprises. However, the competitiveness measure can be used as well at the national, the regional, the city, or even at the local cluster as at the enterprise level.[10] This is useful for an urban manager who realizes that his or her city plays a role at the local and the global level and wants to know how well this role is being played. An application of this theory can be found in Chapter 10 on the competitiveness of Nanjing and in particular of its information technology (IT) industry.

I will indicate that competitiveness has a different meaning at these different levels and that different factors may contribute to its explanation. Comparative advantage used to be the basis for evaluating competitiveness between countries until the end of the 1970s. The difference between competitive advantage and the classical theory of comparative advantage is summarized in Table 3.3. Productivity is an indicator of efficiency. Originally the concepts used were labor and capital productivity. More recently the term total factor productivity is used more often (for example World Bank, 1993). The implication is that competitiveness needs to be stimulated in very different ways at the different levels. Competitiveness is different from comparative advantage and more encompassing than productivity. The change from comparative to competitive advantage is one from an essential static approach (advantages are based on a certain given level of production factors: the land, the climate, etc.) to a more dynamic approach, where the competitive environment is influenced by the managers and policy makers (see Table 3.3).

Table 3.3 Competitiveness, productivity and comparative advantage

Comparative advantage	Competitive advantage
The comparative advantage of a country is based on differences in factor costs of production, such as taxation, labor, energy, land, construction or raw materials. Comparative advantage is static and given.	Competitiveness is the term used to indicate the performance of enterprises, clusters of enterprises, cities, regions and even whole countries.[11] Previously the discussion focused on productivity, efficiency and comparative advantage.
The change from comparative to competitive advantage is one from an essential static approach to a more dynamic approach. The competitive advantage is not inherited but can be acquired through innovation.	Competitive advantage is dynamic and man-made. Comparative advantage is what you have, while competitive advantage is what you could achieve. The source of competitive advantage can be technological progress, just like organizational and managerial innovations.

Competitive advantage at the enterprise level is 'the capacity of a firm to gain, maintain and expand its share in markets for final products' (Visser, 1996). At the cluster level enterprises in the cluster together do better than those who are not part of the cluster (an example is described in Box 3.5). For some Europe examples the reader is referred to van den Berg et al. (2001).

Kresl and Gappert (1996) distinguish at the urban level economic and strategic determinants of competitiveness, such as institutional flexibility, an effective local government and the ability to conclude public-private partnerships (see Table 3.4). These are also important matters for the population, who should participate in the strategic planning exercise, which would lead to an urban strategy enhancing the competitiveness of a particular city.

BOX 3.5 DYNAMICS OF AN AFRICAN URBAN CLUSTER

We have learned that urban small scale enterprises can compete through clustering, networks, interfirm relations and flexible specialization (Van Dijk and Rabellotti, 1997). New technologies have become available which are profitable at a small scale. Interfirm relations in the cluster help these firms to meet the challenges of the new international competitive environment. Modern and traditional forms of clustering and networks exist in Ouagadougou the capital of Burkina Faso. Entrepreneurs take advantage of what is beneficial to them. Different forms of networks distinguished are large, formal groups; small informal groups such as the Rotating Savings and Credit Associations (ROSCAs or tontines in Burkina Faso) and small groups of mutual supporting entrepreneurs, based on family, tribe or regional relations. Traditional clusters can be clusters of entrepreneurs belonging to one tribal group or clusters of enterprises closely located on their own initiative and benefitting from being together. Industrial estates, handicraft zones and municipal markets function as modern clusters.

Clusters and networks can be considered steps towards enterprise cooperation. Statistically the entrepreneurs in these clusters were doing significantly better on a number of variables than their dispersed colleagues. The development of clusters, networks and different forms of cooperation should be stimulated to bring in new ideas in the sector. Innovation, interfirm cooperation and subcontracting are key words for this kind of development. Providing space for economic activities, preferable at the same time for enterprises of different size can stimulate the creation of clusters of innovative entrepreneurs. Female entrepreneurs may need special attention. The development of clusters of economic activities should be stimulated, including the physical grouping of enterprises of different sizes. Subcontracting and other relations between micro, small, medium and large enterprises need to be developed.

At the regional level competitiveness is 'how well regions perform in terms of applying skills, resources, technology and information to production, distribution and trade' (van Dijk, 1999).[12] At the country level we talk about 'the strategy is to ensure the economy's high growth by improving its competitiveness, expanding its export base and tackling the (remaining) reform agenda' (*IMF Survey*, 27 September 1999).[13] For a cluster it would be that firms outside the cluster are lagging behind compared with firms inside the cluster.

Table 3.4 Factors influencing competitiveness of the urban economy

Economic determinants	Strategic determinants
Factors of production	Governmental effectiveness
Infrastructure	Urban strategy
Location	Public-private partnerships
Economic structure	Institutional flexibility
Urban amenities	

Table 3.5 Indicators of competitiveness measurable at different levels

Percentage growth of	Enterprise	Cluster	City	Region	Country
Production	✱	✱✱	✱	✱	✱
Market share	✱✱	✱✱	✱✱	✱✱	✱✱
Exports	✱	✱✱	✱	✱	✱

Note: ✱ means standard information, while ✱✱ means some effort will be required to collect the information.

Box 3.6 gives some examples of the competitiveness between cities in India, namely Hyderabad versus Bangalore and the port of Mumbai (Bombay) versus the ports of Gujarat. For the European situation I refer to Bramezza (1996).

What are the advantages of using this theory of competitiveness? In the first place competitiveness is measurable (see Table 3.5) and provides the urban manager with the possibility to rank his or her city and an opportunity to improve the score. The question can be with which cities do you want to compete? Second, the theory helps to identify the factors explaining competitiveness, measured for example as a higher growth or market share of a region, city, or enterprise. The factors mentioned in Table 3.4 help for example to explain the competitiveness of a city. Much research concerning location factors can be interpreted as identifying the competitiveness of a region or city. Finally, this theoretical model helps to emphasize that different actors are active at the different levels and often have different instruments. At the local level the managers only partially realize the implications of what the higher levels of government are trying to achieve for what they are trying to achieve themselves. Linking these interests and policies could be one of the roles of the urban manager.

Table 3.6 Geographical level and most concerned disciplines

Geographical level	Most concerned disciplines
National	Macroeconomists
State/province	Administrative science people
Regional	Regional economists
Urban	Urban geographers, economists and sociologists
Cluster	Economists and geographers
Enterprise	Business economists and managers

In my own research concerning factors influencing the competitiveness of a cluster (Van Dijk,, 2006a) entrepreneurship, the existence of a business support system and of an innovative environment turned out to be important. At the city level one can add the importance of policies to create the conditions for a dynamic economic development. For local governments this can range from providing land and infrastructure to local government developing an innovation policy.[14] In the third place this theoretical framework has the advantage that different levels of aggregation, which are normally covered by different disciplines, are now linked (see Table 3.6).

Urban management is by definition multi-disciplinary, but very little multi-disciplinary research is actually taking place. That is a challenge for the future. Management science and business economics normally study the lowest level of the enterprise. Geographers, regional and development economists have worked on clusters and urban and regional economists are occupied with the urban and regional level. Finally macroeconomists and international economists work on the other two levels: the country and world region level. Urban managers should study the successful experiences in their field and why they were successful.

4. GOOD URBAN GOVERNANCE AND THE NPM

Which economic theory is the most relevant for the urban manager? I suggest a theoretical framework that can be used to link different levels of analysis in the urban economy, namely the theory of competitiveness. What counts in the global economy is being competitive and improving urban governance. In the latter case the New Public Management (NPM) theory can be used and some experts go as far as saying: good urban governance = applying the principles of the NPM. For that reason we will now discuss the NPM theory. The key ideas are given in Figure 3.1.

BOX 3.6 MUMBAI VERSUS GUJARAT AND HYDERABAD VERSUS BANGALORE

India changes rapidly. A few years ago the Chief minister of a state would not travel abroad to sell his or her state and attract foreign investment. Now there is rivalry between states and cities as will be illustrated below:

Port of Mumbai versus the ports of Gujarat

The state of Gujarat has a tradition of liberal economic policies with respect to the private sector. It stimulated industry when this was not yet done in the rest of India. One of the reasons was that the state had been created as a separate state in the 1960s. Before it was part of Maharastra and many Gujarati businessmen had contributed to the development of Bombay (the capital of Maharastra) but considered it was now time to do something in their own state. The competition with the Maharastri can be illustrated with a text from a special supplement on Gujarat in the Financial Times in 1996. The advertisement said: 'if you have had enough of congestion in the port of Mumbai, try the 173 ports of Gujarat!'. Gujarat consciously wants to compete. Ten ports were privatized and in a number of other ports the state government invested.

Hyderabad versus Bangalore

At present Chief ministers can offer cheap land and tax and investment facilities to investors, or promise to provide the necessary permissions without any red tape. Andhra Pradesh is a good example of this new approach. The capital Hyderabad competes with the city of Bangalore of the neighboring Karnataka. Near Bangalore there is a concentration of computer and software industries, which is exporting its products all over the world. Andhra Pradesh has now managed to convince Bill Gates to invest in Hyderabad. The previous Chief Minister Naidu used the internet to get information from the district capitals in his state and to provide them with instructions.

The good governance discussion is a step forward in urban management, because urban politicians and managers are now more than ever accountable for what they are doing. Accountability is one of the key concepts of the NPM theory, a theory that is revolutionizing public management by putting the emphasis on contracts and autonomy, while stressing the importance of market orientation and customer orientation. I think the challenge for urban managers is to make this theory work.

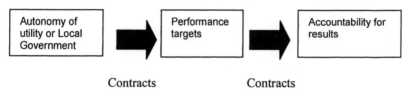

Figure 3.1 Framework for analyzing the relationship between an organization and its environment

The key terms in the NPM are autonomy, accountability, customer orientation and market orientation. They will now be explained.

4.1 Autonomy

Autonomy refers to the ability to make important decisions at a lower level of government or at the level of a government owned company. In our research we made a distinction between (Schwartz and van Dijk, 2003):

- Internal autonomy is within the local government or a utility, which makes the organization more flexible, effective and innovative.
- External autonomy: the service provider (local government or a utility) is shielded from opportunistic political interference to allow the managers to respond to the needs of their customers.

The degree of autonomy is determined by the legal authority of the local government or utility, only constrained by a number of external limitations (see Figure 3.2). Various accountability mechanisms that together form the web of accountability to which a local government or utility is subject (can) include (based on Thynne, 1994):

- The use of performance contracts or the like between the organization and different levels of government;
- Public reporting of performance;
- The application of the regulatory framework to which local government or the utility is subject;
- The application of requirements by financial organizations that lend money or provide grants to local government or the utility;

- The application of customer service charters or the like that the utility or local government is bound to.

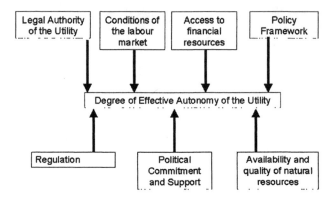

Figure 3.2 The degree of effective autonomy of a local government or utility

Customer-oriented service provision stimulates innovation. If a utility gets its funds from the customer instead of a government agency, the utility is more likely to investigate innovations, which will increase customer satisfaction. Customer-oriented service provision is likely to be more efficient as it better matches supply and demand for services.

4.2 Accountability

Accountability means rendering account of the way public money is spent: for which purposes has it been spent and did this have the expected results? It is necessary for a local government or a utility as a whole, but also within local government or a utility. Local government is accountable to the municipal council and its citizens. A utility is accountable to a variety of actors and groups, including the owner, the regulator, financing institutions and NGOs or special interest groups.

Two kinds of accountability should be distinguished in the case of a government owned company. The first relates to the relationship between the actual service provider and the management oversight agency (say the municipality or a board of directors). The second kind of accountability concerns the accountability of staff within the organization (for example a service provider), and is also known as 'managerial' accountability. Accountability concerns who is holding management responsible for the performance resulting from their decisions. Internal accountability and external accountability follow a similar logic in that internal accountability is based on the link authority with responsibilities – performance targets – accountability.

One of the main accountability mechanisms promoted in NPM is that of the contract. This contract can have a variety of forms such as performance contracts, customer charters, loan agreements, etc. In our research we focused on these more formal accountability mechanisms. The corporate culture of a utility or local government is also important. Is there a tradition of rendering account, or is the organization very top down and reluctant to share its performance results with others?

4.3 Customer Orientation

Customer orientation is in essence the attention paid to customers of the local government service or a utility. It is measured by the attention paid to complaints, representation of customers in different bodies and the frequency (and results) of surveys to find out what the customers (citizens) think of the service provided by local government or a utility.

The advantages an increased customer orientation includes (Osborne and Gaebler, 1992):

- Customer-oriented service provision increases the accountability of local government or urban providers to its customers
- Customer-oriented service provision depoliticizes the provision of urban services

4.4 Market Orientation

Market orientation aims to capture the benefits of competition. The best-known method is private sector participation. Out contracting is one way to achieve it for local governments and utilities. Benchmarking (see Chapter 6.2) and testing the markets are other indicators for market orientation for a local government or a utility.

The introduction of a stronger market orientation is mainly aimed at reaping the benefits of (quasi-) competition between either suppliers working outside the utility or local government, between outside suppliers and internal departments or between internal departments of a utility or local government. Increasing the market orientation of a public sector organization is typically done through a range of contracts, (quasi-) competition between (public) agencies, interagency fee charging, and outsourcing (Burki and Perry, 1998). The main advantage that an increased market orientation is expected to achieve is that of increasing efficiency of service provision. An increased market orientation is also expected to stimulate innovation. Assessing the market orientation of local governments or utilities can be undertaken by looking at:

- The use of out contracting/outsourcing in service provision
- The use of benchmarking practices in the utility
- The use of other mechanisms to introduce (quasi-) competition

Many a public utility does not get its funds from the people they are designed to serve, but rather they depend on government agencies. In addition, most of the public utility's customers are 'captive' customers. Apart from moving away to another service area they have little alternative but to use the services of the utility (Osborne and Gaebler, 1992). The combination of being dependent on government agencies and having a 'captive' clientele, has often led utilities to pay little attention to their customers and more attention to their financiers. Because customers are not 'directly paying' for the services they receive they are not as 'empowered' to hold the service provider accountable (Barzelay, 1992).

The key hypothesis of the NPM is that well-performing local governments or utilities are likely to be subject to considerable accountability mechanisms that contain explicit performance targets. How it can work out in practice will be shown in Chapter 6 where we will discuss the efforts to improve drinking water supply in Addis Ababa.

The analytical framework of the NPM theory focuses especially on the formal accountability mechanisms in the local government or a utility. This means that the urban manager will examine if the departments and staff are accountable to meet explicit performance targets, how the performance of the departments and staff is monitored (reporting requirements), how the achievement of the performance targets is measured, and what the consequences are of meeting and failing to meet the agreed performance targets.

NOTES

1. Different theoretical approaches are possible, mostly focusing on one aspect of the urban economy. For example the theory of social exclusion in cities (Fainstain et al., 1992, call it the divided city), the paradigm of flexible specialization or industrial districts (van Dijk, 1993), or the bridgehead theory of Turner (1986) concerning the behavior of migrants in slums.
2. Without going into detail I believe certain theories are relevant in a particular stage of development or for a specific sector or issue, or for a certain type of city.
3. Demand and supply of industrial land in one industrial estate will be analyzed differently from the problem of higher unemployment rates of different social groups living in the city.

4. These decisions can be divided into four categories (financial management decisions, operational management decisions, human resources management decisions and customer management decisions).
5. IHS and Erasmus University have worked on the topic of decentralization in Indonesia (for example Suselo et al., 1995 and Rukmana et al., 1993) and master students in the joint Urban Management Center (UMC), for example Alisjahbana (1995) and Wahyu Kusumosusanto (1998).
6. In big countries and in particular in federal political systems implementing legislation is required at the State level (India) or workable detailed regulations need to be prepared to determine the division of labor between the provinces and the local governments (Indonesia).
7. As an example of the kind of legislation required for decentralization: Article 8 of the Indonesian law from 1999 states that: 'The competencies of the Province as an autonomous region cover the competencies in the administration sector of a cross District and or City character, along with competencies in certain other administration sectors'. Section two adds: 'The competencies of the Province as an administrative region cover competencies in the administration sector delegated to the Governor as the representative of the government in the scope of de-concentration'. Article 10 specifies as the 'competencies of a district region and a Municipality region'.
8. IHS and Erasmus University jointly developed a research project on decentralization: as new opportunities for managing the cultural heritage of Indonesian cities.
9. It was estimated that Central government grants financed a little over one-third of local government expenditures but contributed over two-thirds of local government revenues.
10. A cluster being defined as a strong spatial clustering of economic activities (for example IT enterprises in van Dijk, 2006a).
11. Van den Berg et al. (1993) on city marketing can be considered as a predecessor of the competitiveness approach.
12. Is there much difference between a region and a city? No, only in administrative or governance terms (see Chapter 10). There are now interesting theories about 'the economy of urban regions' (Kaplan, for example in *NRC*, 2 June 2000), or about the replacement of the nation state by the region state (Ohmae, 1995). The latter theory argues that a city alone can never achieve the dynamics, which a region can achieve because cities are to much preoccupied with solving their specific problems. Kresl and Gappert (1996) conclude that 'the integration of regional and urban economics is the new frontier', because they are usually treated as separate subject matters.
13. At the level of the world region 'The ability of a part of the world to achieve high rates of economic growth, on the basis of suitable policies, institutions and other economic characteristics' (van Dijk, 1999a) is important.
14. Cheema (1993) also emphasizes the importance of 'the generation and transfer of urban innovations'.

4. What is Urban Management?

1. INTRODUCTION

The urban manager now has received the responsibilities. Decentralization has given him or her the task (functions and responsibilities) to run the city. The urban manager has acquainted himself or herself with several useful theoretical frameworks. But what is he or she now going to do?[1] What is urban management exactly? We can now give a more precise definition of urban management. Davidson and Nientied (1991) call the essence of urban management 'taking an active role in developing, managing and coordinating resources to achieve a town's urban development objectives'. This definition is satisfactory, but rather short and general. The same applies for the definition of Tribillon (1985) 'putting planning into practice'. This definition is too simple. Tribillon rightly emphasizes the important role donors have played in stimulating urban management in developing countries.[2] Finally the task of the urban managers can be defined as being responsible for the necessary infrastructure (Lindsey, 1998). Although an important aspect I consider this definition as too limited.

Stren (1993) calls urban management an 'elusive concept which escapes definition'. More importantly Stren stresses that urban management is an integrating concept. This requires an understanding of the transition from 'physical planning' to urban management. Urban management implies an integrated approach of the major issues of cities in emerging economies. In many countries local government's intervention is limited to 'zoning policies' and the authorities trying to impose some minimal building or housing standards. This limited role serves slum inhabitants, who want to build their own houses and no further interferences. However, at a later stage an urban manager is required to intervene, because some problems (sewerage, pollution and health hazards for example) cannot be solved individually.

As an example of the integrated approach one can think of building houses, which not only solve a housing problem, but can also create employment if small contractors are involved and influence the direction in which the city develops and the traffic flows which will be generated.

The urban management approach should take the most important issues in the city as the starting point. These could be poverty, crime or congestion. The literature rightly stresses the importance of participation of stakeholders and the role of different financial actors, the commercial and non-commercial sectors. This is certainly a challenge for urban managers, who should forge public-private partnerships (PPP), or what is known in Indonesia as public-private-community partnerships (PPCP). These institutions and civil society need to be involved. There also exist new opportunities to attract private finance.

BOX 4.1 URBAN MANAGEMENT IN TWO MEGA INDIAN CITIES

In the big Indian cities the relations between the Municipal Corporation, the Urban Development Authority, the district and 'the metropolitan planning committee' are usually underdeveloped. Municipal Corporations (MC) are responsible for drinking water supply and services such as waste collection and they collect local taxes. In Ahmedabad the economic capital of the state of Gujarat the 'urban development authority' is responsible for planning a larger area than covered by the Municipal Corporation. Other parts of the city are not covered by the Ahmedabad Municipal Corporation (AMC) or the Ahmedabad Urban Development Authority (AUDA) but are under the responsibility of the district in which Ahmedabad is located. It is clear that there are coordination problems in this situation.

In the bigger Indian cities a 'metropolitan planning committee' can be created in which all different institutions should cooperate. The committee has only planning responsibilities and can only get political clout if a State level minister takes the presidency as has happened in the case of Hyderabad, capital of the state of Andhra Pradesh. In Ahmedabad there is not yet a metropolitan planning committee, which means that a lot of decision power remains at the State level, which once again undermines the idea of decentralization.

In Ahmedabad local and regional development are clearly interrelated. Ahmedabad is a dynamic city and another example of an integrated approach to urban management. It developed from an industrial to a service-based economy (Box 4.2). The economic dynamics of the city made it very attractive to do research in this city (van Dijk and Shivanand, 1999 and Box 4.3). In the 1990s India changed a lot in general, but Gujarat state in particular underwent rapid development and social transformation. The transformation of Ahmedabad is largely the result of local entrepreneurs going elsewhere when faced with stricter environmental legislation. The old textile industries were no longer competitive and new industries were not allowed in the city center. Hence chemical and other polluting industries found a place elsewhere in this state and service activities were concentrated in this economic capital of Gujarat State.

For several reasons proper urban management in emerging economies is not yet as common as one would expect. In the first place the necessary institutions are sometimes not sufficiently developed. This turned out to be a problem in Indonesia and India. In India the chosen mayor of council as well as the appointed chairperson of the Municipal Corporation could be the urban manager. The Municipal Commissioner is usually a central government official and tends to be in charge for a limited number of years, a problem the urban manager shares with the elected mayors.

Second, the existing institutions are often not sufficiently coordinated. The lack of coordination was mentioned for example when we discussed the need for 'metropolitan government' in cities with several elected local governments (see Box 4.1). Also the development of institutions and rules determining the behavior of urban managers is important and part of putting good governance in place. Urban management is a relatively new discipline, born out of the need to deal with the important issues of cities. No longer is administering what happens in the city enough.

BOX 4.2 AHMEDABAD: FROM AN INDUSTRIAL TO A SERVICE ECONOMY

The development of Ahmedabad is strongly related to the rise of the indigenous industrial sector. At the beginning of the 19th Century the textile industry resulted in the city gaining the name 'the Manchester of India'. The factories were built on large estates in or around the center of the city. Ahmedabad became a city of 5.5 million inhabitants and the factories became islands of noise and pollution because of its narrow streets. It suffered from congestion and had a large number of slums. Hence a law was announced in the 1980s that polluting industries were not allowed in a radius of some 20 km around the city center.

Subsequently industries chose a location in other parts of the state (in particular to the south on the axis to Bombay), or just outside the city. When the textile industry was no longer competitive a recession started from which it took ten years to recover. By then the character of the economy of Ahmedabad had changed to a service economy with a concentration of financial institutions, trading companies and transportation firms.

Finally, the people concerned are often not well trained to be able to manage a city. Good managers often work in the private sector, or prefer to work for central or state government in the Indian situation, which is more rewarding and prestigious. Initiatives need to be taken on very different levels. Urban management requires an active role of the political system at the neighborhood, city and region level. Good economic analyses of the growth potential of urban clusters and of the city, or the region are desired. If people are insufficiently trained they need to be educated.

BOX 4.3 DYNAMICS OF RESEARCH INTO THE URBAN ECONOMY IN INDIA

The IHS of Erasmus University undertook with the School of Planning in Ahmedabad a research project to study the consequences of decentralization and liberalization for slum inhabitants, as well as for all kinds of informal, small and medium sized enterprises. At the national level liberalization started in 1991, but in Gujarat state it started much earlier. A former collaborator of the School had written a Ph.D. ten years ago with income and employment data, which allowed us to determine the developments over time under the influence of liberalization policies. To understand the changes in the urban informal sector, mostly micro and some small and medium scale enterprises, a number of questions were added in the questionnaire concerning the present situation and the situation three years ago. Did your turnover increase, how many people worked with you three years ago and are you earning more? It turned out that the situation of the slum inhabitants as well as the small entrepreneurs has improved after decentralization and liberalization.

In 1995 the State High Court ordered the closure of some 1000 formal sector, mostly medium scale, enterprises because they were too polluting. In particular the chemical industry developed outside Ahmedabad during the 1980s was strongly polluting (Gorter, 1998). Although the industries were rarely sentenced, in general people were satisfied that the High Court corrected the executive branch of government, which is considered corrupt as far as environmental inspections are concerned. Four years later I learned from a MA thesis of a student at the School of Planning in Ahmedabad, which I read as the external jury member, that many cases were dropped because the High Court could not show exactly how much pollution the units produced before closure. According to the law that would have been necessary. The lawyers of the industrialists had become trained in escaping judgment. The only positive result is that the pubic awareness of the pollution problems has increased tremendously.

2. MY DEFINITION OF URBAN MANAGEMENT

What is urban management? Urban management started at the end of the 1980s in developing countries (cf. Devas and Rakodi, 1993 and Cheema, 1993). It meant the end of at least three accepted ideas. In the first place the idea that officials at the urban level would mainly be responsible for administering what was going on in the cities. May be they were also responsible for housing, water supply and sewerage systems, but that was it. Economic development, the environment and poverty have also become responsibilities of an urban manager. Second, urban managers could no longer just blame higher levels of government for not providing urban services and ask money from them. The urban managers are now becoming responsible themselves for formulating a strategy, for raising funds and subsequently implementing the strategy. Finally, the master plan is no longer the most important planning instrument (below Box 4.4).

BOX 4.4 CRITIQUE ON THE TRADITIONAL URBAN MASTER PLAN APPROACH

In the past land use planning, resulting in 'master plans' were considered the key to urban development. The planning system in many emerging economies is a copy of the system of the former colonial power. Often this happens to be England where in 1947 a new 'Town and Country Planning Act' was enacted, which makes a distinction between 'structure plans' and 'local (development) plans'. Structure plans were intended to provide a broader, strategic framework for subsequent local plans, and were to take account of the regional context, and of transportation, housing and environmental issues (Devas and Rakodi, 1993: 84). In the 1980s the emphasis was put on 'strategic planning' and 'planning control'. Counties and regions make a strategic plan and districts produce a 'local development plan'. These recent developments have not been copied by developing countries. They still work with master plans, which are usually approved too late and then applied rigidly. They focus on land use and pay hardly any attention to economic developments, nor do they indicate the financial implications of the plan. These plans are top down and concern physical planning only.

Before giving my definition of urban management I would like to point to three things. In the first place one needs to take into account in emerging economies the interest of a large number of actors. I find in particular the private (commercial and non-commercial) sector important. In the urban context they all play a role: more outspoken inhabitants, but also NGOs, CBOs, project developers, other cities, PPPs, saving associations and financial organizations for infrastructure. To be able to for example involve private financing institutions in an urban project the urban manager needs to have a good network.

In Box 4.5 the example of creating an organization for financing urban infrastructure is elaborated to show that governments sometimes create institutions, which compete with the private sector. Such a financing institution is an important source of finance for urban infrastructure. However, one also creates structures that receive responsibilities that the government then no longer has. These institutions can pursue their own objectives and go their own way, for example if they are privatized. This may not exactly be what the government had in mind when it created these institutions. It becomes another actor, whose interest and role has to be taken into account.

Second, we cannot neglect environmental problems created by cities, they often influence a much larger area. Urban environmental problems have become more and more serious and research focusing on rural urban linkages (as the one mentioned in Box 2.1) can help to identify the 'foot prints' of the city (Rees, 1992), the much larger area affected by the pollution produced in the city. In a positive vein this leads to welcome initiatives such as the UNCHS sustainable cities program and the slogan launched by the World Bank: 'making cities livable' (World Bank, 2000). These initiatives need a prominent place on the agenda of the urban manager.[3]

BOX 4.5 INFRASTRUCTURE FINANCING CORPORATIONS: ANOTHER ACTOR

Since economic development in India is advancing there is an enormous demand for infrastructure. A number of states have created urban infrastructure financing corporations or trust funds. In Tamil Nadu this fund has been created with support from the World Bank and functions at 'arm length' of the state government. In other states this is not yet the case. Recently IHS has been asked by the Asian Development Bank to help to restructure these institutions in three Indian states. This is institutional development; a long-term process and the question is whether each Indian state should try to create an institution within the government sector for infrastructure project preparation, for project management and for financing purposes.

The government sector remains bureaucratic and often does not think in terms of financial benefits. Often politicians influence the decisions and the government cannot afford to hire the necessary financial experts, because it cannot pay the salaries necessary to attract specialists. For that reason the private sector should be used more.

In many Indian states the lack of project preparation capacity is the real issue. If enough good urban infrastructure projects would be prepared, and real 'cost recovery' would be introduced, financing through the private sector, and through international capital flowing into the country would be possible. International capital flows into India, in particular in the present situation where the rate of growth is high and interest is often 10 percent or more, while state governments may provide guarantees for repayment of the loans or bonds.

Finally, urban management requires more than the traditional master plan. The critique on the master plan approach is summarized in Box 4.4. It is necessary to develop a broader vision where one wants to go with the city in the future. What are the opportunities for this city, given its competitive advantages? This requires a strategic planning exercise, which could be based on a preliminary action planning effort (see Chapter 5, Box 5.1).

Urban management is not urban management science in the narrow sense as it is taught in the business schools. For me the relations between the municipal authorities, enterprises, clusters, the citywide and regional developments are too important for that. The toolkit of micro and macroeconomic methods can contribute to understanding the factors determining the dynamics of an urban cluster, a city or a region. Hence the importance of economic and financial analysis as tools for urban managers (see Table 4.1).

My definition of urban management would be 'the effort to coordinate and integrate public as well as private actions to tackle the major issues the inhabitants of cities are facing, to make a more competitive, equitable and sustainable city'.[4] The most comprehensive definition comes from my colleagues van Klink and Bramezza (1995). They define 'modern' urban management as 'the process of developing, implementing, coordinating and evaluating integrated strategies with the help of urban actors, taking into account the objectives of the private sector and the interests of citizens, in the framework of a policy defined at a higher level of government to achieve the potential of sustainable economic development'. A good definition also provides a framework to monitor and evaluate urban management. In the discussed Indian and Indonesian situation there is a lack of coordination and too often higher levels of government are still active in the cities in a sectoral way. They deal with the problems in the housing or public works sector, as perceived at the national level. Often without much vision or political support from the relevant level and without coordination with regional or urban managers.[5]

3. METHODS AND TOOLS FOR URBAN MANAGEMENT

Table 4.1 gives an impression of the most frequently used methods and tools for urban management. There is no direct link between the different columns. Sometimes it is difficult to say what is a method (a way of doing things) and what is a tool (an instrument helping to achieve the desired results). The objective is each time to make the city more competitive, equitable and sustainable.

Urban competitiveness can be improved for example through an action planning or strategic planning exercise in which the people concerned participate, or by using information technology (see Chapter 9 below). It is desirable that such actions are initiated by an official or politician, who will also be involved in implementing them. Personal commitment usually helps.

The different methods mentioned in Table 4.1 are not unique for urban management, but general methods used in this case for a specific purpose.

4. CONCLUSION

I have tried to convince the reader that decentralization provides new opportunities for urban management in emerging economies. Subsequently I have argued that cities in the Third World and Eastern Europe are more and more integrated in the global economy and compete with each other. Good urban managers can play an important role in that 'war of cities', which is going on. A good manager is someone who via an integrated approach, based on a strategic plan, makes his or her city more competitive and in such a way that the social and environmental problems are also tackled. [6]

Table 4.1 Theories, methods and tools for urban management

Theories of urban management	Methods (more abstract)	Tools (more concrete)
Decentralization	Economic and financial analysis (cost benefit analysis) Action planning	Integrated problem analysis Participation of stakeholders Environmental management
Urban competitiveness	Research methods Strategic planning City marketing	Use of private finance and IT Developing integrated solutions
New public management	Policy analysis and evaluation Planning of reforms Comparative analysis	Institutional reform Monitoring Benchmarking

In Egypt the jogger risks to succumb from acute led poisoning because of air pollution. In India the runner may overlook the underlying social issues and in general he risks bypassing the real problems because he is running too fast. I am aware of these pitfalls and I can only say that usually a cold shower follows after jogging and then the urban manager can start refreshed to deal with the major issues. Cities in emerging economies have enormous problems but also huge opportunities. The city is an engine of growth and a source of energy.

The urban manager now has a theoretical framework and an impression of the challenges and the opportunities he or she is facing. In Parts III and IV we will provide case studies illustrating the issues and applying the theories. In Chapters 6, 7, 8 and 9 the issues are respectively improving urban service delivery, caring for the urban environment, financing urban development differently and useing information technology for urban management purposes. In Part IV concerning China, Chapter 10 studies employment in the urban informal sector and in Chapter 11 a dynamic development of the IT sector in Nanjing is analyzed. Such a development will create employment. Theories concerning decentralization are used in Ethiopia and China, competitiveness is in particular illustrated in the Chinese case, while the NPM is used to suggest improvements in service delivery in Ethiopia.

NOTES

1. Important books on urban management are van den Berg et al. (1993), Castells and Hall (1994), Cheema (1993), Cohen et al. (1996), Devas and Radkodi (1993), Fainstain et al. (1992) and Freire and Stren (2001).
2. Post (1996) exaggerates in my opinion when he states that urban management in the limited sense is what the World Bank prescribes and can be considered 'a translation at the urban level of structural adjustment (at the national level)'.
3. The United Nations Center for Human Settlements (UNCHS of Habitat) runs a sustainable cities program; also Serageldin (1994).
4. At a more philosophical level one could take the definition of development of Sen (1999) (development is freedom) and argue that in an urban context this would mean: to provide options to people, which would mean in my words that the actors have the possibility to choose and can contribute in this and other ways to the development of cities, neighborhoods and their habitat.
5. In South Africa many post-apartheid urban problems are still defined in a sectoral way: how can the housing or employment problem be solved as quick as possible with subsidies and with physical planning legislation. There is less attention for the broader issue of how to make the cities more competitive in a global economy. How can the private sector for example contribute to the economic development and employ as many people as possible and do something for their housing problems?
6. This requires developing a 'pro-poor urban development strategy' at the urban level. Promoting the urban informal sector and social development funds would be important just like a different way of supplying services. See van Dijk (1992), van Dijk (1997) and Wegelin et al. (1995).

5. Methods and Tools for Urban Management

1. INTRODUCTION

The urban manager needs to use different scientific methods and tools. Some of these methods and tools will not be discussed in this chapter because they are extensively used in the following chapters, as indicated in Table 5.1.

Table 5.1 Methods and tools for urban management used in subsequent chapters

Methods and tools	Relevant chapter
1. NPM tools	Chapter 3 and applied in Chapter 6
2. Urban environmental analysis	Illustrated in Chapter 7
3. Financial analysis and when to use different financial instruments	Different financial instruments in urban management in in Chapter 8
4. Use of IT in urban management	The topic of Chapter 9
5. Comparative analysis	In Chapter 12 the Pearl and Yangtze River deltas are compared

For urban managers appropriate planning tools are needed, but also communication is a skill that has to be learned. Other methods and tools briefly discussed in this chapter for example are city marketing, the use of urban indicators and monitoring and evaluation. The methods and tools discussed in this chapter are presented in Table 5.2. The list is not complete and the discussion will be brief, but a reference will be given each time, which may help for further study of the topic.

Table 5.2 Methods and tools for urban management

Methods and tools derived from economic theory	Methods and tools derived from management science	Methods and tools based on other social sciences
Neoclassical economics	Overview management theories and skills	Research methods and policy impact analysis
Institutional economics	Planning and marketing	Participation, communication and stakeholder analysis
Tools: economic and financial analysis and monitoring and evaluation	Benchmarking, strength weakness/opportunities threats (SWOT), organizing capacity and asset management	Tools for environmental management and for scenario building

This chapter is divided in three sections: methods and tools derived from economic theory, methods and tools derived from management science and methods and tools based on other social sciences.

2. METHODS AND TOOLS DERIVED FROM ECONOMIC THEORY

2.1 Neoclassical Economy

There are two main streams in economics, neoclassical and institutional economics. In the neoclassical paradigm individual consumers maximize their utility and entrepreneurs their profit. They meet in markets, where the transactions take place. These markets take care that the best solution is obtained in a given situation. Adam Smith suggested that the invisible hand was active and he proved that the market mechanism leads to efficiency. The only imperfections are due to a limited number of market suppliers (oligopoly) or to an extreme case of only one party (the monopolist). Second the theory assumes that all market parties have the same and full information, which is not always the case (Williamson, 1998).

The theory is very useful to analyze the functioning of markets. Unfortunately there are many markets in developing countries, and especially in cities (for example the land and housing markets), which do not always function smoothly. Textbooks summarizing the neoclassical approach are for example Marshall (1920), Richardson (1976) and Samuelson and Nordhaus (different editions).

2.2 Institutional Economics

According to institutional economics markets are often highly imperfect. They are defined and shaped by institutions, but these institutions need to be created and to be modified when a new situation arises. Hence the analysis of markets begins and ends an analysis of the actual functioning of these institutions and the design of a better institutional framework. These institutional changes make the market work and let them function in the desired way. Government policies and agreed regulation play an important role in designing institutions (North, 1993).

Institutional economists do not believe in an invisible hand. They emphasize the importance of rules and regulations. To let a market work parties have to communicate and hence to agree on a common language and adhere to the defined conditions of the deal. Any discussion on how to stimulate competition or whether to deregulate, regulate or re-regulate certain markets makes the importance of institutions clear (Viscusi et al., 2000). Institutions also play a role when trying to keep the government at arms length, or to safeguard the public and private interests. Institutional change is an important issue in developing countries and the central topic when liberalization of markets or of various infrastructures is discussed (van Dijk, 2003a).

The common theme of institutional economists is the rule-based character of social behavior (Coase, 1960). From that perspective the evolution of systems of institutional rules becomes important. Second, the field of economics becomes broader and would include what is currently called economic sociology and uses insights from other social sciences. For example cognitive psychology can help to understand how the brain works. That helps to test whether people really maximize their utility and to understand how people and organizations are learning and why certain people are innovative.

Institutional design and change become even more important when markets are concerned with not just simple products, but complicated goods such as technology and information. In the 21st Century the economy is more and more based on electronic information and communication networks, where the question is whether information should be public or private, shared or privately owned (intellectual property rights), freely accessible or restricted to certain groups. Does the public interest require a monopoly or should in the creative economy (Florida, 2004) a thousand flowers blossom?

The historical divergence in institutional structures proves to be persistent. It influences the present day differences in economic development between China and India. Also informal institutions, such as trust and social capital in a broader sense may influence finance and growth. Informal institutions tend to be substitutes for more formal legal rights. China has made the transition from a planned economy to a much more market-oriented economy in a relatively short period (Chen, 2000). This is an example of institutional change or reform and will be analyzed in Chapter 10 (see also Yiwen, 2004).

2.3 Tools for Financial and Economic Analysis and for Monitoring and Evaluation

Tools for economic and financial analysis are quite standard and a description of these methods can be found in several good textbooks (for example Brealey and Myers, 1996). Cost benefit analysis (CBA) is an important instrument for this purpose. It is basically comparing the stream of investments and production costs of a project with the flow of benefits it will produce. The urban manager should be able to understand the results of cost benefit studies, and the underlying decision rules of economic analysis. Understanding practical applications of CBA techniques are essential for choosing between different investment opportunities (Mishan, 1988).

McGuigan et al. (1999) define CBA as 'a resource allocation model that can be used by public sector and not for profit organizations to evaluate programs or investments on the basis of the magnitude of the discounted costs and benefits'. The possible criteria to be used in the public sector: maximize the benefits for given cost, or net benefits, or minimize cost while achieving a fixed level of benefits. Different CBA need to be compared, because they provide feasible and unrealistic financial options. The implied rates of return on investments should help to prioritize the investments and can be the basis for the negotiations with the private sector, which may be involved in the ownership, the financing, or the management of the project. Even if specialized firms are available to advise the government, government officials need to be trained in what this type of negotiations are about and how these tools should be used.

The leading idea for sustainable cities is that they also need sustainable finance, which requires healthy cost recovery systems. For that reason the financing modalities and cost recovery systems in place in the different cities and projects should be studied and compared (Bohle, 1992). However, we should also look at the socio-economic consequences of urban management (for an elaboration see Chapters 6 to 12):

1. Do the proposed activities exclude certain people (Fainstain et al., 1992)?
2. Do they increase the financial burden of the population to above what is affordable?
3. Do we need instruments to subsidize or cross-subsidize the solutions introduced?

Monitoring and evaluation are tools developed to supervise the progress of a project. They are often called 'tools of management' and are described in detail by Casley and Kumar (1988). To assess the progress it is often necessary to do a base line survey and to specify the progress in the project document as concrete as possible. Monitoring on these quantified indicators is then possible and allows management to take corrective actions when the progress is not as expected.

Mukundum (1998) suggest using a indicators to rank urban local bodies in India, mentioning in particular:

1. A number of financial indicators (tax revenues, debts and the development of income and expenditures).
2. A series of service level indicators (for example water supply, solid waste management and street lights).
3. Other performance indicators (per capita income, cost of collecting tax, etc.).

One can add variables measuring the quality of life: certain environmental indicators (Zhang, 2002), the human development index (which adds education and health to income as an indicator of development) and social indicators, such as poverty and inequality.

Evaluation is *ex post* and can also be carried out independently from the monitoring process. It requires criteria, such as effectiveness, efficiency, impact and sustainability. The meaning of these criteria may be different for different types of project (Bamberger and Hewitt, 1990).

Table 5.3 Overview of management theories and skills

Basic thoughts and theories behind management	Basic skills of management
Management competencies and styles	Managerial decision making and problem solving
Getting the most from employees	Management of time
Organizational structures and cultures	Dealing with people in the workplace
Managing change	Oral communication in the workplace
Managing conflict and stress	
Managing teams and workgroups	Written business communication
Management by objectives	Presenting yourself and your ideas
Quality	Making meetings matter
Ethics	Project or program planning
Managing in different cultures	Marketing management

Source: Scott (2005).

3. METHODS AND TOOLS DERIVED FROM MANAGEMENT SCIENCE

3.1 An Overview of Management Theories and Skills

The Concise Handbook of Management (Scott, 2005) gives an overview of the basic theories behind management. They are listed in Table 5.3.

An important distinction should be made between private and public management. The NPM is typically developed for the public sector, while most of the theories and skills mentioned in Table 5.3 were developed for use in the private sector. More and more however, theories, methods and tools developed for the private sector are also applied in the public sector.

3.2 Planning and City Marketing

Urban competitiveness can be improved for example by action planning or strategic planning exercise in which the people concerned participate, or by using information technology. It is desirable that such actions are initiated by an official or politician, preferably one who will also be involved in implementing them. Personal commitment usually helps. Finally a business plan translates a strategic plan in an intervention, of which the revenues should cover the cost (Mintzberg, 1994). In Chapter 2 Box 2.1 concerning Kaya, can be considered an example of the choices to be made in a strategic plan. The definition given is that a strategic plan translates a strategic vision about the future into a plan, which need to be prepared in an environment in which the actions of one player depend on and affect the actions of other players

---

BOX 5.1 ACTION PLANNING AS A TOOL FOR URBAN MANAGEMENT

Action planning basically refers to ways of solving an urban problem in a limited time frame, in an innovative or non-routine way with involvement of the stakeholders. The emphasis is on participatory planning. Other characteristics:

- Action planning refers to a well defined physical area;
- It should be owned by those involved;
- The problem should be a legitimate one to tackle.

Action planning relates to realistically available resources and those involved can learn from the process.

Source: Baross (1991).

Urban development requires always some kind of planning. World Bank (2000) summarizes it as 'successful urban development also requires strategic city wide or regional planning to guide trunk investments and identify the most appropriate locations for jobs, residences, and transportation'. There are a number of books on urban planning (for example Devas and Radkodi, 1993 and Post, 1996).

It is necessary to develop a broader vision where one wants to go with the city in the future. What are the opportunities for this city, given its competitive advantages? This requires a strategic planning exercise, which could be based on a preliminary action planning effort. For a definition of action planning the reader is referred to Box 5.1 and Baross (1991). The advantages of a strategic plan for a city or region are:

1. A framework of policies setting out the government's planned approach;
2. A choice of areas which will best accommodate urban growth;
3. A statement of expected outcomes planned of a ten year period.

BOX 5.2 CITY MARKETING: REQUIRED INFORMATION AND CHOICES TO MAKE

To prepare the right marketing strategy the following information about your city is required:

- What are important products of the city?
- Who are the producers?
- What market is the production addressed to?
- What is the actual and envisaged image of the city/region?
- Is there a promotion strategy?

Some choices to make:

- What are the main objectives of the city marketing strategy?
- Do you want to market the city or the whole region?

Has the promotion strategy been designed in consultation with urban and regional partners, from the private and public sector?

Source: Van den Berg et al. (2002).

City marketing tries to put a city on the map and is described in some more detail in Box 5.2. A city can be put on the map if people have an association with that city:

for example Porto, was elected cultural capital of Europe for one year, some years ago and still has that name. Similarly, Bangalore is often called the Silicon Valley of the east. City marketing is very common in Europe and the USA, but not so widely spread in developing countries. Box 5.2 also summarizes some of the information required for city marketing and lists some of the choices to make.

3.3 Tools: Benchmarking, SWOT, Organizing Capacity and Asset Management

Benchmarking is a systematic comparison of the performance of one organization with other organizations. It is an alternative for competition and sometimes called quasi-competition. Benchmarking practices introduced in utilities provide a measure of their relative performance. It can be informal benchmarking and sometimes benchmarking takes place at the level of the technical variables only. It can also be obligatory and concern a large number of technical and economic variables. It can be done by the government or could be undertaken by the sector itself. In all cases it makes it possible to detect sources of inefficiency.

We discuss the strength weakness/opportunities threats (SWOT) analysis briefly, since this is one of the most popular research strategies of managers and business economists. This is a tool that reveals the internal strength and weaknesses of a business and identifies environmental opportunities and threats facing the business. This happens through:

- Systematic identification of these factors;
- Developing a strategy to maximize the firm's strength; and
- Minimizes weaknesses and threats;
- Identifying the distinctive competencies;
- Finding a niche in the company's environment;
- Finding the best match between competency and niche.

Although this method is extremely popular I like to point to some major issues:

1. What is exactly the unit of analysis? Is it the region, the city, the municipality, the department, etc.? This makes a big difference as far as the specific strength weakness and opportunities threats are concerned.
2. What is the best way to direct the SWOT? Do you ask the people individually what they consider the SWOT? Do you use secondary sources, organize a group session or interview key informants?
3. Whose opinions did you register and how much weight do you give to the different opinions? Some people are more concerned than others and some may be more vocal than others.

4. How can you give weight to the different factors mentioned? Some factors may be crucial and some may be minor factors, which hardly influence the success or failure of a project.
5. How do you want to move from the analysis to implementing the results?

Once the strengths and weaknesses have been identified and the opportunities and treats are listed, how are you going to proceed to change the situation?

The concept of organizing capacity of regions and cities is often used. According to this theory the success of urban development projects depends on the organizing capacity of a city or a metropolitan area. Organizing capacity means to be able to anticipate, respond to and cope with changing intra and intermetropolitan city relations due to internal and external processes of change at the proper spatial scale level. It can be defined as the ability to enlist all actors involved, and with their help generate new ideas and develop and implement a policy designed to respond to fundamental developments and create conditions for sustainable developments and for sustainable economic growth (van den Berg et al., 2000). The elements of organizing capacity are:

- Vision on long-term sustainable development (for strategies, programs and projects to hold on to);
- Formulation of concrete, measurable objectives;
- Strategic and coherent thinking and acting;
- Leadership qualities to manage processes and projects adequately;
- Creating and supporting strategic networks of relevant partners, needed to develop and implement policies successfully;
- Creating political and societal support;
- Emphasizing communication strategies.

Key elements of organizing capacity for community-based projects that are intended to solve city problems are the organizational tools, represented by 'T' (the instruments with which to achieve an adequate community-based projects) and the project process, represented by 'P'. Moreover, the contexts, represented by 'C', under which cities are operating, are also equally important elements in organizing community-based projects.

This framework can be summarized into a Table 5.4. The underlying assumption is that the success of community-based projects depends on the three important categories of variables (C, T and P). The three main variables (and their components) could be dependent (inversely or directly) or independent to each other.

Capital assets are important for a city. In the infrastructure sector drinking water and sanitation projects for example require huge investments and result in buildings and equipment (the assets). These remain usually public property and need to be maintained. The characteristics of these assets are that they are in use for a long time, they cannot be used for different purposes and they need to be maintained, but the cost must be affordable for the users. Asset management aims to come to an optimal balance between the asset operation costs and the benefits. For that purpose asset modeling is used, where data predicting the residual life of a network or system are used.

Table 5.4 Key elements of organizing capacity

Context variables (C)	**Tools of organizing capacity (T)**
Spatial-economic conditions (C1)	Vision and strategy (T1)
Administrative organization (C2)	Strategic networks (T2)
The social context (C3)	Leadership (T3)
	Political support (T4)
	Societal support (T5)
	Communication strategy (T6)
Project process (P)	**How to proceed?**
Project implementation monitoring and output (P1)	A score can be used for each of these key elements of organizing capacity, to allow a comparison between different projects/cities.
Evaluation and outcome (P2)	

New water and sanitation development projects may require partnerships between the major actors: the public sector, the private sector and civil society. Such a tri-partnership would make use of the strong points of each actor and would help to access the knowledge about water use practices. Smooth cooperation requires the definition of the roles of the private and public sector and an agreement on sharing the cost and on the allocation of the risks between them. The cross cutting theme of risk assessment is very important in this research (Lindfield, 1998).

In developing countries the majority of formal water and sanitation services are provided by the public sector. However, public service providers have often failed to provide consumers with adequate services. Problems that are stated very often for having led to poor service provision include overstaffing, low cost-recovery and poor governance. Problems in water supply and sanitation are usually not the lack of water or the lack of demand for water, but rather a series of non-technical factors to get the water to the users and to develop financial viable and sustainable waste water treatment plants.

The institutional environment is often only gradually developing and should help to deal with risk, and issues like a certain return, volatility, inflation, duration of loans, etc. In many developing countries the World Bank, International Monetary Fund (IMF) and the Basle Bank of International Settlements (BIS) play an important role through their surveillance and financial activities.

Issues which are important in the case of asset management:

1. How are the decisions taken with respect to ownership and finance of major assets in the water and sanitation sector? Are operation and maintenance (O&M) considerations playing a role in the decision process?
2. Can these decisions concerning the lifecycle of assets be modeled and is there scope for improvement?
3. How do the different financing formulae affect asset management?
4. Do different models provide different results?
5. What is the effect of regulation and surveillance?

4. METHODS AND TOOLS BASED ON OTHER SOCIAL SCIENCES

4.1 Research Methods and Policy Impact Analysis

Research methods and techniques (RMT) is the designation of a topic, which could also be called the methodology (the theory of how to do research) of a certain scientific discipline. Research starts with formulating research questions and choosing a research strategy (for these terms, see Box 5.3). This is a way of achieving the objectives of your research by developing a research proposal that could mean doing experiments and surveys; undertaking case studies; using grounded theory, ethnography and/or action research; doing a SWOT analysis, rapid appraisal or a series of case studies. There are also several textbooks on research methods (for example Saunders et al., 2003 or van Dijk, 2004b). Box 5.3 summarizes some of the key terms for a research project.

Policy analysis and evaluation focuses on the process of policy formulation, implementation and evaluation. It is explained in more detail in for example Wallis and Dollery (2001).

BOX 5.3 DIFFERENT TERMS RELATED TO RESEARCH

Action research: research strategy concerned with the management of a change and involving collaboration between practitioners and researchers.

Case study: empirical investigation of a particular phenomenon in real life context.

Ethnography: research strategy that focuses upon describing and interpreting the social world through first-hand field study.

Grounded theory: theory is developed from data generated by observations or interviews in an inductive way.

Hypothesis: a proposition the researcher wants to put to a test.

Operationalization: effort to make concepts measurable in a practical context.

Positivism: works with observable social reality leading to law-like generalizations.

Proposition: untested statement about the relation between different variables.

Questionnaire, list of questions or of topics to be discussed, in research process.

Reliability: degree to which data collection methods will yield consistent findings.

Research methods: surveys using questionnaires, the case study approach and so-called rapid appraisal methods.

Research objectives: statements identifying what the researcher wants to achieve through the research.

Research process: starting with an idea about the topic of your research, put in your research proposal until the end of presenting the results in the final report or thesis.

Research question: a research question is one of a small set of key questions related to a certain issues, which the research will try to answer with the data collected.

Source: Van Dijk (2004b).

4.2 Participation, Communication and Stakeholder Analysis

Participation of stakeholders creates the conditions for consensus and potential conflict resolution. Participation not only makes programs and policies more acceptable they make them cost-effective and enhances the feelings of ownership. The stakeholders, once involved, undertake significant follow-up activities on their own accord and enhance social mobilization.

Low-income groups will make a personal cost-benefit analysis before participating in a program. Deciding collectively which basic need to fulfill first, results in commitment towards a program. It requires dissemination of information towards these beneficiaries. For example if upgrading results in higher rents, as can be seen in the case of Ethiopia, low-income groups will either become a 'free-rider' (waiting till others will do it for them), or will turn their back towards participation.

It is important to plan the sequence of reforms and improve stakeholder participation. To do so it may be useful to do a stakeholder analysis, a tool which tries to determine the interest and power of each stakeholder.

Evaluations of participatory projects can give more insight into the effects of joint efforts between parties have on developing the urban area. Taking into account the increasing demands on urban areas, mutual commitment between interacting parties is likely to become more important in the future. Efforts to improve the living environment of people will benefit from a control mechanism, measuring the impact. In this regard it might be interesting to study more carefully the possibility of institutionalized control mechanisms in a multi-actor-approach program. Jointly undertaken efforts to improve the quality of urban life are highly influenced by political, social and economic circumstances in the country itself. More in-depth knowledge of the influences of these partnerships on urban development programs makes better anticipation of the problems possible.

A clear example of a successful multi-actor approach is also given in the case of Belarus (Baharoglu and Lepelaars, 2002). The citizens of Vitebsk have undertaken a problem analysis together with the representatives of the stakeholders, to define the inner city problem and the causes. A similar approach can be seen in the Bangalore Urban Poverty Program. Slum Development Teams, formed or elected by the slum people, are responsible for identifying local needs and draft action plans.

In her Ph.D. thesis Correa de Oliveira (2003) formulates the essence of the multi-actor approach. No sector acting independently (state, market or organized society), is fully equipped to solve the housing problem for low-income groups. However commitment and involvement of the actors involved are important building blocks for a successful approach of jointly undertaken service delivery. The absence of local ownership felt by one of the actors involved can influence the success of the project. Effective and appropriate reform needs to be expressed through the local political process to reduce the influence of counter forces. How the communication process works can be learned. It will lead to communication strategies, with suggestions both within the city administration and for external communication (to citizens, companies, public bodies, etc.). The challenge for urban managers is also to use improved communication technologies (see Chapter 9).

A finance-oriented example of participation of different actors is also given in the case of Brazil analyzed by Correa de Oliveira (2003). The citizens of Porte Alegre established a permanent control over the use of public resources, called municipal budgeting. The advantages of this approach are citizen's influence on municipal priorities and involvement of the civil society in decision making and control of the state.

4.3 Tools like Environmental Management and Scenario Analysis

Environmental management is necessary to protect the natural environment and produce good living conditions. Examples are given in Chapter 7, Zhang (2002) and van Dijk and Zhang (2005).

Finally scenario methods are interesting to explore possible future actions. One tool for scenario building is using the scenario cross. This means finding two dimensions, which are crucial for the future. The main difficulty with the scenario building tool is finding two uncertainties (or driving forces) that, when combined with each other in a scenario cross, will give four very different scenarios that can then help prepare for an uncertain future. Scenarios have also been developed using other generative techniques (e.g. future imaging).

PART THREE

Examples of urban management

6. Improving Urban Service Delivery: Water Sector Reform in Ethiopia and its Impact in Addis Ababa

1. INTRODUCTION

Key services, like water and sanitation often fail poor people, in access, quantity and quality. Urban service delivery is a task for the urban manager, who can sometimes delegate it to a municipal water, electricity or infrastructure company. Even in that case the overall responsibility and the supervision and regulation will be part of the job of local urban managers.

This chapter deals with urban service delivery in Ethiopia and in particular in the capital Addis Ababa. Public service delivery has been failing in developing countries for a long time. In particular the water supply and sanitation sector is often not on an acceptable level for urban, and in particular for the peri-urban and rural communities in most developing countries. The expectations were that decentralization and regional development would change the situation, which has often not happened. Obviously, decentralization alone is not enough. We will analyze this in Ethiopia, where improved service delivery has not happened, despite decentralization efforts. Experiences with public service delivery in other African countries and South Asian countries are quite similar. The case of Addis Ababa will show how the new public management theory can help to analyze why reforms may not have all the desired effects. It helps to propose detailed measures to improve the drinking water supply in Ethiopia's capital. Principles and instruments will be derived from the NPM theory and then applied to the case of Addis Ababa.

2. ASSESSING THE QUALITY OF URBAN SERVICE DELIVERY

Key words for assessing and improving the quality of urban service delivery are:

1. Specificity;
2. Private sector involvement;

3. Gain experience with small projects;
4. Analyze existing experiences;
5. Benchmarking: measure the performance.

These terms will now be explained briefly, since they are crucial for a discussion about the quality of urban services and will lead to an indication of the need to undertake a drinking water sector reform program in Ethiopia.

2.1 Specificity

Urban service delivery is very different from one service to another and hence specific sector knowledge and experience is necessary. However, at the management level a number of similar processes are taking place and cross-sector knowledge and experience may help to analyze the problems and to come up with appropriate solutions. In the literature the most common examples of urban service delivery are:

a. Water and drainage;
b. Electricity;
c. Roads;
d. Waste collection and treatment;
e. Other urban infrastructure and services such as health, education and telecommunication.

2.2 Private Sector Involvement

There are strong arguments to involve the private commercial or non-governmental (NGO) sector in urban service delivery. A distinction should be made between economic arguments, ideological arguments and historical practices in different countries. It is also important to distinguish privatization in the broad and in the narrow sense of the word. Privatization in the broad sense means promoting private sector involvement in service delivery but not necessarily changing the ownership of the utility.

Outsourcing, management contracts and concessions are different ways to increase private sector involvement without changing the ownership. In the narrow sense of the word privatization means changing ownership by selling the shares or selling the utility as such to a private party. We like to use the term divestiture for outright sales of public property and privatization for other forms of private sector involvement or participation. Roth (1989) provides an overview of the historical practices and theoretical arguments in favor and against different types of private sector involvement (see also van Dijk and Schulte Nordholt, 1994).

The different forms it may take in the water sector are depicted in Figure 6.1, where the emphasis is not on ownership but on the role of public and private finance and the use of public or private management techniques.

Improving urban service delivery 77

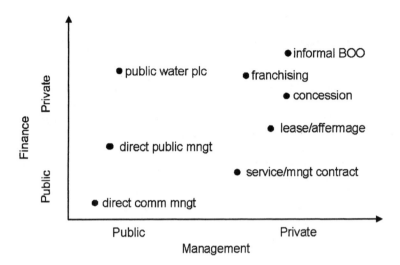

Note: Plc = public limited company; Comm. = community, Mgt = management and BOO = build operate and own.

Source: Janssens and Baietti (2002).

Figure 6.1 Different forms of private sector involvement in the water and sanitation sector

2.3 Gain Experience with Small Service Delivery Improvement Projects

The Chinese approach of testing a different approach to a specific problem on a small scale seems interesting for other countries as well. In most countries there are experiments with improved urban service delivery on a small scale. However, the results have not always been analyzed systematically, with the intention of then applying the insights gained on a larger scale and for example in other cities.

2.4 Analyze Existing Experiences with a Comparative Studies Framework

The advantage of comparative analysis is that it helps to gain insights, which factors are specific and which are of a more general nature. Students in the master course Urban Management at Erasmus University have always been encouraged to look for the existing cases of urban service delivery to find out what works and what does not.[1] The NPM theory provides a good framework for such a comparison. For an application of this framework to a number of successful water utilities in different countries see Schwartz and van Dijk (2003). The results are presented in Schwartz and Van Dijk (2004) and partially used in this chapter.

2.5 Benchmarking: Measure the Performance

Benchmarking is a tool of comparing companies or utilities on a number of key indicators. It is good to use several measures of performance, because the different results of reforms should be clear and the comparative performance of different utilities within the same reform program is interesting. What explains the differences in performance? Even involving the private sector is no guarantee for unlimited supply of the service at the desired price and quality. Hence monitoring the performance and benchmarking (comparing the results with other utilities) are good ways to assess the results. In the Netherlands benchmarking in the drinking water sector is undertaken by the association of water companies on a voluntary basis (VEWIN, 2001). The analysis of these data shows big differences in performance between different actors (van Dijk, 2003a).

3. WATER SECTOR REFORM: ANALYTICAL FRAMEWORK

In order to be able to assess the functioning of a public utility and to make recommendations for better performance we need an analytical framework based on experiences elsewhere. Schwartz and van Dijk (2003) studied: why are some public utilities functioning well, whilst other utilities perform poorly? The approach taken in this research project is to analyze this question in the framework of different approaches to the way in which public sector organizations are managed.

Table 6.1 NPM principles and corresponding NPM instruments

NPM principles	NPM instruments
Autonomy	Influencing tariffs
Accountability	Using contracts
Customer orientation	A service-oriented company
Corporate culture	Incentive programs
Market orientation	Benchmarking/making an inventory of possible Private Sector Participation

The analytical framework focuses on the distinction between the bureaucratic paradigm of management in public sector organizations and the NPM approach. The latter can be separated in NPM principles and NPM instruments, as illustrated in Table 6.1 and Figure 6.2. The hypothesis formulated is that well-performing utilities are likely to be subject to considerable accountability mechanisms that contain explicit performance targets. The study also looked at the corporate culture of the utilities.

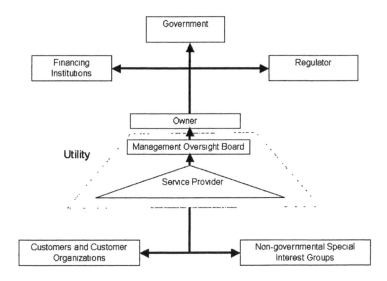

Figure 6.2 Conceptual overview of accountability between utility and its environment

The World Bank is looking for a strategy to engage again on a larger scale with the public water sector in developing countries. That means working with national and local governments and, assuming that the utilities have implemented some reforms in the past, find out:

1. What instigated the reform process in the first place and what were the critical moments?
2. What was the sequence in which the reforms were implemented?
3. Was the sequence of the implementation purposely planned?
4. If so, what was the reason for this sequence of implementing the reforms?
5. What can we learn from efforts to reform in other countries?

We will deal with these five issues in the case of service delivery in Ethiopia. Starting for example after macroeconomic stabilization or restructuring programs, water sector reforms are usually at three levels: at the level of the sector, concerning the ownership and finally the internal reforms in the utility. The internal reforms need to be spelled out in a lot of detail for the public sector reform. If a country does not want to involve the private sector in for improving service delivery, it means government companies have to mimic to a large extent the measures the private sector would take, when the private sector would have been asked to step in.

3.1 The Reasons behind the Reform Process

There need to be opportunities to reform. What can we say about triggers for change? In Uganda the threat of privatization was important and stimulated the management to reform the national water utility. Management expected a lease contract and wanted to show that they could also perform well without foreign private partners. In Singapore the shortage of water led to adding wastewater treatment in an innovative way. Finally, in Scotland the price cap (a maximum price the utility could charge for a liter of drinking water) forced them to improve efficiency and develop alternative sources of income. So a first conclusion concerns the importance of external pressure to reform:

- A water shortage crisis may force utilities to look for other approaches;
- A serious case of pollution or health problems can play this role;
- The threat of privatization can bring about a change;
- Too high prices trigger off political unrest, which may force politicians to change current policies.

3.2 The sequence of reforms

Sequencing of reforms could be for example: start with new management, training of staff, increase the tariffs and build up continuing pressure to perform. Subsequently more customer orientation, the development of internal procedures and systems to measure performance and finally more market orientation will do the job. There is however, the problem of conflicting time horizons: the new management, the politicians and the donor all have different time horizons.

It is also important to look at the capacity requirements for reform: a certain size of the utility makes it easier to find the necessary capacity. Plus the need for funds to train the staff. Capacity building is also needed at different levels. Sometimes the utilities need at the town level trained low-skilled people, to do the manual work. There is a big difference between the single municipal water utility and the multi-utilities and multi-municipal cases, often concerning the whole country (for example in Burkina Faso, Tunisia, Uganda, etc.).

Table 6.2 Functions of the board and the managing directors

Functions of the larger Board	Managing Directors
Hire and fire executive managers	Implement the company policy
Fiscal matters	Manage the institution
Health and safety of personnel	Hire and fire lower level managers
Legal matters: to comply with the law	Prepare corporate plans and budgets
	Prepare financial accounts
Monitor performance and advise management	Assure the necessary finance
Approves business plan	

3.3 Separation of Different Roles

A key message in the reform process is: separate the different roles in a local government or utility. The main roles are ownership, oversight and service provision. After separation it is necessary to define the relations between the different units. NGOs can help to monitor the process and play a role in the web of accountability that needs to be woven. To be able to reorganize (or turn around) utilities the director and the board need some autonomy. We give a list of functions of the board and the managing directors in Table 6.2. The items in the different columns can be used as a checklist for the functions of the board and the directors.

Corporate governance is the issue and the detailed picture of the functioning of the Board and of the management should be based on local legislation and the articles of association of the utility or company to be reformed.

3.4 An Example of Sequencing

The internal reform process could follow the following sequence:

a. Find out what the public sector considers the priorities in drinking water supply;
b. Identify the necessary reforms and link it to what these reform packages would cost;
c. Find out how much money is available;

d. Link different reform packages to different price tags and choose what you can afford, given available means;
e. The package should be concentrated, follow the 20/80 rule, with 20 percent of the means you can achieve 80 percent of the objectives;
f. Make a business plan, which will eventually become a three year rolling annual plan;
g. That requires physical concentration of your activities, choosing: going for standpipes, more connections or more pressure (choose one that is urgent) and refuse exceptions, which jeopardize your planning (the sister-in-law of the mayor);
h. Start higher tariffs as soon as you have something to show;
i. For public companies it may be necessary to reconcentrate activities before you decide on outsourcing certain activities to private or public partners (the South African case of metering, billing and complaints which are still the responsibility of the municipality);
j. Major instruments in the internal reform process are:
   - Internal benchmarking;
   - Internal contracts;
   - Agreements linked to easily measurable indicators;
   - Enforcement of contracts and agreements;
   - Incentivy the agreements and contracts.
k. The challenge is to sequence these measures and then visualize reform tracks, which may be different, depending on the point of departure, the identified bottlenecks and priorities;
l. Then locking in the reforms is extremely important, avoiding that the next government or director can just undo them.

3.5 Experiences in other countries

We found an enormous variety of situations and that there is not one solution for all water companies. Much depends on the past. How much progress has been made with the reform process and what political leadership and commitment there is to improve public water supply. Examples of success are often influenced by accidental factors.

Another factor coming out in a number of cases is what we would call the importance of external pressure. Such external factors can bring about the necessary turnaround because people are ready for the radical reforms that need to be introduced. We also found that the utilities should get some autonomy. Finally, the commitment to reforms is important. The change can come from inside or from outside, but the commitment to change should be inside and outside the utility and here urban managers play an important role.

Examples of turnaround utilities are found in Uganda and in Haiphong (Vietnam). Sometimes a lack of interference by local politicians in the business is already enough to allow for the necessary reforms. For example Singapore functioned well for a long time, although it was only a municipal department, not even corporatized to separate its finance from the regular municipal finance. However, the authorities did not interfere! Linked to this is the need to push eventually autonomy down the line, which boils down to further decentralization. For example dealing with customer's complaints can be pushed down the line and there are examples where this worked. The people who need the feedback would get it and will be able to deal with it. This points to an important point that comes out of a lot of research, namely if management introduces a change it is important to explain it, to introduce it properly to the personnel and to allow them to make it their point.

In certain utilities (Haiphong for example) the management is very centralized, which may work with a director who knows the company for a long time, but it may be a constraint for his successor. It is interesting to note that in Sansa (Brazil) a lot of the decisions were prepared by working groups. This seems a good way to involve different layers in the organization. Providing autonomy also means the utility can introduce incentives and introduce competitive salary scales. It is sure that those utilities that are set up as companies tend to do better than the others. They are companies and start behaving like it.

Another way of formulating this point is that there should be a weak link between the owners and the management. Preferably there is a business plan, with a vision, a strategy and concrete objectives, which guides the management. Leadership and the ability to recruit good people is also an important factor contributing to the success of the utilities studied. This applies for Uganda since 1997, for Haiphong from 1993 to 2003 and also for the case studies undertaken in Scotland and in Philadelphia (USA). The role of the donors can be very positive. They put a lot of money in the water sector, hopefully within a water sector reform framework put in place with the World Bank. However, if 80 percent of the investments are donor financed the question is whether this will be sustainable in the future.

The reform process takes often a lot more time than expected. In Haiphong it required ten years. In other countries it is certainly not going to happen (and become sustainable) in three or four years, the normal period of a project. This leads to the importance of the phase where the utility is in the reform process. Also the sequencing of reforms is very important. A sequencing of the proposed recommendations is necessary. For example tariff increases have to come before more private sector involvement (PSI). PSI is compatible with the public model if forms like outsourcing, concession contracts and build, operate and transfer (BOT) formulae are used. We need to develop a road map of where to go with public utilities. Similarly it would be good to provide practical tools, for example through a comparative analysis of the relevant cases. This involves a prioritization and indications of what to do.

Finally the stability of management is important. In particular the Latin American cases show the importance of the stability of management. In Mexico and Brazil most senior staff are replaced when there is a change in government. When the new mayor has been elected, the board and senior management are sacked! The sustainability of reforms is a worrying point. This is not just in developing countries. Even in the Philadelphia case a lot of senior managers threatened to leave the company and the question is whether the utility will be able to attract good new people. The question becomes how we can lock in reforms. Suggestions to achieve continuity in the reform process of the utility are to stimulate:

a. Multi-ownership;
b. Certification procedure for management;
c. Transparent recruitment procedures;
d. Link loan to performance criteria (this is what the World Bank did in Haiphong);
e. Keep politics away from the water entity, use the Board as a buffer. It would create a weak link with the owners, namely only through the business or annual plan: with general objectives and specific targets);
f. Use working groups to prepare decisions, to achieve employee involvement.

4. DECENTRALIZATION IN ETHIOPIA

In December 1994 a new Ethiopian constitution was promulgated. National and regional elections were held in May and June 1995. The constitution provides for the establishment of a decentralized federal system of government. Ethnically and linguistically fairly homogenous regions (regional states) are defined constituting the federal units of the political and administrative setup. Ethiopia's constitution retains state ownership of the land, while recognizing user rights and opening the possibility of leasing land.

The Regional State Council is the highest organization in an Ethiopian region. The executive body is called the Executive Committee and comprises 24 members. The Chief Administrator of the regional state heads the Executive Committee. The major professional institutions are the social sector, the economic sector, the legal affairs and the Peoples' militia and security sections.

This description does not tell us exactly which responsibilities have been put at which level. In fact the distribution of responsibilities may differ from state to state, like in the case of India. A systematic study could help to clarify this. We found for example that in the Southern State (the SNNPRS province) water is the responsibility of the state authorities, while in the east (Harar) it is a municipal affair. Similarly in most regions municipalities are not allowed to issues bonds, but most state banks can do so.[2]

Is Ethiopia really a federal system with decentralization to lower levels of government? The local journal *Reporter* (28 January 2004) mentions the de facto non-existence of federalism in Ethiopia, given the repeated interventions of central government in regional states affairs. For example the government is controlling the major towns and their financial activities.

The prime minister of Ethiopia keeps telling his ministers that 'utility companies of Ethiopia should bear some semblance of effectiveness following a sweeping administrative reform' (*Capital*, 25 January 2004). In particular six ministries (including the Ministry of Infrastructure) have been selected for reforming dysfunctional institutions. The reform process is designed to introduce efficient and speedy service from a government that is to be reengineered.

The objective of the reform is to bring about a managerial revolution to make service provision companies efficient, competitive and customer friendly. However, the problem with public policy in Ethiopia is that there is no space for private sector in public services delivery. *Capital* (25 January 2004) concludes 'many companies are still under state control and management despite their being out of tune with the times, incurring losses or simply failing to be profitable ... (the administrative reform) has failed to give them a real managerial shake-up to make them competitive or efficient'.

Reforms at the utility level need to be spelled out in a lot of detail. The reforms at the utility level try to mimic to a large extent the measures the private sector would take. Reforms at this level concern a number of actions that are listed in Table 6.3.

Each of the reform actions at the utility level will now be discussed and eventually a number of actions need to be combined to form a reform package. The may be part and parcel of a process of increasing private sector management techniques or bringing in private sector finance, as depicted in Figure 6.1. In the reform process usually four stages can be distinguished (Schwartz and van Dijk, 2004):

a. Pressure to improve the performance in the sanitation sector;
b. Broad sector reform;
c. Service provider reform;
d. Maintaining progress.

If we look to public service delivery in terms of private or public ways of managing and private or public ways of financing utilities (see Figure 6.1) Ethiopia is very much on the left and the bottom in this figure. Reform would mean moving from the left to the right and for the World Bank it also means moving from the bottom to the top of the figure. In terms of type of utility it would mean, going from a municipal department, through ring-fenced utility (a utility that cannot be influenced directly by politicians) and water boards to the water public limited company (PLC). These are different ways of achieving better performance in the utility sector. Another argument for this trend of moving to the right is that the suggested and started reforms cannot so easily be undone, if you are more on the right in this figure.

5. THE WATER AND SANITATION SECTOR IN ADDIS ABABA

Addis Ababa was founded as the capital in 1887 by Emperor Menelik (1899–1913) and gradually became the largest city of Ethiopia. It was given the right to collect and use income derived from the leasing of land within its jurisdiction through proclamation 80/1993. Through proclamation 87/1997 the city obtained a chartered status with all its benefits. The city lies in the center of the country and sprawls over a core area of 28 000 hectares. According to the Central Statistical Authority it generated about one quarter of Ethiopia's Gross Domestic Product (GDP) in 1994. Besides the core area, the so-called metropolis is in total around 7500 km^2, most of which lays in the Oromia Region. The current population is about 3 million people.

Although the Addis Ababa Water and Sewerage Authority (AAWSA) is a separate authority and hence an example of what Rondinelli and Ruddle (1978) would call administrative decentralization through delegation, the AAWSA is not really autonomous. For example it cannot fix its own tariffs. It is loss making and unable to improve its situation, although customer orientation has improved. Tariffs are extremely important, just like customer orientation. In fact one may lead to the other. Successful utilities have generally been able to increase their tariffs and pay more attention to the needs and problems of their customers.

Asset management is important for the water sector, because the assets (the pipes and the pumps) are investments with a horizon between 50 and 100 years. AAWSA depends on the municipality and foreign donors for financing its investments. If the infrastructure is not properly maintained it may generate no return at all. If there is a need for an extension this may be a quantum jump. There is often a grant element in the financing. Cost benefit analysis (CBA) can be measured by the fact that it can satisfy only 60 percent of the current demand for water, while only 2 percent of the urban population is linked to the sewerage system. It is also shown by its high unaccounted for water (UFW), at least 35 percent, and the low coverage. It is also shown by the lack of transparency for customers or researchers to find out what is really going on in the current water sector reform process in Ethiopia. To improve urban water supply a clear reform program is desired, with changes at the policy and the utility level. The formulation and implementation of such a program would clearly also need to be supported by the municipal and local government authorities.

To improve urban water supply a reform program was started and Desta (2003) assessed the progress of the water sector reform in Ethiopia. The importance of water sector reform programs in developing countries is increasing, but very few evaluations are available. The normal objectives of such a water sector reform program are:

- Increasing institutional efficiency;
- Improve the policy context of the water sector;
- Change the financial set-up to make the sector self-financing;
- Establish robust sector and utility governance;
- Introduce new, more efficient and professional management.

It usually implies improved quality of the service delivered and a better financing structure. The Water and Sanitation Program (WSP, 2002) of the World Bank has described the responsibilities in case of water sector reform and the tools for these reforms:

- Institutional changes;
- Tariff reform;
- Improvement of sector governance and regulation;
- Professional management of the utility.

We intend to determine the tools to be used in the water sector reform programs and will try to assess the possible results. It is important to analyze which factors have hindered or facilitated the formulation and implementation of the reform program and which factors explain the eventual success or failure. An evaluation should be in terms of effectiveness, efficiency and impact. Sustainability of the effort can be added as an additional evaluation factor. It should be realized that different objectives imply different indicators for the effectiveness (the degree to which these objectives have been achieved).

Desta (2003) notes a number of structural and tariff reforms, but also concludes that the current tariff does not allow AAWSA to make the necessary investments to improve its performance substantially. AAWSA cannot increase the tariffs sufficiently, but the new organizational set up gives more emphasis to water management and managing public relations.

She describes the current organization and tariffs and lists performance indicators to conclude that the degree of autonomy is very limited. The key powers of tariff setting and investment planning are under control of the Board of Directors (BOD), which authorizes hiring and firing, incentives and so on. The BOD depends very much on the municipality. These are clearly decisions, which according to the NPM should be the responsibility of the management of the utility. Finally Desta notes that the combination of technical and financial problems has affected the scope of the service delivered by AAWSA. This in turn had a negative impact on the willingness of the consumers to pay for its services.

6. WATER UTILITY REFORM IN ETHIOPIA

The following matrix of reform elements (see Table 6.3) lists the most important ones in the light of the research undertaken and the principles and instruments derived from the NPM theory. A combination of these actions allows preparing the best fit in a given situation. It will then be necessary to sequence these actions and we can then visualize reform tracks, which may be different for another utility, depending on the point of departure, the identified bottlenecks and priorities of the concerned water utility.

Second, we want to distinguish between reforms at the utility level concerning their time horizon:

a. The short term crash program;
b. In the medium term reform package;

c. In the long term the institutionalization of reform.

Table 6.3 Matrix of reform actions at the utility level

	Reengineering the utility	Taking the customer serious	Develop market orientation
Internally, develop	1. Business or action plans 2. Corporate culture: incentives 3. Promote internal decentralization 4. Involve staff in preparing decisions 5. Leadership 6. Have ability to recruit staff 7. Human resource development policies	8. Link increasing user fees and improved customer orientation	9. Introduce internal contracting 10. Internal benchmarking 11. Competition between internal departments
Externally, achieve	12. Create an independent Board 13. Define the roles of the Board and of management 14. Increased financial autonomy	15. O&M cost are paid for by beneficiaries 16. Do and use customer surveys 17. React appropriately to complaints	18. External (sub) contracting 19. External benchmarking 20. Assure access to water resources
Monitor success of utility level reforms	In all the stages		

6.1 The Short-term Crash Program

Short-term measures could result in some kind of crash program. For example after formulating the objectives:

a. Find out the constraints and formulate priority actions in the drinking water supply sector;
b. Identify necessary immediate measures to increase water supply, pressure or the number of connections, or whatever else is most needed;
c. Introduce stakeholder participation;
d. Relate actions to what the improvements would cost;
e. Find out how much money is available;
f. Link different reform packages to different price tags and choose what you can afford, given available means;
g. The package should be concentrated. Sometimes the 20/80 rule is followed, meaning that with 20 percent of the means you can achieve 80 percent of the objectives. Hence give priority to these allocations.

If management introduces a change it is important to explain it, to introduce it properly to the personnel and to allow the employees and customers to also make it their priority. This is an important conclusion from our research for the World Bank.

The role of donors can be very positive in putting together these short-term packages. They put a lot of money in the water sector and are sensitive to short-term immediate needs. If such actions can be undertaken within a broad water sector reform framework put in place with for example the World Bank the assistance from different donors may be much more effective.

6.2 In the Medium term: Develop a Reform Package

In the medium term more substantial reform packages can be developed combining the following reform actions (Table 6.3), which will each be discussed below. The implication of the separation of functions at the utility level is more autonomy for the utility. A key message in the reform process is: separate the different roles in a utility. Another way of formulating this point is that there should be a weak link between the owners and the management. The main roles are ownership, oversight and service provision. After separation it is necessary to define the relations between the different units.

6.3 In the Long run: Institutionalization

In the long run a combination of reform actions of Table 6.3 can be implemented. If progress is monitored properly, corrective actions can be undertaken if the desired results are not achieved.

6.4 Develop Business or Action Plans

Once the objectives have been formulated and the constraints have been identified a business plan needs to be prepared. It should have a vision, a strategy and concrete objectives, which can guide management. Such a business plan may eventually become a three-year rolling annual plan. The plan would have to specify the minimum acceptable level of access to water supply and sanitation. This may vary from country to country depending on the level of development and the available water resources.

The plan needs to distinguish the implicit goals of the past (the utility is there for employment creation) from explicit ones (the utility is also involved in nature conservation). The cost of the second type of reforms can be calculated and the bill can be sent to higher levels of government for activities like nature conservation or water resource protection.

6.5 Develop a Corporate Culture and Promote Decentralization

Autonomy needs to be exercised. A corporate culture can be developed and there is the need to push autonomy down the line, which boils down to further decentralization. Promote a businesslike culture with business plans, a vision and mission, focus on what you try to do, tell your staff where you want to go, devolve decision making as far as possible, etc.

As an example of decentralization, the dealing with customer's complaints can be pushed down the line and there are utilities where this worked very well. The people who need the feedback would get it and will be able to deal with it. Decentralization may also involve the transfer of responsibility from traditional local government utilities or agencies to other stakeholders.

Providing autonomy also means the utility can introduce incentives and introduce competitive salary scales. It is sure that those utilities that are set up as companies tend to do better than the others. They are companies and start behaving like it. Examples are:

- a bonus is paid;
- staff gets opportunities to follow training programs;
- possibilities for promotion are provided.

6.6 Create an Independent Board, Define Roles of Board and Management

We can now discuss the implications of separation of functions. Corporate governance determines the actual functioning of the Board and of the management of the service provider. Proposals will be based on local legislation and the statutes, or the articles of association of the utility or company. Sometimes a lack of interference in the business is already enough to allow the necessary reforms to be successful.

The division of authority between the owners of the service provider, the corporate oversight agency or board and the service provider itself need to be specified in detail. One of the main problems facing public service providers is the intervention by the government-owner in the day to day functioning of the service provider. A corporate oversight agency (like a Board of Directors or a Board of Commissioners) should provide a buffer between the owner and the service provider. That can be achieved by modifying the articles of association, if incorporated or by changing the statutes.

6.7 Involve Competent Staff in Preparing Decisions

In some of the utilities studied a lot of the decisions were prepared by working groups. This seems a good way to involve different layers in the organization.

6.8 Leadership

Leadership is important for successful water utilities as our research has shown. In several cases a visionary leader made the difference.

6.9 Having the Ability to Recruit Staff

Having the ability to recruit staff and in particular the ability to recruit good people, who can be offered a rewarding package is also an important factor contributing to the success of the utilities studied.

6.10 Develop a Human Resources Development Policy

It is important to develop a human resource development (HRD) policy, which is broader than just a training plan.

6.11 Link Increasing User Fees and Improved Customer Orientation

Usually a set of reform measures is introduced simultaneously. Often 'new' management (with considerable management skills) is introduced. The new management team also receives considerable autonomy to manage the service provider. Staff of the service provider are trained to improve skills as well as to introduce a new company culture in the utility. Tariffs are increased to levels that (at least) cover operational expenditure. There is a link between increasing the utility's income from user fees and the necessity to improve customer orientation. Successful utilities have generally been able to increase their tariffs and pay more attention to the needs and problems of their customers. Involve the utility in the price fixing process, because they are the only ones knowing the real cost. Subsequently these proposals can go to the Board for approval.

6.12 Introduce Internal Contracting

The separation of responsibilities in the sectoral adjustment phases requires some form of 'contractual' agreements. The use of contracts has its limitations; the required capacity to formulate them and the required capacity for enforcement and the political will to do so need to be in place.

Major instruments in the internal reform process are internal contracts. However, there is a need for agreements linked to easily measurable indicators, enforcement of contracts and agreements how to incentivy the agreements and contracts. The incentives at the utility level can be:

- permission to do certain investments;
- freedom to negotiate salary levels;
- bonuses.

6.13 Internal Benchmarking

Introduce internal and if necessary in first instance informal benchmarking between the present and the past, between departments and between stations in different locations.

6.14 Create Competition within the Utility

Besides the introduction of benchmarking one can go further and introduce competition between different departments on various subjects: cost, efficiency, quality, customer orientation, etc.

6.15 Create an Independent Board

The implication of more autonomy and a separation of functions is a more independent Board, staffed with professionals rather than politicians.

6.16 Define Roles of the Board and of Management

After solving a governance problem by separating ownership, oversight and the service provider it is necessary to clearly define the role of the board and of management. This involve issues such as:

a. Who nominates board members and the director;
b. Candidates are suggested by different stakeholders?
c. For how long;
d. Who nominates the Managing Director;
e. With which mandate?
f. How many politicians, how many specialists;

g. Investments above a certain level are not left to management, but have to go to the Board;
h. Who signs of on price increases?

6.17 Increased Financial Autonomy

Increased financial autonomy leads to a drive for increased customer orientation. By cutting out subsidies and price distortions decision-making is facilitated. With financial autonomy of the utility a series of mechanisms are triggered which are likely to lead to:

a. Increased customer orientation as the service provider needs to generate its income from the customers;
b. Increased managerial autonomy;
c. Increased accountability to local institutions;
d. A drive for increased efficiency as the pressure to reduce costs increases.

Financial autonomy implies the utility can look for different sources of finance. This does not have to come just from the government, but could also be provided by donors or result from direct access to capital markets (van Loon and van Dijk (1995).

6.18 O&M Cost are Paid for by Beneficiaries

It is suggested to start the reform with having at least the O&M cost paid for by beneficiaries. If no full cost recovery is yet possible, a short-term goal could be that the operation and maintenance (O&M) cost are paid for by beneficiaries

6.19 Organize and use Customer Surveys

Customer surveys help to find out what customers really want and what their problems are.

6.20 React Appropriately to Complaints

It is important that the service provider reacts promptly and adequately to the complaints raised by customers.

6.21 External (Sub) Contracting

After gaining experience with internal contracting and benchmarking these instruments can also be used to involve the private sector, or to compare with other (private) operators.

6.22 External Benchmarking

In some countries utilities are legally obliged to submit their performance indicators to allow the government to follow the development of the efficiency of these utilities.

6.23 Assure Access to Water Resources

Sometimes access to sufficient water, or water of a sufficient quality is the key problem and the reform package should deal with this element of the reform process.

6.24 Monitor Success of the Utility Level Reforms

The progress of the reforms needs to be assessed at the sector and the utility level. Improvements should be monitored using clearly defined indicators. If the projects are formulated in a logical framework format monitoring on verifiable indicators is usually a lot easier. NGOs can help to monitor the process of separation of functions and they can play a role in the web of accountability that needs to be woven.

7. SOME RECOMMENDATIONS

The data collection and analysis we did in Ethiopia leads to some recommendations for sector reform in the urban drinking water sector in Ethiopia:

1. Stability of management can be improved by going for multi-ownership. If several public bodies own the shares and are represented on the board it becomes more difficult to change management after an election. In Mexico water managers are even thinking about a certification procedure for management in the water sector; to avoid those political nominations would spoil the reform perspective. In this line of thought the State Commission for water would certify certain people for such jobs.
2. Introduce effective benchmarking, sometimes informal benchmarking, sometimes at the level of the technical variables.
3. Develop more performance related rewards for the utility and the people working in the utility. Given the current very low levels of salary every possible improvement may lead to more effort to achieve better service delivery.
4. Promote a clear separation of the owner and the operator to avoid political interference and changes in the policy after elections.
5. Use the principles of the NPM theory and translate those into instruments and reform actions. It is not necessary to insist on implementing all elements of the theory in an integrated way. However, the NPM is a powerful way of convincing utilities of the need for change and to suggest tools to achieve the objectives.

6. Involve the staff of the utility in the price fixing process, because they are the only ones knowing the real cost.
7. Plan the sequence of reforms carefully and improve stakeholder participation.
8. Solve the governance issues by separating ownership, oversight and the service provider and by clearly defining the role of the board and of management.
9. Promote a business like culture with business plans, stating a vision and a mission, focus on what you try to do, tell your staff where you want to go, devolve decision making as far as possible, etc. If the utility is set up as a company it can also be mapped against a normal business: is a business plan produced, what are the standards you aim for? Are the directors appointed in a normal way, what is the level of services, etc?
10. Use the board of directors. They have a few hard controls: strategy, business plans, financial supervision and performance monitoring.

8. CONCLUSIONS

Urban service delivery for the poor gets more attention since the Millennium Development Goals (MDGs) have been formulated. The relevant ones to be achieved by 2015 are listed below.

1. Improve the situation of slum inhabitants, reduce their number by 100 million.
2. Decrease (urban) poverty by 50 percent.
3. Halve the number of people without access to clean water.
4. Halve the number of people with no access to sewers.

The MDGs are very clearly calling to halve the global incidence of poverty and they specify what this means for the water and sanitation sector by 2015. Ethiopia has a long way to go to achieve these goals. Urban service delivery can be improved by putting poor people at the center of service provision, by enabling the poor to monitor and discipline service providers, by amplifying their voice in policy making and by strengthening the incentives for providers to serve the poor (World Bank, 2004). Designing proper water sector reform programs is an important step in the right direction. An analysis of experiences in different countries helps to bring out the critical factors to look at. In this chapter we suggested based on the NPM a number of reforms that in practice would help urban service delivery and hence help Ethiopia to reach the MDGs.

The major MDGs mentioned are clearly related. Urban management provides a framework to deal with the more important MDGs in an integrated way. Their achievement can be made part and parcel of the city development strategy.

NOTES

1. A number of theses at ECSC, RLDS and the UMC in Rotterdam have analyzed experiences in different African cities with urban service delivery (for example Ndimo, 1998).
2. A bond is a standardized loan that can be bought and sold. More formally it is a financial asset that promises a stream of known payments (the interest) over a specified period of time (see Chapter 8 below).

7. Urban Environmental Management in Cities in The Netherlands

1. INTRODUCTION

We asked our students from Third World and Eastern European countries what the major problems concerning industrial pollution in their countries were. They mentioned in the first place the lack of clean air and second water pollution (including rivers and lakes). Other problems frequently mentioned were pollution from traffic and hazardous waste dumping. Less frequently mentioned were sewerage problems and excessive noise. We would like to add the problems of draining a city, of waste collection and treatment and of industrial pollution in the urban areas. In particular small and medium enterprises can be very polluting as has been analyzed by van Vliet and Frijns (1997). Finally, it is important to point to rural environmental degradation as the result of a neighboring city.

In the Netherlands the National Environmental Policy Plan notes that originally environmental problems were largely local and regional in scale (noise, odor, local air pollution, regional water pollution, household refuse). However, currently we are also confronted with problems on a world scale (CO_2, climate change, damage to the ozone layer), on a continental scale (acidification and diffusion of environmentally dangerous substances) and at the level of river basins (accumulation of environmentally dangerous substances, waste streams of various kinds, eutrophication) (NMP, 1988).

The importance of environmental problems is summarized in Box 7.1. Environmental problems are typical urban management problems. No single department can solve them alone. Air pollution caused by a more intensive use of private cars requires legislation concerning the use of cars and of unleaded fuel, but its reduction also requires the development of alternative means of transportation and an information campaign to influence the general public.

There is a general neglect of the environmental consequences of industrialization in developing countries. Environmental policies may discourage investments. However, the lack of such policies may hinder the export of these industries in the future, particularly when green protectionism becomes stronger in the developed countries (Wiemann, 1996). The case of the Netherlands will used as an example in this chapter.

BOX 7.1 ENVIRONMENTAL PROBLEMS AS URBAN MANAGEMENT PROBLEMS

In general one finds in cities: the dirtier the poorer! In every Indonesian city one notes that the sky is colored because of pollution. Air pollution is the result of factories, but also old, poorly tuned engines, which do not get the best quality fuel. In New Delhi, the capital of India, there are days one knows the sun is shining but does not notice it because the dirt in the air functions as a filter. According to an American expert breathing the air in New Delhi equals inhaling two packages of cigarettes on a day. In Jakarta people often put a special filter before their mouth. In Surabaya the water cannot be drained quickly enough during the rainy season and complete neighborhoods are flooded. Third World cities were known for their sun and nice atmosphere. After some scouting a visitor could find a slum and open drainage systems. At present traffic congestion and pollution seem to be the most visible problems of these cities.

---

2. ENVIRONMENTAL ISSUES IN THE NETHERLANDS

The interest in environmental problems in Europe increased after the publication of the report of the Club of Rome in 1971. The title of the report was *the end of growth*, referring to shortages of raw materials which were becoming scarce and expensive as a result of rapid economic growth. In the Netherlands a first policy document was published a year later and in 1973 a European Environmental action program was launched.

In this chapter we concentrate on industrial pollution in the heavily urbanized western part of the Netherlands, often considered one big city: Randstad. It will be assumed that clustering of industries provides an opportunity to coordinate environmental policies, to involve the industrial sector directly in the discussion about the desired measures to reduce industrial pollution and to make the required investments collectively.

It is useful to distinguish between industrial estates and industrial districts. UN (1994) defines an industrial park or estate as a geographic area, which contains several businesses of an industrial nature. These industries may be similar or diverse, light or heavy, modern or unsophisticated, etc., but the industries will usually be small to medium-sized. Other terms used are business parks or industrial estates. However, not every industrial park, estate or business park is an industrial district.

An industrial district can be defined as: a specific geographic area where a group of related industrial firms (often including small ones) are located, which have developed strong relations between them (implying vertical disintegration), which fosters innovation and contributes to higher efficiency (van Dijk, 1993). Marshall (1920) mentions three reasons for localization (or external) economies of industrial districts: a pooled labor market; the concentration of industries allowing provision of non-traded inputs specific to an industry in greater variety and at a lower cost; and information flows more easily locally. Such a district is supposed to have a dynamics of its own, brought about by agglomeration and localization economies (van Dijk, 1993). What determines the dynamics of such an industrial district?

Coordination in a dynamic industrial district is not planned but quasi-spontaneous. But the innovative atmosphere and the entrepreneurial dynamism is certainly part of the secret of the success of these districts. Flexible productive networks mean that the enterprise can satisfy rapidly increasing demand. The flexible specialization (Piore and Sable, 1984) and the new competition (Best, 1990) concepts, which are very much related to the discussion about industrial districts, all stress the importance of a strong division of labor, interfirm relations, competition and cooperation, innovation, flexibility and a local value system.[1] In general environmental policies can be implemented with less cost if enterprises are clustered.

Industrial estates allow specific policies, because all enterprises are near and the problem of free riders can be attacked easily. The industrial districts require policies at a larger geographical scale. However, they also allow for the target group or branch-specific approach, since usually one finds sectoral specialization in the district. The point of departure for environmentally sound management in industrial districts in Europe and Asia should be the objective to achieve sustainable development (van Pelt, 1993). 'Sustainable development is development that meets the needs of present generations without compromising the ability of future generations to meet their own needs' (NMP, 1988). Environmental management boils down to preventing or abating the undesired effects of human activities or operations on the environment (NMP, 1988). Waste management means reducing waste discharges from industry in this case.

3. THE OPPORTUNITIES PROVIDED BY CLUSTERING

How do industries in the Netherlands, usually located near urban centers, deal with environmental problems? The fact that they are clusters of industrial activities makes it easier to undertake environmental investments collectively. In the Netherlands parliament has accepted several national environmental policy plans, which stress among others:

- Abatement at the source;
- Information diffusion;

- The use of covenants between the government and the private sector;[2]
- The polluter pays principle.

The importance of clustering of economic activities for a dynamic development of the industrial sector has been stressed very often (for example van Dijk, 1992; 1993). Collective activities to diminish pollution in industrial estates are rare, however. Besides the well-known advantages of clustering, also some disadvantages should be mentioned. In many industrial estates in the Third World one notices that industrial pollution only increases when industries are brought together, although industrial estates would provide the best opportunity to do something about the environmental problems of industries.

Waste management is only one aspect of industrial pollution. The choice of the technology, the raw materials used, the organization of the production process, the sources of energy used, the specification of the final product and the packing of products are also important from an environmental point of view. The issue concerning industrial pollution is not to produce less, but to produce differently.

BOX 7.2 PRINCIPLES OF THE NEPP

1. The stand still principle: environmental quality may not deteriorate;
2. Abatement at the source: remove causes at the source instead of treating symptoms on the 'side effects';
3. Prevention of unnecessary pollution and the polluter pays;
4. Application of best practicable means: follow the development of abatement technology as rapidly as possible;
5. Isolate, control and monitor waste disposal;
6. Two track policy: more stringent source-oriented measures on the basis of effect-oriented quality standards;
7. Environmental aspects are integrated into activities of target groups;
8. Keep pollution as low as reasonably achievable;
9. An international approach: solutions by preference in the framework of the EU or the UN.

---

4. DIFFERENT APPROACHES TO ENVIRONMENTAL ISSUES

In the Netherlands different approaches have been suggested to get industrial producers to internalize the external costs of polluting the environment. It would usually work better if the government and the industrial sector cooperate. The Netherlands parliament discussed the first National Environmental Policy Plan (NEPP) during its 1988–89 session (NMP, 1988). It contains a strategy for environmental policy in the medium term. The principles of this policy document are summarized in Box 7.2 and can be considered the foundation of modern environmental policies.

Urban environmental problems are tackled through a different approach, stressing the need of strengthening governance by strengthening the institutional capacity of different layers of government to deal with the issue. Other new elements are the efforts to:

- Provide positive incentives to participating industries;
- Promote participation of the concerned industries in policy formulation and implementation, this is preferred over just enforcing laws and regulations;
- Involve industrial estates. This would provide an excellent opportunity for tackling industrial pollution on a collective basis in the future.

Sustainable development is pursued in the Netherlands through feedback at the sources directed at a combination of closing substance cycles, saving energy and quality improvement. Source-oriented measures are to be preferred to effect-oriented ones because the possibility to control is greatest at the source, one source can cause more than one effect, uncertainties about the cause effect chain can exist, irreversible effects can occur and because it generally costs less to intervene at the source. Box 7.3 gives a list of source-oriented measures. These are preferred when the pollution has already taken place, when effect-oriented measures are not sufficient and cannot be implemented in the short run.

BOX 7.3 SOURCE-ORIENTED MEASURES IN THE NEPP

1. Emission-oriented measures: add-on technology, which reduces emissions and waste streams without changing the process of production and consumption;
2. Volume-oriented measures: legal and organizational measures which reduce the volume of raw materials and products without changing production and consumption processes as such;
3. Structural source-oriented measures (structural changes of a technological or other nature which change the process of production and consumption) directed at:

    - Integrated life cycle management;
    - Energy extensification;
    - Quality improvement.

For the industrial sector in the Netherlands special emission ceilings for acidifying and eutrophying substances have been formulated for 1994 and 2000. Emissions in 2000 had to be reduced by 50 to 75 percent relative to 1985. Second, industries are asked to contribute to soil clean up on industrial sites, curbing waste streams and modifying the use of pesticides so that unacceptable risks are prevented. Finally, all industrial sites with installations causing high levels of nuisance must be zoned by 2000. The disturbance in the residential environment from noise and odor and the chance of catastrophes needs to be brought to acceptable levels.

The promotion of environmental concern in particular in firms and the screening of different industrial sectors together with private industry are important spearheads of the policy relating to industry. Box 7.4 summarizes different approaches to industrial environmental problems. Guiding principles for environmental action programs have been developed among others by USAID (1994).

In Western Europe the environmental police covers everything from one-man auto-paint shops to sprawling petrochemical plants. They have to keep up with the listing of emissions permits held by thousands of local companies and to uncover operators who hold no licenses (*WSJE*, 19 January 1994). In the Netherlands the urban population itself is the best environmental police. The so-called 'blip' system refer to the habit of starting an investigation once the people have alarmed the authorities.

BOX 7.4 RECOMMENDATIONS HOW TO DEAL WITH URBAN ENVIRONMENTAL PROBLEMS

1. Systematic involvement of the population concerned, or organizations of the major actors, after identifying the key actors in each and every environmental issue.
2. Increase the awareness about the sources of pollution. Launch information campaigns and awareness programs to influence consumption patterns.
3. Introduce emission charges or fees, requiring the determination of an optimal tax level. A system of marketable permits has a number of advantages over emission fees.
4. Define environmental property rights properly.
5. Advocate the pollution prevention pays concept to encourage an integral approach to pollution.
6. Move from regulation to incentives, responsibilization and conscientization.
7. Prevent unnecessary pollution and internalize environmental cost.
8. Promote participation of potential victims of environmental degradation.
9. Use alternative technologies, which are environmentally friendly and energy efficient.

The annual report of the Rotterdam area environmental authority (Milieudienst Rijnmond) in the Netherlands does not publish data on pollution by individual companies. However, it does publish a list of companies about which the population complained most often. The people mainly complained about bad smells, something everybody can assess.

5. RECENT DUTCH ENVIRONMENTAL POLICIES

The following measures are implemented to limit environmental damage in the industrial sector in the Netherlands:

a. The preparation of a code of conduct for the execution of covenants (voluntary agreements with a target group) between government and industry.
b. Guidelines for determining environmental priorities by enterprises and the institutions giving permission for production.
c. Special attention for free riders, enterprises that profit from environmental policies without being active themselves.
d. Improved information dissemination by setting up an organization for this purpose and by using branch organizations.
e. Intensification of energy saving and policies to prevent climate change.
f. Consultation with target groups on acidification to prepare measures to reduce the emission of nitrates (in line with the covenants and expected implementation by the year 2000).
g. Reinforce waste prevention interventions through a branch approach using the methods of PRISMA (Project Industrial Successes with Waste Management)
h. Environmental policies for specific products.

The Dutch approach of reaching negotiated environmental agreements is very different from how other countries impose environmental regulation. In China the system is characterized as 'command and control'. However, in many countries covenants have become more and more important. According to the WSJE the Dutch decided they would have needed an army to legally enforce their environmental plan. So the government is now emphasizing environmental 'covenants' (19 January 1994). Under these covenants companies voluntarily pledge to reduce their emissions to certain levels within a specified period. Enforcement remains in the hands of eight 50-member regional inspectorates 'which are not expected to grow much anytime soon' according to the newspaper.

The metal industry signed one covenant at the end of 1991. This group of 32 big industries (responsible for 95 percent of the emissions) employs more than 27 000 people and now takes its own responsibility for the environment. Both sides (government and industry) are quite happy with the covenant. The industry considers they get more flexibility in executing the covenant, while the government considers monitoring of covenants easier than implementing (and controlling) environmental laws. Covenants can concern a branch or sub-sector of industry, or a specific product. As early as 1985 it was for example decided not to produce batteries with mercury oxide any more. The covenants are linked to a permit system, which defines detailed emission standards for each industrial site. The system is administered and monitored by local bodies.

In the decade after signing the first covenant 52 agreements have been reached in the Netherlands. 18 concerned the environmental quality of products, eight concerned emissions of the production process and 26 the saving of energy. Subsequent agreements concerned specific industries such as the paper, leather, meat processing, rubber and plastic products industries. Eventually an agreement would be reached with all 14 industrial sub-sectors distinguished in the Netherlands, such as the chemical, wood, graphic and metal industry. One of the advantages of the covenants is that there will be social control by members of the group. Hence free riding becomes less easy.

In 2001 issues like climate change and bio-diversity became more and more important. A long way from the original concern about the negative environmental impact of fertilizers in the 1960s! The change of ideas went via the pessimistic report of the Club of Rome to ideas on sustainable development. After the UN Conference on the Environment and Development (UNCED) in Rio de Janeiro, the definition of sustainability of the Brundland report became more generally supported: 'we should not use the environment at the expense of future generations'.

6. ENVIRONMENTAL PROBLEMS IN URBAN ASIA

Europe is not the only continent with environmental problems. Travelers in Asia mention as examples of urban pollution: traffic congestion in Bangkok, air pollution in New Delhi and flooding in Dhaka. The following urban environmental issues are on the so-called Brown agenda (Bartone et al., 1994): lack of a safe water supply; sanitation and sewerage problems; drainage problems; inadequate solid and hazardous waste collection and management; uncontrolled emissions from factories, cars and low-grade domestic fuels; accidents linked to congestion and overcrowding; and the degradation of environmentally sensitive lands; as well as the interrelationships between these problems.

Environmental issues tend to be aggravated by a rapidly growing population in the urban areas and they tend to increase with the level of economic development. In Asia, more than in other continents, one feels the impact of the large number of people and the very rapid economic growth on the environment.

Environmental problems also have a lot to do with poverty. ADB (1994: 192) rightly mentions substandard housing (slums), squatters (illegal settlements), no access to drinking water, no daily garbage collection and no human waste disposal systems as indicators of poverty.

A number of special problems hinder the solution of urban environmental problems. Because of these special problems the discussion about urban environmental problems is sometimes confusing and the responsibility for tackling these problems is not always clear. There are several reasons why the environment is not as prominent on the agenda as it should be:

1. The classification of environmental issues is also not always unambiguous. Sometimes environmental issues are classified in a sectoral way:

- Urban pollution, due to the industrial sector;
- Pollution due to transportation;
- Pollution due to different sources of energy used in the households or the industrial sector.

Sometimes the issues are classified by type of pollution: air pollution, water pollution and land pollution. Others classify pollution by effects, such as: affecting the health of people; affecting the productivity of people; threatening permanent damage to the urban ecosystem; and those resulting in a low quality of urban life.

It means water as an environmental problem may mean the lack of a good urban water supply system, a poor water drainage system, the problem of ponds (standing water allows mosquitoes to breed for example) or the problem of the lack of clean surface water. Clearly different institutions may be involved in all the four cases distinguished, ranging from the water company to the health department.

2. It is not always clear, who is the responsible organization for these different environmental issues. In fact most urban authorities are organized in a sectoral way, meaning that the responsibility is spread over a number of different departments or institutions, as shown in the case of drinking water before and for other examples below.
3. Different actors are involved in the effort to tackle urban environmental problems: the national or local authorities, the population, entrepreneurs and organizations of people (for example NGOs) or of entrepreneurs. They need to be reached in different ways and may have to cooperate in a way that is new to them.
4. Then there are many different ways to achieve a better environment, ranging from regulation to incentives, from government involvement to involving NGOs and from imposing taxes to changing the habits and attitudes of the population, entrepreneurs or government officials. Choices are not always made and the effectiveness of different approaches is not always clear.
5. Much of the literature is on rural environmental degradation (for example ADB, 1994: 49), while urban degradation and the role of industrial pollution tend to get less attention. Some developing countries considered, as became clear during the Uruguay Round (van Dijk and Sideri, 1996), the right to pollute their own environment part of their comparative advantage.

7. WHY SHOULD GOVERNMENTS INTERVENE?

Some agreement may exist on the list of urban environmental issues, but what about the solutions? Countries should set their priorities and define their standards. Subsequently the major instruments for environmental policies are: charges or taxes, variable license fees and incentive based policies. However, one could ask why should the government intervene at all?

Economists have suggested several reasons why governments need to intervene in the economic process. Market failures and external effects (like pollution) or spillovers are among them. The market does not always solve the problem, despite Coase's theorem that if the property rights would be well specified there would be no environmental problem because the parties involved would solve their problems between them. We must conclude that very few situations are satisfying the conditions of Coase (1960).

Governments wishing to do something about environmental problems can choose between: using specific regulation, applying the judicial system, introducing a system of fines or providing incentives or subsidies. Stiglitz (1988: 235) argues convincingly that when there is good information about the marginal social cost of the pollution and the fines can be adjusted to reflect those costs, then a fine system can attain a Pareto-efficient outcome. The number of economic distortions introduced is limited in that case.

The difference between using specific regulation and applying the judicial system is not very big. Usually enforcement is easier if the judicial system is involved, while regulation may be more convincing for the sector concerned, particularly if it is developed in discussions with for example the industrial branches concerned. In the Netherlands another government instrument is often stressed: information diffusion. Information dissemination becomes easier when the industries are concentrated in industrial estates or industrial districts, or when information uses branch organizations to reach the entrepreneurs.

The chemical industry is important in the Netherlands. The factories are often clustered and the industry has made large environmental investments in recent years. The chemical industry has declared its willingness to start consultation with the government on production within the frame of sustainable development in the chemical industry. Joint projects will be prepared in the framework of these consultations. The chemical industry can make significant contributions with respect to the following points:

- Researching how the use of chloride can be reduced or completely controlled;
- Analyzing environmental effects when developing new products;
- Holding international consultations to move the European chemical industry in the direction of sustainable development.

8. CONCLUSIONS

Environmental provisions for the industrial sector are important and are part of the responsibilities of an urban manager. The chances to provide such an infrastructure in the framework of an industrial estate or district are generally better, but in practice a lot remains to be done. Second, positive incentives and participation of the concerned industries in policy formulation and implementation seems to work better than just enforcing laws and regulations.

Joint efforts to reduce industrial pollution can be achieved easily in the case of a cluster of industries, because the enterprises can be contacted easily and the costs can be shared among a larger number of entrepreneurs. Evidence suggests, however, that the contrary can also happen. In Pakistan and India locating industries together has not yet been an argument to invest in environmental facilities. There is a danger that the industrial estate or park is considered so important for the local economy that the authorities will not dare to intervene. Even in the Netherlands cooperation between clustered industries is limited.

Finally, developing countries should be aware of green protectionism in the future, if they do not tackle the environmental problems of their export industries in time (Wiemann, 1996). Green protectionism may still increase in the world, if only because of all the European Union green laws. There are some 200 pieces of such legislation in Europe and many more in the pipeline. Soon this protectionism will not only concern the production, but the whole product cycle, including cleaning up what is left at the end. However, a used television will not be shipped back easily from Manila to Amsterdam (where Philips has its headquarters), to be recycled. Developing countries will have to take these additional costs into account. Finally, they should not leave cleaning up of industrial sites to donor organizations or countries, but rather provide the proper incentives to their industries at an early stage.

A number of risks with respect to introduction of environmentally sound norms for industrial production must be mentioned:

1. The international competitiveness of an industry may be harmed by excessive zeal as far as the environment is concerned. Countries not taking these measures may be able to sell a cheaper product at the world market, but may also face green protectionism. The dilemma between employment and the environment may prevent many countries from taking the necessary policy measures.
2. Industrial estates and districts have often been created long before the environmental awareness of the general public has led to the conclusion that such a park provides a good opportunity for attacking environmental problems collectively and from its inception stage.
3. The focus of many governments is on creating an enabling environment for industrial development. Consequently environmental policies may become less of a priority. In Europe the argument is often used that an individual country cannot do much if the European Union does not take action. The same may play a role in

Asia and the World Trade Organization (WTO) may have to deal with the matter, as agreed when the Uruguay Round was concluded.
4. The UNCED Rio conference has stressed the need to transfer clean technologies to Third World countries on favorable terms. It seems even more important to develop local environmentally friendly technologies, rather than importing them.

Additional environmental projects and programs are needed to solve the issues in the industrial sector. Donor countries and organizations can play an important role in the attack of urban environmental problems in Asia. The German and Dutch support to the heavily polluting leather industry of India is an example of that type of assistance. ADB (1994: 217) mentions an interesting approach to urban environmental problems stressing that the solution for Asian cities must reflect Asian problems. The next step will be to provide assistance to interested developing countries, as suggested by the ADB and promised by the developed countries during the UNCED Rio conference.

Urban managers will have a problem to define their own environmental policies, because these policies are often formulated at higher levels of government. In that case their role is limited to implementing these policies and supervising to what extent the agreed environmental norms are not violated. Good consultation of urban managers by higher levels of government is necessary. They are the experts that can give feedback on the experiences with implementing such policies at the urban level.

NOTES

1. Key terms of flexible specialization concept are:
- Multi-purpose equipment and innovation, skilled labor, with an innovative mentality use general purpose equipment to produce whatever is in demand.
- Clusters of enterprises or small firm communities (industrial districts), the seedbed for an exchange of ideas. Besides that physical nearness facilitates the exchange of ideas, it also makes the development of institutions and their interventions more easy and effective.
- Interaction/networking, the whole set of subcontracting and collaboration efforts between small enterprises and between smaller and larger ones.
- Collective efficiency, the result of the physical presence nearby of other innovative producers.
2. The agreement in the framework of a covenant sets a stringent timetable for achieving pollution abatement targets. They now exist for over 200 substances in the Netherlands, with the intention of bringing the economy towards sustainability (OECD, 1999).

8. Financing Options for Urban Infrastructure in India

1. OPTIONS FOR FINANCING URBAN INFRASTRUCTURE

What are the options for an urban manager to finance the necessary investments in urban infrastructure? In particular what are financing options for roads, wastewater treatment and sanitation or power generation? The issue will be illustrated for two Indian states (Gujarat and Karnataka) and a program to link local governments and capital markets will be discussed. All local government bodies in India could eventually be linked up to capital markets (van Dijk, 1999b). This requires for most local governments a substantial improvement of their municipal accounting and other financial management system reforms, which will also be discussed.

There are usually several options to finance urban infrastructure. The major ones are listed in Table 8.1, but we will deal with issuing bonds mainly in this chapter. It may not be efficient for the municipalities individually to issue bonds, but some organization could do it for them, to pass on the money in the forms of loans for bankable infrastructure projects. State Level Financial Institutions (SLFIs) currently function as an intermediary between the local governments and the capital market (van Dijk, 2004a).

The difference between using a Bond Bank (indirect issuing of bonds) and direct issuing of bonds by local governments will be presented. The latter model is known as the United States model and that country supports introducing this approach in India. A good functioning SLFI (for example the Karnataka Urban Infrastructure Development Finance Corporation or KUIDFC) can be used as a model of how such a Bond Bank would function. In Gujarat for the contrast, at present no institution seems to play the role of an intermediary, providing loans to local governments and issuing bonds on their behalf to allow them to invest in infrastructure.[1]

2. FINANCIAL MANAGEMENT SYSTEM REFORM

Decentralization requires more local revenues. However, the need for financial reform at the municipal level should be mentioned as a condition if municipalities want to qualify for loans to finance their infrastructure. Decentralization is the trend, but the financial means also need to be available at lower levels of government to carry out the tasks assigned to them. These means are often lacking. A solid and sound financial management system should comprise an improved municipal accounting system, but also a better budgeting system and budgetary control, improved internal control systems, internal audit systems and modern data processing facilities. A number of reforms at the municipal level are necessary for example to qualify for support in the framework of an urban infrastructure project in Andhra Pradesh (Box 8.1).

The Andhra Pradesh Urban Services for the Poor (APUSP) program supports the decentralization process in India because the finance made available under the program goes to cities. At the same time the state formulates clear conditions concerning the required reforms at the municipal level. Cities wanting to benefit have to reform their urban management (see Box 8.1). These cities will have to prove to be willing to do something for their poor, to be ready to put order in their financial situation and they have to put all these intentions on paper. The program supported by British development cooperation (DFID), and similar programs supported by the Asian Development Bank and the World Bank in Karnataka, show that development cooperation, which until now was often used to help people not benefitting from the development of the economy, can also be used to stimulate private initiative to invest in infrastructure.

Table 8.1 Instruments for infrastructure finance

From more traditional finance	To more alternative finance
Loans or bonds	Microcredit to finance water connections
Municipal Infrastructure Development Funds, for example	
	Rotating savings and credit associations (ROSCAs) to link traditional savings with credit
• Investment/capital funds	
• Trust fund	Private sector involvement
• Endowment fund	Project finance
BOT (Build Operate Transfer)	Design, Finance, Build and Operate (DFBO) and ROT (Rehabilitation Operate Transfer)
Subsidized entry fees	
Higher levels of government financed out of general or specific tax revenues	Hedging (futures/options) to cover risks
State Level Finance Institutions	Pooled Finance Development Fund

> **BOX 8.1 REFORMS AT THE MUNICIPAL LEVEL TO QUALIFY FOR FINANCIAL SUPPORT**
>
> a. Improved financial systems, such as a better budgeting and accounting system. In particular the introduction of double accounting (going from cash based to an accrual-based system) and of cost centers.
> b. Improvement of the planning capacity, resulting in the preparation of a Municipal Action Plan for Poverty alleviation (MAPP). The population needs to be consulted and involved in the formulation and execution stage of the project (participatory planning and execution).
> c. Improvement of the project preparation and appraisal capacity.
> d. Reform the municipal finance system to generate suitable indicators allowing a comparative assessment of the financial capabilities of the municipality.
> e. Setting up a monitoring and evaluation system, which generates information on the extent to which the activities undertaken are actually benefitting the urban poor.
> f. Improved personnel management and human resource development Cooperation with the program to achieve human resource development at the municipal level is required.
> g. A clear delineation of tasks and responsibilities of the nominated executives and elected bodies.
> h. A plan for the operation and maintenance of the urban infrastructure, resulting in improved maintenance of assets.
> i. Improved cost recovery for the services provided.
> j. Improved management of service delivery.
> k. Restructuring of Andhra Pradesh Urban Finance and Infrastructure Development Corporation.

User fees directly related to the service provided are to be preferred over general taxes. To achieve repayment people need to perceive a relation between their payment and the service concerned. In the same way real repayment to the State or National level is better than repayment through deduction from future loans or grants. This requires the authority to raise fees, or increase taxes and often necessitates a reform of municipal finances: to be able to pay for the infrastructural activities that a city now has to undertake. Introducing reforms at the municipal level, improving the accounting standards of all Indian local governments and developing uniform financial reporting standards will take time, but are necessary to meet the increasing demand for urban infrastructure.

3. THE NECESSARY ACCOUNTING REFORMS

Good governance requires a good basic accounting system and financial reporting. Local governments need budgets and to prepare them they need to take decisions where they want to go. There is the complication that most municipalities in India are still using cash accounting systems. The disadvantage of this system is that debts are not reported and that rating agencies require more time to provide a rating if the municipality is accounting on a cash basis. This is an argument to move to more modern accounting methods, for example accrual accounting, even if the state governments continue with cash accounting.[2]

The financial sector may not really care whether the customer has accrual or fund-based accounting. In the Indian situation the banks are at present only interested in providing finance to the five major Municipal Corporations in India. However, with the existing accounting system it takes four to five months to assess the financial system of local governments. Gaining access to capital markets requires more than just moving to accrual accounting. The change also requires training people at the state level, training people at the local level and involving chartered accountants. It is a good occasion to check on all assets and to see that all properties are brought into the tax net. Local government finance reporting is meant for very different users, ranging from the local SLFI to ADB and from the World Bank to the Housing and Urban Development Corporation (HUDCO), or a commercial bank.

At the moment no one asks a municipality for a balance sheet except for the ADB and HUDCO. Municipal councilors often do not know what the numbers mean. If the president of the Municipal Council would also ask for it, then there is an incentive for the people doing the daily management of the reformed system to provide this information. Local governments should require accounts that give the information they need. This requires training and consultancies, but there are a number of problems, which keep coming back. In the first place training and consultancies tend to be one time things and improved accounting is only useful in a different organizational context where people value information. Second, local councilors also need to be trained in which information they should ask for at what moment in time. Such training would contribute to local ownership of the improved system.

Before a financial statement can be issued all information has to be available. Second, there are often poor and inappropriate procedures; there is a lack of basic records and no information on fixed assets and long-term liabilities. Sometimes there is no property register, or the register has not been updated since 1975. It is impossible to produce the final result before such a register would be in place.

Another problem is that the personnel at the municipal level tend to change jobs quite often. The incoming officials are often not trained and if someone who is familiar with the system leaves its use will stop. One municipality in Gujarat has not produced a single financial statement in ten years. It would take two to three years to implement what TCS-IHS (2000) has recommended. The basic new accounting model looks very different from the budget format that local governments are using.

They have to be taught to start all over again. At the moment there is no transition strategy: who will carry on this work for the next four to five year? Who will pay for it? The State government will have to provide incentives because otherwise the local government will build up resistance to change and just forget about it.[3]

Some problems can be solved, however, if an appropriate accounting system is designed. The basic accounting model is a fund accounting model used in the Netherlands, the UK and the USA. However, there are some differences. One, a government is a not for profit organization. This has implications for the type of information and the order. Second, the purposes for which you report are different; and finally the basic structure of urban local government finance is different.

Local governments are free to use funds for statutory purposes such as street lightening, etc. Some resources can be spent by law or government order, or because of a contract. Financial support from higher levels of government has to be spent in a prescribed manner. These expenditures are reported in a special revenue fund. Because the envisaged infrastructure investment project may be the most important thing for the whole municipality it may require the creation of a separate fund, which is almost run as a private corporation. The books show what is available for expansion and one can follow closely what is available for daily operations. The recommendation for Indian local governments is to set up the general fund and make it operate for the commissioner and councilors so that they have increasingly better information to monitor their budget for their existing responsibilities. The general fund shows you which funds are currently available and once the information on the fixed assets and long-term debt are available the balance sheet can be produced.

4. THE ROLE OF THE PRIVATE SECTOR

An important issue is what can be the role of the private sector in infrastructure development? The Indian government creates and has created SLFIs, which will eventually compete with the private sector, unless further privatizations are carried out as we have recommended (van Dijk, 2004a). In many states the lack of project preparation capacity is the real issue. If enough good urban infrastructure projects would be prepared, and real 'cost recovery' would be introduced, financing through the private sector, and through international capital flows would come forward, in particular in a situation where the rate of interest is relatively high and state governments are often quite willing to provide guarantees for repayment of the loans or bonds. That situation should not be continued once real commercial infrastructure projects are prepared as is already happening in Rajasthan State for example by PDCOR (the Project Development Corporation of Rajasthan).

It is good to stimulate the involvement of private financial institutions for infrastructure urban development. In the course of our research we gradually became convinced that governments could not do a number of the things they did in the past (Roth, 1989). This certainly applies for complicated and expensive infrastructure, which also needs to be maintained afterwards. The government does not have the money, but should also not be involved heavily in infrastructure development, but rather create the conditions for private sector involvement. At the same time it may be necessary to strengthen and leverage certain existing government organizations, in particular if they monitor the process of private sector involvement.

India will have to choose between the dominant European model of Bond Banks and the dominant USA system of each city issuing bonds for urban infrastructure. Although India may be big enough to try both! Because of the 74th Constitutional Amendment local government and higher levels of government have become equal partners. To make that real, local governments need to have the financial information to allow them to be an equal partner. We also suggest to use to the maximum different 'user charges', local taxes, intergovernmental income transfers and possible contributions of the private sector.

With the introduction of the City Challenge Fund (CCF) in India a new approach is emerging, which is not replacing the capital market.[4] The Challenge Fund approach tries to bring about the necessary reforms at the municipal level and promote project preparation qualities to prepare local governments for eventually submitting themselves real financially sound infrastructure proposals to financial institutions. The CCF is a novel approach, probably very much fit for the bigger cities, which may have access to the capital markets already (for example Ahmedabad through its bond issue). The question is to what extent the smaller cities would also benefit from it? They may have more problems to come up with competitive proposals. However, the preparation window of the CCF may allow them to make a start with the reform process and access more funds in a second round. Local governments in states that have already similar projects, like Andhra Pradesh Urban Services for the Poor (APUSP, 1998) will find it easier to prepare a proposal combining the reform and infrastructure plans.

5. INVESTMENTS IN URBAN DEVELOPMENT IN INDIA

There is a clear need for investments in urban development in India, given its population growth and increasing urbanization. The required funding for urban infrastructure has been estimated (Expert group, 1996). Increasingly efforts are made to tap private funds, but a number of conditions need to be satisfied before cities can access the capital market. The efforts to help local governments in India to obtain infrastructure range from creating municipal infrastructure development funds to establishing SLFIs. In this section some efforts made by Indian municipalities to finance urban infrastructure will be reviewed.

According to Satyanaranya (2006) only 50 percent of the population in urban areas had water taps within the compound. Approximately 65 percent of households had some sort of water facility, be it a tap, well or hand pump within the compound. The remaining 35 percent of the population depended on outside sources. On the sanitation front, 61 percent of households had access to either pit latrines or water closets.

State governments are responsible for urban development and local governments are considered to be responsible for water, sanitation and sewerage. The 74th Constitutional Amendment in India promotes decentralization and suggests strengthening and establishing SLFIs to help states to finance their investments. A number of State Level Infrastructure Development Corporations have been created in India since 1992.[5] Their mandate is to provide financial assistance (loans and advances) to Urban Local Bodies (ULB) for financing infrastructure and services.[6] The SLFIs were often used to channel Central Government grant money to municipalities. Later also HUDCO loans were channeled through them. Private or semi-public institutions have indicated that they are willing to finance urban infrastructure.[7]

6. FINANCIAL INSTITUTIONS REFORM AND EXPANSION PROJECT VERSUS THE BOND BANK APPROACH

Municipal bond markets are a growing market in developing countries and a convenient way to finance urban infrastructure. The United States Agency for International Development (USAID, 1996) intended to help Indian cities to prepare projects in such a way that bonds can be issued in the American capital market, using a partial USAID guarantee. In principle water supply, sewerage, roads, land development, education and health facilities could be financed under the FIRE project (FIRE, 1996) supported by the USA. The formula is that each city would issue bonds itself.

Table 8.2 Example of a Bond Bank: the Bank of Dutch Municipalities

History and approach	Examples: sectoral interventions
Incorporated in 1914: a financial specialist of and for the public sector, such as municipalities, provinces, their joint local authority undertakings, regional police forces, housing associations, education & health care organizations and businesses allied to the public sector The BNG being a triple A institution pays a low rate for the bonds it issues	Loans for housing programs
	Investments in waste treatment
	Cash management for local authorities
	Financing sport facilities in municipalities
	Arranging project finance for major renovation of business park projects
	Streamlining rent payments for housing associations

Source: BNG (1999).

Bonds have been finding favor with Indian borrowers and investors since 1994. In that year the primary market issuance by Indian companies exceeded the volume of offerings on the Indian share market (*Financial Times*, 28 April 1995). However, if the SLFIs issue the bonds it would not require the individual municipalities issuing bonds, but a state level organization would do it for them. This is just like a Bond Bank in the USA or like the Bank of the Dutch Municipalities (BNG) in the Netherlands. Bond Banks issue bonds and pass on the money in the forms of loans for bankable infrastructure projects to the municipalities. The USA Bond Bank is described in Petersen (1999) and the Dutch BNG model in Table 8.2.

The BNG centers on lending and project financing, often very long term. It stopped being just another capital market institution in 1989 when it became a full credit institution subject to the full supervision of the Dutch Central Bank. In 1994 BNG was awarded the Triple A status by no fewer than three credit rating agencies. Total assets are approximately US$ 500 billion. It has 300 staff members and just one office. The key to BNG's success is the knowledge of municipalities it has built up over the years and the rule in the Netherlands is that municipalities are not allowed to run a deficit, otherwise they will loose their financial autonomy. Ninety percent of monetary transfers between central government bodies, semi-government bodies and municipalities take place through the BNG.

7. FINANCING INFRASTRUCTURE IN GUJARAT

There are important differences per state in India as far as legislation and the type of intermediary financial institution that has been created are concerned. An institution similar to KUIDFC does not exist in the state Gujarat for example. The Gujarat Infrastructure Development Board (GIDB) is the state institution to facilitate investments in advanced infrastructure such as ports, electricity and major roads. It is a high level nodal agency, falling directly under the Chief Minister of the state, but is not necessarily working with local governments.

In the case of Gujarat urban project development and project financing activities are best suited to the private sector. The state could learn from the PDCOR, which is a relatively small outfit with the majority of shareholders being private sector financial institutions, which prepares projects and links them to potential investors. The private sector is better able to package and pool important projects, while the government could take the necessary policy reform initiatives. State governments are in a better position to push local governments to adopt the necessary reforms and to undertake the project preparation activities. The State's role should be enabling, deploying strategies to ensure confluence of the financial institutions needs with the local government offerings.

Infrastructure development in Gujarat is hindered by limited borrowing capacities rather than by limited fund availability. It can also be noted that restrictive municipal laws need amendment to allow private sector participation and capital. Finally, there is a lack of contract documentation for evolving project vehicles with private sector participation. There are a number of challenges concerning infrastructure in the state and the sector seems to be ripe with opportunities.

There is a certain sector preparedness in Gujarat. In this state the biggest city, Ahmedabad, has already gained experience with obtaining a credit rating and issuing bonds to finance water and sanitation projects. Also several toll roads have been built with the help of the private sector and private financial institutions are eager to get more involved in infrastructure. The State government has prepared and launched an Infrastructure 2000 Plan, which gives a vision and a strategy (Gujarat, 2000) and the Government of Gujarat prepared a note on regulatory framework for water. The state was the first one in the country to draft a BOT law and has experience with giving concessions to the private sector. Inherent is the entrepreneurial spirit, which can be proven by the number of private consultants and specialized NGOs in this field.

Accessing the market for financing urban water and sanitation has caught on in the country, since it was promoted under the Financial Institutions Reform and Expansion (FIRE) project since 1996. The advantages of market access are ushering in fiscal discipline in operations of the service delivery, additional financing sources, and creation of incentives for better performance. The AMC (an intermediary in charge of managing the core of the city) was the first one to access the capital market through direct access through the issue of municipal bonds in 1998. Since then, 12 more municipal bond issues aggregating to Rs 12 700 million (US$ 270 million) have been issued in India to finance infrastructure. The Government of India provided an impetus to this process through tax exemption for municipal bonds in 1999. Models for enhanced services to the urban poor are gradually emerging in the country. They include demand creation and institutionalization of citywide strategies such as the slum-networking program in Ahmedabad.[8]

8. FINANCING INFRASTRUCTURE IN KARNATAKA

Bangalore, the capital of Karnataka state, has the Bangalore Water Supply and Sewerage Board (BWSSB) which is responsible for the provision and management of water supply and sewerage services in the metropolitan area of Bangalore. Only one-third of the metropolitan area is covered with a piped sewerage system and there is treatment facility for only two-thirds of the wastewater generated. The remaining wastewater still goes untreated into surface waters. In comparison to sewerage, about 52 percent of the total area is provided with a well-developed water supply system.

BWSSB is undertaking various projects to enhance its water supply and sewerage network and improve upon the services offered. Caution is required when considering adequacy figures, as there remains an important degree of qualitative judgment involved in deciding on the adequacy of a particular type of sanitation technology for a specific city. The choice of the technology to be used is largely determined by the size of the population to be served, the required investment and whether the commercial private sector or an NGO/CBO is involved. Another issue is that of the integrity and effective operation of the constituting components in the chain of conveyance, treatment and disposal. This issue can best be illustrated by the Bangalore case, where the capacity of wastewater treatment plants approximately equals the volume of waterborne sewage, but remains largely unused because of the huge losses in the sewer system.

An array of corporate and community approaches is being increasingly used to deal with these issues. Initiatives by CBOs are assisted by large NGOs. Likewise, in Bangalore, a remarkable 15 percent of the population make use of communal toilets that have been set up both by local government and by NGOs. The latter also operate these facilities on a 'user pays' principle. In Bangalore, the corporate sector has also participated in the improvement of urban management and subsidized entry fees as practiced in the water and sanitation sector. The BWSSB completely subsidizes the access charges for the urban poor and is moving towards individual facilities in the case of water supply. The consumption charges remain the same for all users in the city. An overview of some creative financial activities in the water and sanitation sector is given in Table 8.3. The table indicates that they are not always successful. Satyanaranya (2006) gives a number of reasons why such projects may fail.

Table 8.3 Failed private sector participation efforts in Bangalore

---

BOT Project for Cauvery Bulk Water Supply. Initiated in 1997 and abandoned.

ROT (Rehabilitation Operate Transfer) of existing system. Initiated in 1997 and abandoned.

BOT for two sewage treatment plants (two separate projects). Initiated in 1997 and abandoned.

Source: Satyanarayana (2006).

However, Bangalore has been able to issue bonds to finance the necessary investments. This required good accounting methods, which increase transparency. Hence the population, the councilors, the donors and the ADB all want to see better accounting methods used. That is exactly the reason why so many initiatives to introduce improved accounting methods have already been taken in India. TCS-IHS (2000) has detailed the procedures for Karnataka. The Institute of Chartered Accountants of India (ICAI) plays a crucial role in working out the details and sanctioning the proposals for new accounting systems. Also there is a need for involving regulators at different levels of government.

Direct access to financial markets will be applicable only for large cities in Karnataka state. Small and medium cities will need to pool their resources to attract capital and reduce the transaction costs. Satyanarayana (2006) suggests in these cases that based on the experience of USA Municipal Bond Market, USAID and the FIRE project pooled finance is an interesting option. The first pooled deal concerned 14 small cities in Tamil Nadu, with a credit enhancement through a Development Credit Authority (DCA) guarantee from USAID. The second pooled finance deal is expected to follow suit, providing another eight cities in the Bangalore Metropolitan Area in Karnataka with a similar type of credit. Meanwhile, the Indian Government is in the process of establishing a Pooled Finance Development Fund at national level to provide support to states for credit enhancement and grants for reforms. The case for a pooled finance framework also for peri-urban and semi-urban settlements is strong, as demonstrated in Karnataka and in other states (Tamil Nadu).

Bangalore is considering the involvement of the private sector in the water sanitation sector. Negotiations for a management contract were initiated in early 2001 for two pilot areas of 1 million people each. The contract covers operation and maintenance to improve the service quality and efficiency. Vivendi and Northumbrian Lyonnaise International jointly submitted a proposal in 2001. Negotiations followed in 2002, but collapsed in 2003. The Chief Minister at that time kept saying that he would be interested to involve the private sector more and a leakage detection and reduction contract for a pilot area was awarded to Thames Water in April 2003.

Satyanaranya (2006) notes that the Government of Karnataka is currently working on the development of urban water policy and a pooled finance framework for 8 cities in the Bangalore metropolitan area. There are certain lessons that can be learnt from the sewerage and sanitation sector development through various projects in the past:

- Administration and coordination shortcomings have resulted in investments in additional capital works for water supply ignoring complimentary investments needed for sewerage systems, sewage treatment plants (STPs) and recycling.
- There is a lack of coordination between BWSSB and other institutions as a result of which storm water drainage and sewage cannot be managed in a comprehensive manner.
- The absence of a comprehensive master plan of the city resulted in sectional development of Bangalore and non-integration of sewerage with other developmental schemes.
- There is a need to link or ratify the master plan as a component of comprehensive development plan. Even though in the present scenario, the Bangalore Development Authority (BDA) is responsible for the City Master Plan, the BDA should be under the overall control of the city and its elected body.
- Water supply, wastewater treatment and sanitation need to be dealt with in a more integrated way, involving more actors and private capital.

Obtaining the finance is only one of the worries of an urban manager, using it properly is another challenge.

9. CONCLUSIONS ON THE FINANCIAL OPTIONS

There is a need for more urban infrastructure in Third World cities. For example the urban population is interested in getting sanitation facilities, although the people may not be very much concerned about the treatment of wastewater or the necessary off-plot sanitation facilities. This lack of concern usually means a limited willingness to pay and a negative attitude towards involving private parties because people expect to be obliged to pay higher prices. Governments need to provide information to explain possible advantages of involving private partners if this is the way the authorities want to go. Otherwise one risks delays in the implementation stage of the project because different stakeholders oppose implementation.

The cases in Karnataka and Gujarat state show that an array of public, private and civil society actors and individual households take on responsibilities for the provision of infrastructural services. In the case of sanitation many developing countries have opted for on-site solutions such as septic tanks and pit latrines. In these cases it may be a question of infiltration in groundwater or there may be a discharge to an open watercourse. Too often one finds uncontrolled disposal of the sludge and no institution taking the responsibility.

Second it can be learned that the degree of private sector involvement varies from city to city. It ranges from outsourcing in the public mode to a concession to a private firm or a user cooperative. However, NGOs may also play a role, for example in Bangalore, in activities like solid waste collection sanitation and public awareness programs. We have also learned that the link with some kind of cost recovery system is extremely important. The underlying assumption is that people are willing to pay for water and other services if they know they will get them and that they will get good quality services. Only then there is a chance that a cash flow will be generated by the investment, which allows the local government to supply the service on a sustainable basis and to repay loans or service bonds. An effective and equitable tariff system for urban infrastructure is a real priority in most countries studied.

The main issue coming out of these two case studies is the division of responsibilities between the government and the private sector. Ideally the government sector would set the framework. In practice there is often market failure and the government gets involved and finds it difficult to pull out. Second, the type and scale of technology is important and has consequences for the management and financing water and sanitation facilities. The larger the scale of the projects, the bigger the financial implications. In that case governments will also be more inclined to involve the private sector. The private sector may find it easier to arrange the financing and may be better equipped to manage the facilities.

It is also desirable to think of water supply, sanitation and wastewater in an integrated way. The cost of an integrated solution will be much lower than a solution at a later stage by a separate institution based on different cost recovery system. In big cities the integration between dealing with wastewater and offsite sanitation is often the case. However, from the Indian case we also learned that this tends to be limited to the area of the Municipal Corporation, leaving the rest of the city to the development authorities or even district authorities, who tend to have less money and no money raising authority.

The conclusion about private sector involvement in urban infrastructure activities (telecommunication for example) is that the development of new technologies, combined with unbundling and more competition has led to much lower prices for consumers (van Dijk, 2003a). The government would still play an important role as the supervisor, who would see to it that prices remain affordable, in particular for the poor and that the quality of the services remains at a certain level. India has launched some interesting initiatives to finance urban infrastructure and may be able to try different models at the same time: the CCF, the fully-fledged SLFI in Karnataka and the network-based approach to preparing and financing infrastructure projects in Gujarat. A good regulator for infrastructure will be necessary, applying the principles of regulatory economics (for example Viscusi et al., 2000). Under these circumstances viable and sustainable infrastructure finance institutions should be possible, like in so many other countries.

NOTES

1. A distinction should be made between the general obligation bonds, carrying full faith and credit of the issuing government and revenue bonds, which rely on specified sources of revenues from facilities and services which are financed out of the bond proceeds and are usually issued by specific service or functional authorities. The latter (revenue bonds) require user charges to generate the cash flow necessary to service the bond.
2. What is needed at the state level in India is a Coordination committee with all state agencies involved, for example under guidance of the Urban Development Department (UDD). The Committee should establish the accounting standards for local government.
3. The preparation of the opening balance is a well-known problem. It is sometimes relatively easy if a good property register exists. Otherwise there is a need for procedures, there are problems of identification and sometimes legal experts have to come in, or the State government needs to formulate policies.
4. The Government of India has decided to establish such a demand driven centrally sponsored CCF to help municipalities to finance their infrastructure. The CCF will assist cities to achieve creditworthiness through structural reform. It will draw from

experiences with Challenge Funds worldwide. The fund will assist cities and larger class 1 towns to address the major challenges they face. The CCF will create a competitive process, where cities indicate policy reforms and submit model projects. The CCF is intended as a catalyst for a new generation of urban reform activities that focus on large scale restructuring of existing governance arrangements, of fiscal systems and current urban management practices. On the basis of a number of pre-specified criteria the projects eligible for finance will be selected periodically.
5. A number of states have created Urban Infrastructure Financing Corporations or trust funds. In Tamil Nadu for example this fund has been created with support from the World Bank and functions at 'arm length' of the state government. In other states this is often not yet the case.
6. The Asian Development Bank helped to restructure ULBs in three Indian states (TCS-IHS, 2000).
7. Three other banks (IL&FS, ICICI and IFCI) also issued bonds, which would be used mostly for infrastructure.
8. In the case of Ahmedabad, the Municipal Corporation has been implementing a Slum-networking project in several settlements with the partnership of communities and contributions from industry groups. The Corporation has been playing a pro-active role in developing these partnerships and streamlining, simplifying procedures for implementation of community level projects. The Corporation is currently in the process of scaling up of this activity to all low-income settlements in the city.

9. The Use of Information Technology in Urban Management

1. INTRODUCTION

The Urban management course at Erasmus University constitutes an intensive professional education package in urban management combining theory and practice with the latest information technology (IT) innovations to solve different issues, such as planning, land registration and the monitoring of public works. A module on basic Geographical Information Systems (applications of GIS) and the integration and application of Urban Information Systems (UIS) has been taught for some years.

A lot of experience has been gained recently with the use of IT and UIS to deal with issues ranging from health care to transport control. The need to construct a common database, to keep it up to date and to use it in a variety of applications, should be stressed. The challenge is to design an integrated UIS, which allows urban decision makers to preview the consequences of their decisions and to monitor the results of implemented policies and investments. Such an integrated UIS will not only represent a powerful educational tool, but will also be of great practical value for urban managers.

International organizations, such as the World Bank have made available state-of-the-art information and communication technology (ICT) facilities to a number of developing countries. Efforts are made to develop educational and training packages that are suitable for use in distance learning (DL, for example through the PoWer project at UNESCO-IHE Institute for Water Education in Delft the Netherlands). A large number of institutions worldwide in the field of international education, sometimes in collaboration with industry, are making efforts to develop training packages and make them available digitally. Some of these packages can be also used for training urban managers, while others may have to be adjusted for that purpose.

New technologies and means of communication have become available for urban managers in developed and developing countries. This changes the functioning of the urban economy, of cities and of urban management (Castells and Hall, 1994). This also has effects on the way people communicate with authorities and the way officials and inhabitants can be trained and organized. In this chapter I will analyze what new technology combined with existing UIS (or IS for short) can mean for urban management and how different means of communication can be used in urban management. The use of computers and IS can certainly help to improve urban management. Access to digital data allows more transparency and more participatory decision making in urban affairs by inhabitants and other urban actors. Computers also facilitate the provision of training and information to urban managers and the population at large.

For a long time development workers were not very enthusiastic about using computers in developing countries except for the most evident things. The technology was considered too capital-intensive and vulnerable. Urban planning and management traditionally did not make much use of computers except maybe for producing a map, for preparing a computer-based infrastructure survey, or for preparing a text. There are some interesting new possibilities for applications of IT in urban planning and management, which justify rethinking the issue. As early as February 1995 The journal *Urban Age* came out with an interesting issue on Information and cities (Vol. 3, No. 1).

ICT ranges from electronic mailing (e-mail), video- or teleconferencing, intranet and internet, distance learning to ICT-based discussion platforms and electronic databases. A distinction can be made between computer-aided, integral management systems and the use of computers to improve the functioning of local government in single, specific fields. In the latter case one can think of improving municipal finance, or tax registration and collection, just as processing of other urban databases could be useful for tackling other urban management problems (England et al., 1985).

Three arguments can be considered to substantiate why it is interesting to look into new applications of IT for urban planning and management. First, computers can help to integrate different data sets, which would otherwise be a difficult task. Second, they can help in cases where corruption could creep in easily, since computers are objective and transparent, if properly programmed and secured. Finally, some leapfrogging may be possible with modern ICT. In this chapter some of these opportunities will be explored by describing a number of promising applications.

The problems of Third World cities are well known and are often larger than problems of cities in developed countries. This is not just because of the size of the population and a more rapidly growing urban population, but also because of a smaller formal sector, which usually generates fewer funds for local governments while a large section of the population is living below the poverty line. A different approach to these problems may be possible using IT and UIS available in many cities. IT allows us to combine different information systems. Integrated analysis of urban issues, which is then possible, can help to improve urban management and hence reduce urban problems. Utilizing these databases in a proficient way in the urban areas may be a challenge.

I will first ask the question what UIS are. Some examples of their use will be given, partially taken from the approach to physical planning in the Netherlands, and some illustrations of the use of IT in a Third World context will be given. These examples show advantages, but also allow us to identify some problems, which can be expected if local governments would opt for this approach and increasingly make use of IT-based urban planning and management.

2. WHAT IS AN UIS?

An UIS can be defined as an ensemble of discrete sets of digital data concerning all relevant aspects of a city, accessible to computer processing and analysis. Most often, such data sets are arranged in (relational) databases. In a more intuitive way an IS can be described as a collection of data, or data sets, which could be combined in an intelligent way to solve a problem related to a city. For any useful UIS to be constructed, three conditions must be fulfilled: there must be a clear idea on the purpose(s) for which to use it, balanced decisions must be made regarding what data needs to be collected, and there must be a well-defined set of precise, useful applications. If these conditions are not met, confusing and potentially harmful conclusions may be reached. It should be emphasized that the usefulness of the output of an UIS depends on the quality of the input data.

Urban managers must have an idea of what the relevant issues are and to what extent analyzing different data sets in an integrated way could help to solve these issues. Types of data, which are important for urban management, include demographic data, data on economic development, on poverty, on land ownership, health and service delivery, tax revenues, etc.

Second, a database, once generated, needs to be updated regularly. This again requires decisions on which data needs to be collected, how often and for what purpose. Criteria to be used are: usefulness of collection of such data, cost of their collection and their reliability. In practice this is a costly and time-consuming task. Many local governments change the type of information they collect regularly.

Finally, there should be clear ideas on specific applications. One such application, for example, might be a land registration system as a basis for urban planning, property tax and housing policies. Another application could be related to taxing in general. Computers may be used to identify all the assets of an inhabitant and tax him or her accordingly. Applications could also concern the monitoring of the spread of certain diseases, the effects of certain policies on target group or the impact of credit programs on the development of economic activities by poor people.

3. INFORMATION SYSTEMS AS BASIS FOR PLANNING

In this section an overview of ten applications of IT and UIS will be provided, which are listed in Box 9.1. At the end of the chapter the question will be asked: what is specific about applying UIS and IT in urban management? The short answer is that UIS and IT have become a tool for urban management if different data sets are intelligently combined to solve an urban issue. The first example concerns using IT for urban planning purposes.

BOX 9.1 APPLICATIONS OF INFORMATION TECHNOLOGY IN URBAN MANAGEMENT

1. Urban planning: planning becomes easier by using computers, but computers also allow the planners to use geographical and socioeconomic or demographic data and combine these data through GIS.
2. Social development policies: the use of IT and IS allow cities to define and implement social development policies tailored to the needs of the population and to monitor their effects.
3. Land information systems can become tools of urban management if also used for planning and social policy purposes. Computers allow an objective and transparent registration of land ownership and changes in it.
4. Participation can be promoted through IT: increased participation is possible through new technological opportunities. People can use the internet to collect information and provide feedback or household data to local authorities.
5. Monitoring locational changes: combining GIS software with data on the movement of people/businesses allows municipal authorities to monitor locational changes and to assess their urban management consequences.
6. Dealing with urban congestion becomes easier if the transport department has good IS about the traffic movements and instruments to influence them.
7. Monitoring environmental developments: data on air and water pollution can be transferred easily to a central computer, which can warn if certain thresholds are passed.
8. Other urban management applications: a number of applications, which can only be mentioned. For example, using the internet to inform small entrepreneurs about new technologies/products.
9. Single sector specific applications: in practice computers and data sets are often used for simple management purposes, such as registering the taxes or keeping track of the municipal finances.
10. Capacity building: computers provide great opportunities to train people and using computers effectively requires a lot of training.

The possibility of combining spatial and socioeconomic data through GIS can make urban planning a lot easier. If it is known how many people live and work at a certain location it becomes much easier to plan water supply, sewage disposal, waste collection and public transportation. The socioeconomic level of the relevant neighborhoods can easily be incorporated in such analyses.

Paulsson (1992) studied the use of satellites, remote sensing and GIS analysis for urban planning in the Third World. Other examples of the use of GIS in urban planning have been studied by de Bruijn (1987) and Turkstra (1998). The Dutch consultancy firm DHV used computers as early as 1972 in a 'Sites and Services' low-income housing project in Dakar for data collection and processing and in particular to organize the selection of candidates for a certain kind of housing, in an effort to make it an objective process. Also, interestingly, urban water management, with particular attention to the distribution of water between poor and middle class neighborhoods, could be improved by making use of automated systems programmed to take into account minimum water supply requirements for poor urban households (a certain quantity of water per person times the number of persons in the household).

Senter (1997) mentions three ways in which the application of GIS can be important for urban planning in developing countries. In the first place this is in background studies, in which an analysis of the problems of the city has been undertaken. De Wit (1992) uses for example GIS and remote sensing to find out how a slum neighborhood developed over time. His work deals with Bangalore, an important center of the Indian software industry. One-fifth of the 4.6 million inhabitants live in one of the 1000 or so slums or smaller irregular settlements that can be found in Bangalore. The data allows the authorities to track what the slum population has been doing (in terms of building new houses and increasing the densification) and to take initiatives concerning the most important issues identified by them in a consultation process.

GIS is also important for physical planning studies. Turkstra (1998) uses GIS to analyze the physical development in Villavicencio in Colombia. The technology helps to present several alternative development plans to improve, in this case, housing. Because of the application of GIS different scenarios for the city can be compared. He presents a trend scenario, a scenario based on higher density and one scenario combining the two approaches.

Turkstra stresses that maybe more important than the scenarios, is the insight into the problems which can be gained by the population through GIS. This is also the link with urban management. The urban manager looks at the development of the city from different points of view, aims at consulting all parties concerned and at coming up with an integrated perspective. The development of scenarios was made easier through GIS and allowed the plans to be more comprehensible and easier to discuss with the population.

Finally, GIS is important during plan implementation. The case discussed below, of monitoring urban poverty, would be a good example. One will then ask the question: what are the results of implementing the plan for the urban poor? Senter (1997) notes that in this case many data are required to be able to really monitor developments. On the one hand spatial data are needed on where people live and under which spatial and infrastructural conditions and on the other hand there is a need for socioeconomic data concerning households in that part of the city.

4. SOCIAL DEVELOPMENT POLICIES

Under this heading we can think of very different applications of IT. The focus in this section will be on urban poverty alleviation efforts and how these can be monitored better. However one could also monitor the labor market (through a labor market information system; Sparreboom, 1999). In fact, every social policy can be monitored and in this way feedback can be provided to the authorities on its effectiveness. Examples could be the monitoring of health policies or continuously following the uptake of loans in a small and micro enterprise employment program.

UIS can also be used to try to alleviate poverty, a major challenge for urban managers. Poverty is a complex phenomenon. Many factors co-determine the state of poverty in a region or a neighborhood. Appropriate IS can be used to keep track of such factors, which are often only studied in a sectoral fashion. There is normally information on health and education but not on how the activities in these sectors contribute to poverty alleviation. Using the right approaches, the monitoring of different factors can be integrated in larger IS, which – in turn – may become instrumental in defining general, integrated managerial strategies for combating poverty.

Van Dijk (1997) tries to establish the relationship between a qualitative poverty assessment and an UIS. To do so three questions need to be asked:

1. Why qualitative poverty assessments?
2. What insights do you gain from them?
3. How can you link these insights using an UIS?

First we need to know what is to be expected from an UIS. The challenge is then to see which available data can be used to answer the above questions. In the case of urban poverty, the following questions are generally put forward by the municipal authorities:

1. How many poor people are there and where do they live?
2. What is the extent of poverty in quantitative terms?
3. How serious is the problem in more qualitative terms?
4. What are the changes over time? The monitoring of developments.
5. What are the effects of policies and programs? The assessment of their impact.
6. How to measure the success of poverty consultation efforts?

The available data usually comprise a census, some household surveys and hopefully some in-depth poverty studies on the topic. The type(s) of data to be collected depend on the determination of the final properties and possibilities of the IS desired.

The UIS suitable for assessing urban poverty would in fact be a monitoring system using GIS to map the location of the poor, using socioeconomic surveys to indicate the intensity, and requiring periodic updates to monitor the developments. UIS can do more than only identifying their location. It can record the incidence of poverty related variables and measure them over time. A monitoring system can be equipped with alarms, which are triggered if certain variables attain an unacceptable value.

To build an UIS for poverty control more indicators are required than the number of poor and their degree of poverty (a measure of variation). Qualitative surveys would provide additional data on:

- Access to health, education, services, etc.;
- Employment opportunities of the poor;
- Housing and shelter information;
- The wage level of casual or day labor;
- The health conditions of the poor measured by the impact of certain diseases;
- Prices and availability of food: nutritional status of the poor;
- Health situation of children;
- School attendance;
- Family situation;
- Occurrence of misfortune, indicators of vulnerability.

Poverty is an important problem and the authorities in developing countries will have to monitor the situation of their population. Newly available technologies provide new opportunities, which need to be used to the maximum, to monitor and to integrate policies affecting the poor. An example of the latter would be a land tax system that would provide exemptions to poor households. In this example, the value of the information system is obvious: the use of GIS allows linking a certain plot to the socioeconomic status of its occupants.

There is a risk of a digital divide for certain people, as noted by a number of authors (for example van den Berg and van Winden, 2000). It requires conscious policies of urban management, to avoid large numbers of inhabitants, who would have no access to information and communication technologies and who would be excluded from certain services or from relevant information. In some of the cities van den Berg and van Winden (2000) studied, free internet services were provided in public places on an experimental basis to avoid exclusion. Local governments will have to make extra efforts to reach poor people, who need information on for example employment opportunities, on free or low priced services and on the subsidies to which they may be eligible.

Similarly, housing policies can be monitored to find out to what extent poor people benefit from them and labor exchanges can provide information about job opportunities in the city through computers and the internet (Sparreboom, 1999). Inhabitants can also use these technologies to monitor the performance of the authorities in developing or executing local development plans.

5. LAND INFORMATION SYSTEMS

Land information systems can help to find out who owns the land and how land prices develop and what the consequences are for the poor or for urban planning. A digital cadastre could become a part of a computer-aided urban management system, if also used for tax purposes. The latter would be the case if the system could be designed in such a way that the poor would pay less or no tax for the land they occupy or own, while the better off would be billed at the going rates.

A conference of the United Nations Institute for Training and Research (UNITAR, 1998) focused on the experience with urban information systems for urban management purposes in the Third World. Many Third World cities use computers, but does this improve urban management? The conference was held in Cebu in the Philippines, a city that uses GIS for land registration and for levying property tax. Corruption can be diminished; all tax rates and types of land are in the computer by owner. If a secured computer produces a tax bill for a land owner, it will be less likely that the department head, the person collecting the money, or the person paying the bill has a possibility to alter the amount to be paid.

A digital land registration system would certainly be a big step forward from the physical land registration system, which usually requires painstaking registration of all changes. It is typically a case where developing countries can do some leapfrogging, skipping a traditional technology, which is costly and outdated (Paulsson, 1992).

6. PARTICIPATION PROMOTED THROUGH IT

A number of examples can be given of promoting participation by the population in policy making through IT. An impression of the kind of policy making the available data may be used for (i.e., the purpose) can be formed during a strategic planning exercise (Baharoglu and Lepelaars, 2002). The digital city in Amsterdam the Netherlands provides internet services to all kinds of organizations. It is an example of the use of creating discussion groups, but also allowing people to vote or to make payments (Delvecchio, 1999).

Elections and registration of the changes in the urban population are highly relevant but the application of IT in this case will not be discussed.

> **BOX 9.2 ACCESS TO THE TOWN HALL IN DAKAR THROUGH INTERNET, A UNESCO SUPPORTED PROJECT**
>
> Present situation:
>
> 1. An UIS is a real need, which helps authorities to better target the problems that need to be addressed.
> 2. The project in Dakar was implemented in one out of 19 districts with the help of a local association called APESCY.
> 3. They established a grass root popular IS.
> 4. It was achieved with active participation of a part of the population, in particular young people.
> 5. They received training in using computers, which is important for them.
> 6. An urban profile has been determined by a non-municipal, local institution.
> 7. Dedicated popular information centers have been created, which allow top-down information circulation as well as a bottom-up.
> 8. A web site has been created.
> 9. Surveys were undertaken, but not yet finished.
> 10. A strategic planning exercise took place on data-harmonization for a development plan.
>
> Deliverables are:
>
> 1. A popular information system.
> 2. Trained youngsters (16 webmasters and 15 popular journalists).
> 3. A web page.
> 4. Information technology, which can be used outside the project for commercial purposes.
> 5. An example for other districts and African cities.
>
> Needs are:
>
> 1. Assistance for finishing the surveys.
> 2. Support to achieve institutionalization.
> 3. Assistance for structuring the project (see above).
> 4. A well trained GIS specialist.
> 5. External funding for a second phase.

Computers can also be used as a register for complaints and to allow the population to give feedback on urban services delivery. The use of the internet will increase participation substantially (van den Berg and van Winden, 2000).

The question these authors raise is which factors make people decide to connect to the net and how local governments can promote more intensive use of the internet for participation, information and other purposes? In Dakar, the capital of Senegal, the internet is used on an experimental basis to allow the population of one neighborhood, located far away from the center, to communicate with the Town Hall (Box 9.2). The next steps could be:

1. Institutionalize the initiative.
2. Structure the project to obtain a well-established UIS.
3. Integrate activities of the district in larger entity.
4. Make UIS a division or department of the mayor's office.
5. Let other districts of Dakar come and see, but also invite other Senegalese and West African interested parties.

The internet can help to give content to participation of the population at its most basic level (see also Nunn and Rubleske, 1997). In general the information system allows the authorities to monitor pollution and to follow the treatment of urban waste more precisely (Juppenplatz, 1991). Sensors can be put at critical points and digitally inform the authorities about air pollution, noise pollution, or concentrations of toxic substances in surface water. Integrated urban waste treatment programs can be developed to minimize the negative effects of waste on the urban environment.

BOX 9.3 RECOMMENDED USE OF COMPUTERS IN MYSORE, INDIA

1. Financial management and financial control;
2. Registration of urban expenditures and revenues;
3. Generating income from taxes and control progress;
4. Calculation of bills for drinking water;
5. Registration of information for property tax collection;
6. Release of building permits;
7. Administration of wages;
8. Inventory of city assets;
9. Registration of socioeconomic data;
10. Registration of births, deaths and illnesses;
11. Registration of public complaints and how the city has dealt with them;
12. Public grievances and follow up.

Source: Adapted from TCS-IHS (2000).

10. OTHER URBAN MANAGEMENT APPLICATIONS

One can think of many more applications, which will only be briefly mentioned here. Applications of information technology for urban management in developed countries range from creating a 'virtual town hall' (Zoetermeer in the Netherlands, for example) to registration of the movements of companies (Deventer in the Netherlands, for example). The virtual town hall can be important in developing countries where people do not easily go to the town hall to investigate matters (see the Senegalese example mentioned in Box 9.2).

Computers can also be used for the purpose of city marketing, to attract businesses, or to provide tourist and other useful information. Besides there are a number of sector specific applications, which will now be discussed.

11. SINGLE SECTOR SPECIFIC APPLICATIONS

Box 9.3 lists such sector specific applications in the case of Mysore (India). In practice, a lot of the applications of computers have been at this sectoral level. The applications listed are among the more regular applications of computers, for example to register population data, socioeconomic data or land use data at the municipal level.

12. WHAT IS SPECIFIC ABOUT IT IN URBAN MANAGEMENT?

The use of IT and UIS becomes an urban management application if different data sets are intelligently combined to solve an urban issue. The use of IS for urban management implies the combination of information in such a way that several interrelations between issues are taken into account. In cities in emerging economies the challenge lies in using UIS and IT for solving the specific problems of these cities, such as poverty, unemployment, health, congestion, pollution, planning and housing problems.

Modern information technology allows the combination of different sources of data. The kind and number of different data to be included in an UIS are dependent on the scope and type of utilization of the system. The construction of a useful UIS requires a clear view of the problems it is intended to help solve. The advantage of the use of UIS for urban management purposes is that it allows an integrated approach to urban problems. The data contained in computer-based IS can – in principle – be widely accessible to the public. As a result, urban government may be run in a more transparent fashion. In addition, the high data processing capacity and velocity of such systems is likely to contribute to the efficiency of government. Given the scale of the problems in many Third World cities these applications deserve increasing attention in the future.

The use of IT and UIS in for example Cebu and Dakar showed different but very promising applications. It can be concluded that IT and UIS can be used for dealing with a range of urban issues, such as unemployment, poverty, participation, supplying urban services, etc. The challenge is to assess how existing data from larger IS can be combined for this purpose.

A large-scale introduction of IT in the administrative, educational and training systems of developing countries will most likely translate into a boost to their economies. It will create jobs, may open new markets and lead to marked cost reductions in fields such as education and training. The necessary investments may be substantial, but if properly used, the gains would also be important. I have shown that sometimes it is just a question of using existing data differently, which may now be possible because of the availability of more powerful computers. The effects of IT on the local economy will be discussed in more detail in the chapter 11.

PART FOUR

Chinese cases in urban management

10. Urban Employment Promotion, the importance of Micro and Small Enterprises

1. INTRODUCTION

Urban employment promotion includes stimulating the development of micro and small enterprises. A considerable percentage of urban employment in China is in small scale and microenterprises. The latter term is used for economic activities involving less than five workers. In this chapter we will illustrate that urban managers can take a more positive attitude to these activities, which are often neglected or even discouraged by the authorities. However, they are very important from the point of view of employment or income generation for poor people and migrants.

A lot of economic activities in Chinese cities would fall in the category of informal micro and small enterprises. They have no legal basis and sometimes are part of the underground economy. More importantly the legal minimum wage is not paid and the workers have no social security in the modern sense of the word. One only has to think of the bicycle repairman on the corner of the street, the many small traders along the roads and all kinds of small-scale transportation that can still be found in Chinese cities. Problems of unemployment, low skill levels, illegal presence in the city and poverty are often related.

Therefore an integrated solution needs to be developed to solve some of these problems and to contribute to a better life in a more competitive city. In general employment creation in modern industries receives much more attention in China's cities. We will also deal with that issue in chapters 11 and 12.

China is known for its high rate of economic growth. Because of a growth rate of almost 10 percent per year over the last 25 years the number of jobs in the manufacturing sector is increasing rapidly. There is clearly a need to create more urban employment in China. Despite the economic growth rates, the growth of employment has not been so spectacular. It is estimated that a few hundred million workers are no longer needed in the rural areas and are available for employment in the cities. In most cities there is a surplus of these migrant workers and they tend to make a living through street vending and other types of informal work.[1] Very little is known about this 'informal' sector, if only because the Chinese government does not publish figures on these activities. However, there is also no tradition of empirical research in China. The number of empirical studies on street vending and informal work is for example very small. We will bring together available literature, observations and anecdotal evidence to try to give an impression of the importance of the activities that are significant in the urban informal sector. Devas and Radkodi (1993) conclude that 'the discovery of the informal sector' ... 'has had a profound influence on the thinking about the urban economy' and particularly it helped to recognize the importance of these activities for employment, poverty reduction and urban development.

The official unemployment figure for towns and cities in China was 4 percent in 1995. The figure increased to 6.1 percent in 2002 (figures quoted in the *China Daily*, 10 December 2004). Unemployment may not have increased, but the authorities may just be willing to admit in 2002 what they were not yet ready to admit in 1995, that urban unemployment is the result of migration to the cities and a very slow and careful process of restructuring of the state-owned enterprise sector in China (van Dijk, 1998). An important policy objective of the central government is checking the rise in urban unemployment. In particular the authorities are very much afraid of political unrest. This is one of the reasons why the reform of the state-owned enterprises is going at such a slow speed. It is also an argument for restricted traveling from the rural areas to the towns. Those traveling without the required permissions do not get a residence permit in the city and hence have no access to housing and social services.

The evidence presented in this chapter is limited to some of the major Chinese cities, where the phenomenon of the urban informal sector and street vending is widespread. It has not been possible to interview informal entrepreneurs and street vendors in a systematic way, if only because of the suspicion with respect to 'officials'. We have made systematic observations and discussed with a number of small entrepreneurs and people knowledgeable about the urban informal sector.

The big increase in the number of these informal activities was possible only after the economic liberalization process started in China after the death of Mao in 1976. It proves the openness to small-scale capitalism in this country. However, the urban informal sector is also part of China's globalization process, since it provides an outlet for the unemployed for which there is no work in China's industries. It also allows, through its cheap products and services, to pay lower wages in the formal economy, enhancing the country's and in particular the urban competitiveness. Before dealing with the impact of the reforms on micro and small enterprises, we will first describe China's economic reforms after the death of chairman Mao.

2. CHINA'S ECONOMIC REFORMS AFTER MAO

The general economic climate in China before Mao's death in 1976 was characterized by a hierarchical system of state-owned enterprises (SOE) tied to a centralized redistributive system. These enterprises were not subject to hard budget constraints. Central government would bail out inefficient units. The SOE were constantly engaged in a struggle to gain access to scarce resources, such as equipment, parts and foreign exchange. Because of perennial shortages in the planned economy, a vast informal economy came into existence that entailed the exchange of the necessary inputs.

The question raised in this chapter is how did the economic reforms influence the micro and small-scale sector in general and street vendors in particular? To answer this we first review the relevant economic reforms. Subsequently the theory about different variants of petty capitalist production will be summarized to check whether micro and small enterprises are examples of a proto capitalist mode of production. Alternatively, have the reforms and the economic development led to a variant that Gates (2005) calls the off-the-books, or black, or underground economies, commonly called the urban informal economy.

Buechler and Buechler (2005: 121) argue that it is a mistake to focus too narrowly on the contrasts between economic systems such as capitalism and communism. They recommend instead examining variations in the position of persons and productive units over time within the system. This is a more anthropological and institutional perspective that will also be taken in this chapter. Institutions play a role when trying to keep the government at arms length, or to safeguard the public and private interests. Institutional change is an important issue in developing countries and the central topic when liberalization of markets or of various infrastructures is discussed. The common theme of institutional economists is the rule-based character of social behavior. From that perspective the evolution of systems of institutional rules like it happened in China is an important contribution to the development process.

Reforms started after 1978 and can be described as the 'three waves of reform by Mr. Deng' (*Economist*, 'China Survey', 1992) to create a market economy. Liang (2004: 13) even distinguishes a fourth phase in the reform process. The first phase runs from the Third Plenum of the 11th Congress of the CCP in 1978 to the Third Plenum of the 12th congress in 1984. In 1978 Deng outlines his plan for enacting the four modernizations: decentralization of control, stronger divisions in the respective roles of the CCP, local government and enterprises. There was to be no interference in enterprise development, business managers are to be given greater authority over labor management and production operations. In this phase we see the rapid development of the Township and Village Enterprises (TVEs) and the beginning of the SOEs reform. In the rural areas reforms started to eliminate the shortcomings in the Stalinist model of development. They concerned the economic system, rather than the political structures. Second, the reforms started with experiments on a small scale, repeated on a larger scale if successful. Third, the economy was opened up to obtain investments and with it foreign technology and management and access to foreign markets.

Deng started by freeing prices for food and abolishing the agricultural communes. Family farms took over and produced much more than the communes before. He also introduced the open door policy, which was inaugurated by the establishment of four special economic zones (SEZ) in the Guangdong Province: Shenzhen, Zhuhai, Shantou and Xiamen. These zones were designated as territories for accelerated economic development and the controlled import of foreign technology and capital.

The current success of the Chinese economy can be explained by a number of factors, such as the low level of development in 1979 and the decentralization of decision power to lower levels of government. The farmers received more autonomy at the expense of the communes. In 1979 the SOEs also received increased autonomy and a number of city states with economic autonomy were created. Finally, the important inflow of foreign capital should be mentioned and the strategic vision on economic development of the leaders and in particular the late Mr. Deng.

In the second phase of the reform process began in 1984 with the industry reforms. Fewer goods were flowing through the hands of planners and competition became more widespread. Prices were coming closer to true scarcities. In 1987 a number of managerial reforms were announced. Companies began to select managers on the basis of commercial rather than political grounds. SOEs started with management contracts, specifying performance targets. Rewards were linked to sales and profits and managers were fired for poor performance. In this phase we also see a banking market emerging.

A third phase started in 1992 with Deng Xiaoping's southern tour. He delivered a speech on speedier economic development (*Financial Times*, 20 November 1995), in which he encouraged party members to go into business and to make themselves rich as pioneers of reform. Companies were now allowed to retain a large share of their foreign exchange and then to trade this on currency markets. Systematic market reforms were undertaken and a rapid development of joint-stock and joint venture companies can be noted.

The last stage started according to Liang (2004) after joining the World Trade Organization (WTO) in 2001 (Lardy, 2002). It implies more respect for international property rights, but also more competition from imported goods. Second, China will be required not to subsidize industries that compete internationally and the country has been asked to abandon discriminatory taxes and regulations that are hurting foreign companies (*Financial Times*, 17 March 2004). Finally, China will have to be careful with developing standards that deviate from international standards that may be considered a form of protection (*China Daily*, 27 April 2004) and hence lead to complaints in the WTO framework. The importance of the WTO membership is that China is locking in its reform. It cannot just change its economic policies any more. Recognizing the importance of small-scale economic activities would be a last step in the economic reform process. As we will argue there are a number of reasons for urban managers to take a more positive attitude towards these activities, if only because they provide employment often to poor and marginal inhabitants. Another reason is that they help to keep the cost of living low.

3. INSTITUTIONAL CHANGES AND THE ECONOMY

China has made the transition from a planned economy to a much more market-oriented economy in a relatively short period. An analysis of the institutional changes can be based on the four-layer scheme suggested by Williamson (1998). Institutions guide the behavior of economic actors, but they also influence which form these institutions take. The first layer distinguished by Williamson is traditions, norms and religion. The second layer concerns the rules of the game and the third is how the game is played. Finally, at the lowest level of the firm and the households resources are allocated, under the influence of the three higher levels.

Yiwen Fei (2004) analyzes informal institutions in China at the first level under the heading Confucianism, Chinese Familyism, collectivism and equalitarianism. The formal institutions after Mao's take over in 1949 are those of the Centrally Planned Economy, where prices are determined by administrative rather than market mechanisms. Similarly, resources are allocated by planners, rather than by the forces of supply and demand. The transition process was characterized by less importance of the communist formal institutions and a possibility of older value systems reemerging (Chen, 2001). Hard working, valuing education and the importance of networks are certainly among those new 'old' values. They impact the second level of the formal rules (which now reflect the importance of these values) and the third level of the governance structure (where the government is now serving the interests of these entrepreneurs and households). Finally at the fourth level the resource allocation is influenced. It has now tried to get the marginal conditions right to achieve proper functioning markets in China.

The reforms in the urban areas started with the so-called 'responsibility system', which gave managers of enterprises more autonomy. Managers would sign a contract with local authorities or the ministries concerned specifying how profit would be shared. They would sign a contract about the profits to be made and the taxes to be paid. Production above the agreed quotas could be marketed at floating rates between the minimum and maximum fixed by the state. The TVEs would act as independent legal entities with specified rights and obligations. Because production above the quotas could be marketed at floating prices the earnings depended on fulfilling the quotas and on the profits made. In 1985 a reform was introduced allowing the enterprises to nominate their own managers.

The Jiangsu Provincial Committee of Chinese Communist Party and the Provincial institutions are for example responsible for urban development, including the plans for the downtown area of the provincial capital Nanjing. The city consists of a number of districts and has a municipal government, but the districts also have their own layer of government, the district authorities. They play a more active role in creating an enabling environment for the economic activities in their district (van Dijk, 2006a and Chapter 11 this book). The major institutional changes are that mandatory planning changed to 'guidance planning' and the introduction of market forces. Although the big and medium-sized SOEs still received mandatory production plans from the state planning commission the managers' obligations and rights are almost the same as those of the TVEs under the responsibility system. Meanwhile private foreign enterprises, in particular small Hong Kong run industrial enterprises started to invest in China, playing the game by the new rules.

Zhang (1989: 41) lists the shortcomings of the reforms at the end of the 1980s. The urban reforms were only half way through. The system of dual pricing was still heavily distorted. Second, the credit system still did not work and inflation was quite high in the 1980s. Finally population pressure was high leading to high unemployment figures while China lacked natural resources, except coal and iron. It was self sufficient in energy until 1994, but currently has to import about 50 percent of its fossil fuels. This required Deng's third wave of reforms, which made China a very successful export-oriented economy.

4. IMPACT OF REFORMS ON SMALL ENTERPRISES

These reforms had consequences for micro and small enterprises. China's economic reforms opened the country up to capitalist investment. Preferential treatment for joint ventures included a tax holiday during the first two years and a 50 percent tax relief in the following three years. In addition, according to Smart and Smart (2005), access to cheap labor and land across the Hong Kong border encouraged Hong Kong's small entrepreneurs to develop a so-called Kirznerian adaptive response. Rather this implies adaptation to the local situation, rather then upgrading of technology and attempting more Schumpeterian approaches to innovation (the entrepreneur as an innovator). They stress that small and medium-sized Hong Kong's entrepreneurs have been active investors in China in the first decade after opening up in 1979 (Smart and Smart, 2005: 10).

Many small Hong Kong run industrial enterprises in China are either subcontractors, or dependent on orders from import export firms, and act as a buffer between volatile market demand and large well-established businesses. Hong Kong entrepreneurs are sometimes doing business in their home villages in China and are hard to notice without an ethnographic approach (Smart and Smart, 2005: 12).

The suggestions made by Deng after 1978 were taken up quickly in particular by the southern provinces. The Pearl River Delta (PRD) region (close to Hong Kong) played a privileged role as the testing ground for China's market-oriented reforms. The region had access to cheap migrant labor and was closely located to capitalist Hong Kong. Liberalization started much earlier in the PRD, which is sometimes called a cluster of specialized commercial districts (Hong Kong Trade Development Council, 2003). High levels of social capital facilitate these effective networked clusters of small enterprises. The region has endowments such as being located close to international markets via Hong Kong and having a good infrastructure. Studwell (2003) mentions that at a certain stage the TVEs were just reclassified as private enterprises, formalizing their transition to more autonomous capitalist production units. However, the PRD region is now facing growing competition for investments from other regions, in particular the Yangtze River Delta (YRD) industrial complex around Shanghai. Studwell (2003) describes the positive effects for small enterprises of the economic reform process. They started booming in this region.

Tian (1996) examines the role of Shanghai in China's economic development between 1949 and 1995, comparing it with Guangzhou. Guangzhou in the PRD received the lion's share of foreign investment since the reforms in 1978 and its growth of exports has outstripped that of Shanghai. Was this due to the Guangdong's natural advantages (its comparative advantage in cheap labor combined with a cultural affinity and geographical location close to Hong Kong), or to the fact that economic reforms and special policies were carried out there first, while Shanghai remained under tight central control?

The Chinese government is dedicated to economic development and willing to test reforms, but at the same time the legal system leaves much to be desired. For example it is quite difficult for a joint venture partner to put a conflict with a local partner to an independent judge or to get a legal statement (cf. Clissold, 2004).[2] However, the overall effect has been a much more enabling environment for all kinds of enterprises.

5. BACKGROUND AND THEORETICAL FRAMEWORK

The emerging small and micro enterprise sector can be analyzed by using the theoretical framework developed by Gates (2005: 26). She looks to relations between petty capitalists and the surrounding political economies. She defines petty capitalist production as 'a set of relationships always subordinated to another mode, which sets broad political-economic and cultural limits on it'. She argues that there are five main contexts within which Petty capitalist production has been analyzed:[3]

1. The domestic mode of production;
2. Petty capitalism under the tributary modes;
3. Proto-industrialization, or proto-capitalism;
4. Petty bourgeoisies/old middle class; and
5. The informal (off-the-books/black/underground) economies.

The question is to what extent are micro and small enterprises in China examples of these different forms of petty capitalism? We consider in particular whether micro and small enterprises in China have made, because of the economic reforms, the transition from proto-capitalism to a more capitalist informal urban economy. To substantiate this claim we will consider the characteristics of proto-capitalism and of the urban informal sector. Frank (1990) defined proto-capitalist as the extensive presence of commodity production and the existence of producers and traders who sought profit (see Box 10.1). There was investment in capital and there was the use wage labor. However, although the appearance of these micro and small enterprises were consonant with capitalism none of them had quite crossed the threshold of creating a system whose primary driving force was the incessant accumulation of capital. The reason why capitalism did not yet emerge was an insufficient technological base, but not an absence of an entrepreneurial spirit: something was preventing these enterprises making the transition. Is this also the case in China? The question is whether we can also speak of proto-capitalism in China's micro and small enterprise sector.[4] We will look at the evidence on the points mentioned by Frank (1990) and summarized in Box 10.1.

BOX 10.1 PROTO-CAPITALISM AS DEFINED BY FRANK (1990)

Proto-capitalism is defined as a stage between feudalism and full capitalism, where we notice the following elements:

1. Often extensive commodity production;
2. And an important role for traders, who seek profit;
3. Considerable investments in capital;
4. An increasing important role for wage labor;
5. However: not yet accumulation of capital as the primary driving force.

The context of the urban informal sector would be characterized by Gates (2005) as being subordinate to a capitalist economy, but with limited wage labor, receiving usually less than the legal minimum wage and not benefitting from social security.[5] The entrepreneurs are often self-employed and have no access to formal credit. They tend to evade taxes, but are increasingly integrated in the formal private industrial export-oriented economy. Also the authorities take the existence of this sector more and more into account and reserve for example space and provide some infrastructure to allow its development.

6. AN EXAMPLE OF PROTO-CAPITALISM?

Certain authors estimate that there are up to 500 million people who are no longer needed in the rural areas in China, but are not officially allowed in the urban areas either. Although some cities (for example Shanghai) have started to recognize the presence of millions of such 'illegal people', in many cities the discrepancy between official census figures and registered population remains very big. These farmers turned migrant workers do not have the skills required by the modern manufacturing sector and hence get involved in street vending and other informal sector activities to make a living.[5]

Are micro and small enterprises in China an example of proto-capitalism? One certainly notes the important role for the (small) entrepreneur and there is certainly an entrepreneurial spirit among them. However, certain factors constrain the further development of these small productive units before 1976 and even after this date.

Reviewing the parameters of Frank (Box 10.1) for the micro and small enterprise sector in general and street vending in particular one notes in the first place that there is considerable commodity production in China, however not just in the micro and small enterprises sector. Currently this sector is mainly involved in trading, transporting and all other legal and illegal services to the formal private industrial sector and coming from it. Before 1978 the micro and small enterprises were linked to the SOE.

Concerning the role of traders, the second of Frank's points, it is quite clear that they are important. However, they make up only one marketing channel, besides the formal marketing channels and the international value chains in which the formal sector is more engaged.

Is the third characteristic mentioned in Box 10.1, the lack of continuous capital accumulation, also the case in China? It seems not so much the lack of technological infrastructure or entrepreneurship seeking profit, but rather the lack of recognition and of government support, which has been withholding the further development of indigenous entrepreneurship. All the official support went to the modern export-oriented industrial sector and to the stagnating government-owned enterprises. This contributed to a dual development model and resulted in a large urban informal sector.

The role of wageworkers in micro enterprises is limited, but increasing. The low wages paid in China's cities have a lot to do with the large number of migrants from the rural areas looking for work in the cities. They are often second-hand citizens in these cities, but their number is almost endless given that almost three-quarters of China's 800 million rural population are expected to become superfluous in agriculture in the near future (*Financial Times*, 11 December 2002). In the PRD, with cities like Guangzhou (Canton) and Hong Kong, 40 percent of the population are migrants rising to 5-to-1 in Shenzhen, located closely to Hong Kong. According to Enright et al. (2003) real wages have not risen substantially in 15 years in this region because of the unlimited availability of cheap labor. The question is of course how long the workers will accept to work for these meager salaries.[6]

So it is not so much the lack of an incessant drive for accumulation of capital, but rather a political and economic system that made this further growth impossible for such small-scale entrepreneurs and explains the current dual structure of the economy. In these circumstances street vendors and other micro and small enterprises could not take up more labor and accumulate more capital. The dominant forms of accumulation are now in the formal manufacturing and trade sector and in particular the private and joint venture part of it. In the current situation one finds hardly any example of graduation from street vending and other forms of informal activities to more formal private sector enterprises, participating in the current boom of the Chinese economy.

Hence, contrary to Frank's theory investments in the micro and small enterprise sector are relatively limited and currently not encouraged by the authorities or the formal sector for that matter. Also the role of wage labor is limited if only because most of the micro enterprises are one person or family undertakings (what is also called self-employment). Hence the conclusion that accumulating capital is not yet a primary driving force in the micro and small enterprise sector. In fact this is much more the case in the formal manufacturing and services sector, where the government is also actively encouraging it.

Since the 1990s many jobs have been created by small and medium enterprises in the formal private sector. One problem is that China's foreign investments often go into large-scale operations, which are not labor-intensive. Public sector investments go into transport, communication, environmental protection, agricultural irrigation, grain warehouses and other (Zhang, 2002). Many cities in China consider the IT sector a source of economic growth and employment, but this is clearly all formal sector employment and provides opportunities mainly to high skilled labor (van Dijk, 2006a). Most potential employees are low skilled and low wage migrants in the city, who do not qualify for these kinds of jobs. They depend to a large extent on the urban informal sector or work as casual labor for example in the construction sector. The more formal enterprises tend to take the better skilled and younger people, who are more productive and may have the adequate training or experience.

7. IMPRESSIONS OF CHINA'S INFORMAL SECTOR

In front of Nanjing University women have parked their bicycles and exposed a limited number of CDs and DVDs with computer programs, ready to leave as soon as a policeman arrives on the scene. Besides illegal computer programs, they sell illegal copies of recent movies and recent music albums. Men on the sidewalk sell toys, such as plastic electric trains or cars that can rollover against the side of the box in which they are demonstrated.

Behind the rapid growing formal economy there is a huge informal economy where many of the urban poor and illegal migrants from the rural areas make a living with small-scale trade and manufacturing. There are no official sources on the number of people involved, nor the activities that they are carrying out. Table 10.1 gives an impression of the type of economic activities, subdivided in trade-related activities, services and manufacturing activities. One could calculate the number of people involved by taking the total labor force, unemployment figures and subtracting the workers in the formal sector. However, this would require rigorous assumptions about the size of the labor force and about labor force participation of men and women, young and old people.

Typically a large number of the people involved in informal sector activities are older people who have never had a chance to obtain a proper education and a formal sector job. It should be noted that the distinction between the informal sector and unemployment may not be as absolute, given that most unemployed have to make a living by developing some kind of (informal) economic activities, because there is no social security system for most unemployed in China.[7]

Table 10.1 Examples of urban informal sector activities in Chinese cities

Trade related activities or services	Manufacturing activities
All kinds of mobile traders: - All kinds of food and drink - Newspapers - Software - CDs and DVDs - Selling live animals: puppies, turtles, etc. - Children toys: balloons, cars, trains, etc. Unofficial markets[8] Waste collectors Small scale transportation	Tailors Shoe manufacturing and repairmen Woodworkers Bicycle repairmen Waste recycling Food processing Masons, painters and plumbers Fortune tellers Hand reading and medical advice *Maybe formal/maybe informal:* Daily workers in the construction sector

8. WHAT KIND OF ACTIVITIES?

The activities listed in Table 10.1 are characterized by high mobility (people move in and out easily) and flexibility (they may change the products sold or the activity they were previously involved in). In fact whole markets may come up at one place and later be found at another. The manufacturing activities are very much manual work, involving one person or using family members and shying away from the officials, which may try to tax them or flatly make it impossible for the urban poor to be involved in these economic activities.

There is usually a subtle game between the traders/vendors and the local government authorities (van Dijk, 2002). The traders have to find out in practice what they are allowed to do and what not. In the center of Nanjing it is not uncommon to find street vendors in front of the modern shops selling sometimes similar products. They may find it difficult during the day, but often they are allowed to be there when the night falls and many of the formal sector shops close their doors.

In the early morning in Nanjing street vendors sell newspapers, fruits and vegetables and one finds strange sellers on the sidewalk of the streets, leading to the center, selling for example turtles. One man had a big turtle and two small ones, which possible is his only source of income on that particular day. Other men are offering to predict the future for you or a woman provides medical advice at the corner of the street.

A complete market may be built up without official recognition by the local government and functions in the morning hours, or only after 6.00pm. This happens in particular in the old neighborhoods where the streets are narrow and the people are living in four floor apartments without an elevator. There one does not notice many formal markets or official shops, which could be outlets for these kinds of goods. All kind of vegetables, fruits, meat, fish and birds (besides snakes, insects and other typical Chinese food products) are sold on the street.

When you arrive in Nanjing at night, you see vehicles crossing the streets that you hardly see during the day. For example a bicycle with a cart attached to it, which holds two drums. They are used to transport the remains from restaurants; often oil used for baking, or leftovers, which are then used to feed the pigs raised in the periphery of the city.

A woman using a similar bicycle crosses the street looking for useful waste or leftovers from the many building sites. In particular bricks are always reused elsewhere, but also wood and windows and doors are very popular and endlessly transported out of the modern center to be re-used elsewhere. Also used cement bags, tiles and corrugated iron are very much in demand.

The informal sector is everywhere in China's cities. One notices in the morning traffic flows lots of traders using bicycles and motor carts to transport their merchandise into the city. Usually their means of transport are hugely overloaded, which makes parking more difficult and contributes to urban congestion.

In the popular neighborhoods many small shops are private and their goods are often infringing on the public space, which is not always appreciated by the authorities. Most small entrepreneurs were pushed out of the center once the renovation process started and the three to four floor houses of the Mao period are replaced by ten storey office buildings or even bigger apartment blocks. One notices the new city being built, while other people still live in the old houses on the other side of the street.

The same process of pushing activities to the periphery takes place with respect to small-scale transportation. The rickshaws and scooter taxis are no longer allowed in the center of Beijing, Nanjing or Shanghai and can only operate in the peri-urban areas. Modern taxis or the public buses provide trips to the center. The buses and remunerative auto taxis deprive many hard-working small entrepreneurs from their main source of living.

On the sidewalk a man is selling books in boxes from the back of his bicycle-cart. These are traditional Chinese books. Under a tree a woman is selling pornographic DVDs from a small box tied to her bike. The display can easily be folded up if the police show up. The pornographic movies she sells are sold at five times the price paid for illegal DVDs in the local shop. In such shops one can also buy illegally reprinted books, like Harry Potter or Clinton's memoirs.

Older people are in particular heavily involved in street vending. They also organize dancing lessons in the park early in the morning. The classes range from ballroom dancing to more modern dances and the participants take the lessons very seriously. Other groups are involved in all kinds of traditional sports, making gymnastic movements with toys or weapons under the inspired leadership of a usually old and mostly female trainer. In the evening people are collecting used building materials around the many building sites located in the cities, where most old buildings are being replaced by high rise residencies or office buildings.

9. MAYORS' PROMISE TO IMPROVE LIVING CONDITIONS

Under the head 'Mayors' Promise to Help Their Residents' the *China Daily* (9 March 2004) carried a story about the two major Chinese cities, Beijing and Shanghai, which revealed the circumstances under which many migrants and small entrepreneurs live. The Mayors observe that 'Behind the skyscrapers there are poor and shabby shelters'. The Mayor of Shanghai admits 4.5 percent unemployment in his city, or some 300 000 people unemployed. About 350 000 people are living in poverty in Shanghai, while hundreds of thousands of people are still living in 'dangerous and shabby houses' according to him. The Mayor of Beijing declared that nearly 350 000 local households in his city, or 1.1 million people, are living in houses with a per capita living space of under 6 square meters and without toilets.

More importantly large numbers of migrant workers are living outside the Chinese social security system. The municipal government of Shanghai announced in 2004 'for the first time, at least 2 million migrant workers will be put under the city's social security system by the end of 2004' (*China Daily*, 10 March 2004). The municipal government 'will strive to offer better protection to all employees who are not native to Shanghai and strengthen measures to standardize the labor markets'. The estimates are that out of a 20 million population in Shanghai there are at least three million migrant workers. They represent one third of all workers in Shanghai and are not coming in large enough numbers to satisfy the demand for labor. This is one of the reasons why the municipal government decided to allow parents to have two children. Such a policy would also result in a more even age distribution of the future population, which currently tends to be skewed because of the one child policy implemented rigorously since the 1970s. On a trial basis by the end of 2002 already 770 000 such workers had received an integrated assurance, covering medical expenses, occupational injuries and allowances for retirement paid by their employers.

Subsequently other authorities announced better protection of their migrant workers. The wave of promises to do better was triggered off by a discussion in the National People's Congress in early 2004 on a constitutional amendment to protect human rights. The Guangdong Province subsequently announced plans to safeguard the rights of more than 23 million migrant workers and their families in the province. This floating population of about 23.3 million temporary workers should be compared with 78.5 million permanent residents in the province. The floating population in China is defined as people who are not entitled to be registered as permanent residents according to current laws and regulations. It usually implies that traveling is more difficult and no access to services such as housing, education and health are possible in the city where the migrant is working. The urban residency rules were designed after the founding of the People's Republic in 1949 and intended to restrain farmers from entering the cities and have the same status as permanent residents (*China Daily*, 11 March 2004).

Migrant labor is often misused in the cities, for example in Shanghai, although officially rights of migrants are inviolable. The *Shanghai Star* (9 December 2004) gives an example of seven migrants from the countryside who had been working under a labor contractor who was in charge of the construction job but fled without paying the workers' wages when the project was almost finished. They then attempted to commit suicide by consuming large quantities of drugs in their temporary shed in the city of Shenyang in Northeast China. The solution the Chinese have found for these kinds of problems is that the workers should start registering themselves in the city, which is not very likely for most migrants, who know they are not supposed to leave their rural areas.

A Beijing Court helped migrant workers to get money that had been owed to them for six years (*China Daily*, 10 December 2004). A 180 workers received the overdue pay from a food company which mounted up to US$ 135 000. Another firm was fined for low salaries (*China Daily*, 10 December 2004), but this was the Shenzhen government imposing it on a Hong Kong firm. The case is interesting because the workers were paid less than the US$ 74 a month, which is the minimum fixed by the Minimum Salary Regulation of the Shenzhen Special Economic Zone.

Currently the average salary of unskilled workers has increased to US$ 109 per month. Assuming six long days of work, this boils down to US$ 3 per day, while the average wage of unskilled labor in China is estimated to be US$ 5 dollar per day (van Dijk, 2004c). The number of stories are endless and they are the only source of information as long as independent researchers are not organizing surveys among these informal workers and street vendors.

10. PROBLEMS BETWEEN THE INFORMAL SECTOR AND THE AUTHORITIES

One can also find lots of stories about problems between informal entrepreneurs and the authorities. Concerning food sellers in Shanghai, Ms. Lu Chang reported in the *Shanghai Star* (9 December 2004) on a confiscated food stand. She started by saying that the most touching and sad image for many years was the face of a weeping farmer, whose small food stand, along with its tables and chairs, was confiscated by governmental officials of the Industrial and Commerce Bureau. It was noted that the stall was probably the sole basis of her livelihood in Shanghai and that her cry 'was the sound of a person whose last hope had been destroyed'. Ms. Lu Chang continues that a lot of food vendors were lined-up outside the school gates when she was a student, but had disappeared one day. They found out that they had been fined US$ 6 each by inspectors that would come by regularly. Instead of trying to destroy these activities Ms. Chang suggests that the government should use a project called 4050, which helps middle-aged laid-off workers to find jobs with a series of special measures to assist them. Why not provide the same opportunities to street vendors?

The examples given show that the authorities can be tough, but they are not insensitive to the situation of large numbers of people who they have very little to offer. In general what the people in power in China fear the most is popular unrest, which could wipe them away as has happened in so many other communist countries. That means that the authorities will give in if a situation becomes threatening. The other side of the coin is that those street vendors and other informal activities help to keep wages low, because they make it possible for formal sector workers to increase their purchasing power. In the market your yuan may have the value of two![9]

Yasheng Huang (*Financial Times*, 2 February 2005) makes the point that the Chinese authorities have always benefitted from the foreign enterprises more than the local enterprises. In fact this applies even more for the informal sector. Huang adds that the institutional context is unfavorable for Chinese companies since they have to pay a lot of tax and continuously face all kind of corruption. The enormous amount of bureaucracy, while all credit goes to SOEs or foreign ventures, means further institutional reforms are necessary that would favor in particular the local enterprises and hopefully also those in the informal sector.

11. THE LINK WITH THE FORMAL AND GLOBAL LEVEL

The urban informal sector is alive and kicking. Compared to the informal sector in Maoist times, it has more links to the current formal, private industrial sector and the world market. Street vendors and the broader urban informal sector are very diverse but make up a dynamic sector, although usually not recognized nor supported by the authorities. Their activities may be tolerated because the authorities are painfully aware that they have no alternative to offer to these usually older people with limited skills and a low employability. Second, it is partially a sector of the night, illegal, semi-legal or tolerated because you cannot arrest so many people trying to earn a living by working hard and long hours. We may call it China's informal or the shadow economy, but the size of this sector is huge in employment terms and the sector will not disappear, but probably change further and eventually largely be formalized.

China has undergone a transition from a traditional command economy to a market economy after Mao's death in 1976. The current economy has become increasingly globalized, with an important role for a few metropolitan cities, such as Nanjing (van Dijk, 2006a). However, there is an urban informal sector, which may eventually become less important, if the current increase in manufacturing employment continues. Also the trend towards more supermarkets and shopping malls becomes a threat for mobile vendors and informal sector traders. China is certainly a country where competition is widespread, where activities come and go and where people need to have the flexibility to find other types of employment, if they do not want to lose their income opportunities.

It is easy to indicate the links between these street vendors and the global level, where China is more and more active through selling abroad its products and by buying abroad the necessary inputs and equipment. The number of migrants and the fact that their low level of skills does not match the demand for labor in the dynamic export sector means that many migrants end up as small traders in the informal sector. However, they help the formal economy in three ways. In the first place, by keeping the wages low, by providing cheap products and services to formal sector workers. Second, they help by creating a reserve army for the formal sector. Even if currently many informal sector workers are old and low skilled, in times of labor shortages they will be brought into the formal sector labor force. Finally, wages can be low because the street vendors buy and sell the cheap (and often rejected for exports) products of China's formal sector.

Through the liberalization process China became more and more export-oriented. About 30 percent of the national product in China is exported; this figure can be compared with about 10 percent for the USA. This strong export-orientation has led to rapid economic growth, in particular in the eastern part of China where the growth is largely concentrated. Hence the demand for cheap products of small entrepreneurs and mobile vendors has increased strongly.

Chinese industries make at least two qualities of most products. They produce cheap products for African and Latin American markets, but some of that is also sold locally. However, they also produce more sophisticated goods to be exported to the USA, Europe and the East Asian region, each buying about one-third of China's export.

In terms of purchasing power parity China is one of the countries where your dollar has the highest value. A factor of 4 to 5 applies, meaning that with the current per capita GDP of US$ 1000, Chinese people can buy the equivalent of what we would buy for US$ 4500! This is only possible because the prices of local and informal sector goods sold through street vendors and small shops. Although an export-oriented economy, more than two-thirds of the industrial output is sold locally! If through more regulation, competition, formalization and a further separation of the modern city center from the popular neighborhoods life will be made more difficult for street vendors and mobile traders, and the cost of living may increase substantially in China.

12. CONCLUSIONS

Capitalism has always existed in China, but the nature of the micro and small enterprises has changed in the transition process. These enterprises are an important part of China's economy and play a role in the current transition process towards a market economy (Chen, 2000). Unlike in many African and Latin American countries these enterprises are not just selling products from the global markets. Street vendors, small shops and mobile traders outside China often get Chinese products through smuggling and dumping, while Chinese mobile traders can get these products locally from the formal and now often private sector. They play an important role in their distribution process. The evidence suggests that they would like to accumulate capital, but that there were too many barriers to allow them to do so. However, small-scale economic activities help to solve the unemployment problem and help to ensure that China remains a low cost economy, which provides arguments to promote further development of these activities.

Looking at the Chinese economy in this way, the environment of micro and small entrepreneurs in China has changed over time from a situation where these activities were illegal, to one where they are tolerated. The Chinese government has even started to recognize the importance of these activities. In the meanwhile the dominant form of ownership has changed from public to private. Also labor relations have become more capitalist and the opportunities to sell products and services have increased. The open door policy of Deng was the beginning of China's participation in the global economy. As argued elsewhere, China has benefitted more from this than for example India (van Dijk, 2005b).

If the authorities want to take a more positive approach towards employment creating activities they could start with recognizing their role. The formal sector develops because entrepreneurs want to make a profit and try to increase their profits by investing and expanding their businesses further. This process of capital accumulation is promoted by the government by allowing investments to be written off prematurely, or by not taxing certain investments of the benefits from these new investments. Similar benefits do not exist in the informal sector. In fact most informal entrepreneurs fear policemen could capture their investments, their illegal constructions could be destroyed and a bigger stock may attract the attention of tax inspectors. For sure these entrepreneurs would benefit from a more positive economic environment. For urban managers this means trying to remove some of the factors currently constraining the development of these activities. Politicians should make it clear, like the Mayors of Shanghai and Beijing, that they are willing to help these informal microentrepreneurs. It is their ability of generating autonomous growth, which needs to be used. This can happen in the following ways.

In the first place, it is good to review municipal legislation and regulation to find out which rules hinder the development of these activities. Respecting their property rights is important for the urban informal sector, to allow these entrepreneurs to expand their businesses. Second, space could be made available and some elementary infrastructure established to allow mobile vendors to sell their products. Some of them may be helped by micro loans. The regulatory and tax system could be adjusted to the reality of these people. It could be made easier to register and to comply with the existing rules. Finally, some of these activities may develop further if they can develop relations with medium and large-scale enterprises or government departments for which they can act as a supplier or subcontractor.

In actual practice the examples shown give the impression that the authorities are rather tough with micro and small entrepreneurs, while their workers depend on what and whether their employer will pay. Fortunately some Mayors and some courts in China have become aware of the unequal treatment given to these people, who mainly try to make a living in a society that has very little to offer them.

NOTES

1. Informal work is defined here as jobs without a legal basis in the Chinese system, which only recognizes state owned, official private (with a legal status) and all kinds of community-based enterprises.
2. For example on a piracy question as General Motors found out when it wanted to file a complaint about a model, which Chinese automobile producers seemed to have copied from their Korean partner (*Financial Times*, 2004).
3. She argues that many analysts would include a sixth variant of petty capitalist production, one that puts flexibility in flexible accumulation, and, together with improved information transfer technology significantly raises productivity. However, she considers this to be just a small and overemphasized difference (Gates, 2005: 26).

4. Proto-capitalism is a constitutive element of all the redistributive or tributary world empires the world had known.
5. Many also work in the construction sector, where the distinction between legal and illegal workers and formal and informal subcontractors is more difficult to make.
6. In June 2005 several newspaper articles mentioned the shortage of labor in the PRD in China and the need to set up factories in the interior where more skilled labor is available. For example: Shaanxi rises minimum wage for city workers (*China Daily*, 10-6-2005), or Scramble for Asian textiles workers (*Financial Times*, 8 June 2005).
7. Workers laid off by SOEs are probably the exception (van Dijk, 1998).
8. Some of these markets are not allowed by the municipal or district authorities, but have the permission of the lowest administrative level, the community level.
9. 8.2 RMB equaled US$ 1 during the period of this research.

11. Urban Management in Nanjing and the Role of the IT Sector[1]

1. NANJING A METROPOLITAN CITY

Urban studies have focused on the metropolization process or the evolution of large metropolitan areas within the context of globalization.[2] In this chapter I analyze the impact of globalization and the information revolution on the urban economy of a medium sized city in China. Nanjing is the capital of the Jiangsu Province and counts some 6 million inhabitants. I will analyze the reaction of the urban managers to the challenge to create a dynamic city. Nanjing is linked by road, air and river to Shanghai, which is located some 300 km away and serves as a dynamic regional economic center. Shanghai can be considered at the top of the urban hierarchy in Eastern China. From Shanghai a number of neighboring cities, which are closer to the regional center, receive a growth impetus. This is for example the case with Suzhou and Wuxi, which are part of Jiangsu Province. However, Nanjing is big enough to develop its own economy, using the concentration of Research and Development (R&D) institutions in the city and its important regional market.

In this chapter I will link three geographical levels: the global, the regional and the urban through IT and IT-related economic activities. It will be argued that in a first effort to develop IT in Nanjing a cluster of shops and workshops selling hardware and software developed in the inner city. However, in a second wave a number of software producing companies located in different clusters grew rapidly under favorable local, national and international conditions. An international value chain was developing in the case of the software sector of Nanjing. What explains this process of metropolization and the development of a regional capital into a global economic player in the IT sector? To what extent is this government led development? What is the role of labor productivity and of information technologies and what of the locally developing innovative milieu? Can we conclude that Nanjing is at the edge of becoming a global city based on modern technologies and the development of a citywide IT cluster?

2. NANJING: PART OF THE YANGTZE RIVER DELTA OR ITS OWN MEGALOPOLITAN AREA?

In the Yangtze River Delta (YRD) a supra regional cluster is developing around Shanghai, a kind of region state. Ohmae (1995) argues that it is no longer the nation state that is dynamic and an engine for prosperity, but that regional economies are reshaping global markets (see van Dijk and Koppels, 2004). Ohmae's argument is that region states do not have to pay much attention to less favorable regions or social groups, which may lead to the wrong investment decisions (from a financial point of view) in the nation state. To be successful the region state should have the authority to attract capital itself. Second, it should be possible to finish big infrastructural projects independently. Finally, the region state should be able to attract foreign investments. The national authorities can then still play a role in the field of offering military security, a stable currency and general standards. Examples are Hong Kong and in Japan the Tokyo and the Kansai region, which are often competing with each other.

According to the Jiangsu Province authorities, Nanjing is also considered the center of a so-called megalopolitan area. This is an area around the city including six cities in east China's Jiangsu and Anhui Provinces. It reflects the ambition not to become totally dependent on Shanghai, a huge growth pole that is only at 300 km from Nanjing. Shanghai is at the top of the urban hierarchy in the east of the country and an enormous center of development, with a population of 20 million people and an annual economic growth rate of 11.8 percent!

The development of such a megalopolitan area around Nanjing has been given great importance by both government officials and experts since it was first planned in March 2002. The megalopolitan circle around Nanjing contains Zhenjiang and Yangzhou in Jiangsu Province and Wuhu, Ma'anshan and Chuzhou and part of Chaohu in Anhui Province as well as the southern part of Huai'an in Jiangsu Province (*China Business Weekly,* 9 September 2003). The development of this idea is important for Nanjing since the city plays the role of center of this urban hierarchy and as such it is an important market place for more advanced products such as computers and software. If this is considered the future role of Nanjing, it is doubtful whether efforts will be made to integrate more in the YRD. A conference of concerned Mayors decided, 'cooperation in economic development is the key point in building the Nanjing megalopolitan circle'. All cities and districts in this area intend to make joint plans for their different industries and environmental protection. They also intend to build coordination mechanisms among governments, agencies and experts from all the cities.[3]

Nanjing is made up of a number of urban districts. Two important districts in the center of the city are Xuanwu and Gulou. The latter has taken the initiative to start a science park and an industrial estate for IT companies, while the Xuanwu district is hosting several software parks. These two district level initiatives will be discussed below as an example of urban management. Nanjing has become an important business center in the eastern part of China. Historically it was a center of administration for the southern part of the country. It was the national capital until the Japanese conquered Nanjing in 1937. Ever since it has a more regional function, but was never one of the special economic zones (SEZ), which have been booming so much in China after 1978.

Originally the borders of Nanjing were natural borders: a river in the north and east, a small lake and a mountain in the northwest and a smaller river in the south. The historical development of the city can be traced from any map showing the old walls. The walls defended the center and only at the beginning of the 20th Century the real expansion across the walls started. A relatively old industrial area is located towards the northwest and in fact the Nanjing Economic and Technical Development Zone, which is located there still regroups mainly traditional manufacturing industries. This part of the city was less well connected until recently, but a second bridge, a tunnel under the lake and a complex of ring roads north of the lake have improved access.

Between the two world wars the extension of Nanjing to the south started and resulted in the 1990s in the incorporation of the rural district in the south, Jiangning, which is located on the way to the airport. This district now has the most developed high tech industry development zone, with companies like Ericsson and Siemens. More recently the city has expanded across the river, stimulated by the building of the first and the second Changjiang (or Yangtze) river bridges in 1968 and 2001 respectively. The second bridge over the Yangtze river, in function since April 2001, may help to solve the traffic congestion problems on the first bridge. Currently new extensions of Nanjing also go further in the direction of the airport which is located in the southeast. The southern part of the city is popular for enterprises because of the available space and infrastructure.

The Nanjing government did get more autonomy after 1992. The municipal authorities started in 1993 to formulate positive economic policies, also with respect to small and medium enterprises. Economic growth between 1991 and 1999 was above 13 percent per year. The economic growth is attributed to three factors: technological innovation, investigation of the world market and investment from overseas. The city per capita GDP reached US$ 2229 in the year 2000 (*China Daily*, 15 February 2002) and US$ 3000 in the year 2003. This is three times the national per capita average of about US$ 1000.

Already in 1989 the Nanjing municipality decided to start the 'Zhujiang Road', an electronic road where more than 1000 computer and computer-related enterprises are located. After the green light from Beijing and the provincial authorities, municipal actors start to work out the necessary policies. In Nanjing different levels of government formulate different policies to attract investment in the IT sector, which will be discussed below. Without four rural counties (and Jiangning) Nanjing covers 976 km2, the whole metropolitan area is 6515 km^2.[4]

Enterprises occupying plots along the Zhujiang Road were notified that this road would be reserved for IT companies and that they would have to move if hardware or software was not their core business. Alternative locations were offered and empty plots and buildings were allocated to IT firms. In due course over 1000 enterprises found a place on this road or along neighboring streets.

Local government reinforced this concentration process by building and reserving a number of buildings as 'enterprise buildings'. These were primarily meant for information technology companies. Usually some common services are offered, such as accountancy, security and cleaning. The nature of the firms concentrated in Zhujiang Road is very mixed. One can find the regular sellers of specific software and hardware, but also specialized firms providing hospital information systems, software for system integration (including installation and adaptation) or companies repairing monitors or other parts of a computer system. IT consultancy firms can be found side by side with firms recycling old computers. Most enterprises sell hardware or software or a combination of the two. Usually the production of hardware takes place in the high tech development zones in the periphery of the city. Similar companies in Beijing's Zhongguan Chun have developed into major IT companies. That is what the entrepreneurs in Nanjing hope as well. The parallel with the Dell Company of the USA is often suggested.[5] Nanjing has the skilled manpower for IT development and is working on developing its own software sector.

3. URBAN MANAGEMENT IN METROPOLITAN CITIES

Urban management in China is not as developed as in a number of other countries. Three reasons can be mentioned why this is the case:

1. The Revolution had a clear rural origin;
2. The status of the very big cities can be very different, ranging from a special economic zone to being just a big city in a province;
3. The political and administrative system is not always clear: the Party, the administration and People's Committees are active at different levels of government.

In the first place the revolution had a clear rural origin and Spencer (1990) mentions that in the beginning the communists had a difficult time running the cities. The Chinese government remained skeptical about certain cities until the 1980s (for the example of Shanghai, Tian, 1996). Second, the status of the very big cities can be very different. Shanghai and Chongqing are for example city-states, while Nanjing is a regional and Beijing a national capital.

Finally, the political system is not always transparent. The national level instructs the provincial level, where the political leaders instruct the big cities.

However, there are Party people and People's Committees at the different levels of government, which each have their administrative departments. Their opinions and activities are not always known and clearly coordinated as will be illustrated below.

Table 11.1 Different urban social issues/dominant sectoral approach in China

Social issue	Sectoral approach, issue handled by
Poverty Unemployment Corruption Security Education Health	Social service Economic bureau Committee Police/army Ministry/ bureau Ministry/ bureau

The government in China is the major director of change, but the government has different faces, at the national, the provincial, the city and the district levels. What one finds in urban management is a very sectoral approach. The major sectors in China are indicated in Table 11.1 and 11.2

Table 11.2 Different urban infrastructural issues/dominant sectoral approach

Infrastructure	Sectoral approach, issue handled by
Drinking water Improved transport Housing Electricity Environment Sewerage and waste water	Municipal service Bus company Construction depart Electricity company Environmental protection agency Municipal department

4. SECTORAL APPROACHES TO URBAN MANAGEMENT

Urban management would prefer to deal with these issues in an integrated way as depicted in the following figures, which illustrated the possible interrelations between issues. The sectoral approach deals with such issues separately under the responsibility of the sector organizations.

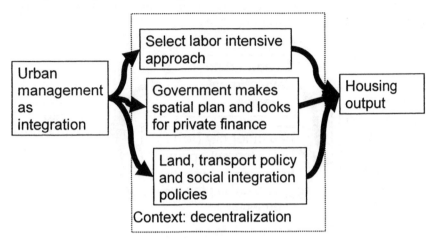

Figure 11.1 Example of an integrated instead of a sectoral approach to urban management: the housing supply system

Figure 11.1 describes an integrated instead of sectoral approach to urban housing, resulting in a housing supply system, which takes into account the existing physical planning and the need for employment creation. It would make the project fit in the current land and transport policy of the city and promote social cohesion instead of separating different groups. In Figure 11.2 the example of an integrated approach to urban infrastructure development is explained, distinguishing new development schemes, inner city development or slum improvement. The suggestion is to go for network improvements instead of an endless series of ad hoc small repairs.

The more common approach in China is the sectoral approach, which deals with economic development land and infrastructure as separate issues, dealt with by separate departments or bureaus each with their own objectives and ways of working. In the same way for Water supply improvements, they can be undertaken as part of new development schemes/inner city renovation/slum improvement, rather than additional individual connections. In fact sustainable water supply solutions: choice individual or collective supply (standpipes), a decision how to deal with the poor (lifelines or cross-subsidies) and introducing repayment formulas (increased tariffs or betterment tax).

The functioning of some of the departments can be illustrated by a number of case studies. The functioning of the economic bureaus is described in a paper on the contribution of the IT sector in Nanjing (van Dijk, 2003b). Housing is described regularly in the press, stressing the problem of over supply (IHT,

August 2004), while the way migrant labor is dealt with is also a subject of public debate (Van Luyn, 2004). The environmental policies of the authorities were the subject of Zhang (2002) and analyzed critically in our paper (van Dijk and Zhang, 2005). So let me take now land policy as an example.

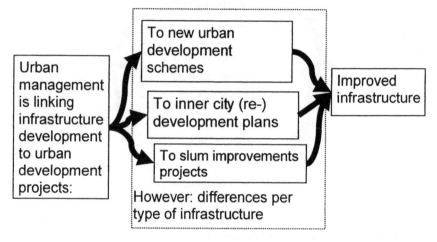

Figure 11.2   Example of integrated urban infrastructure

Agricultural land is scarce in China and this is the reason why in the big cities the six floor Mao housing caserns are gradually replaced by 40 storey apartment buildings in Beijing and Shanghai. However, the municipal authorities break down houses without much consultation of the population. The authorities seem to prefer prestige projects over low cost housing and concentrate on developing business parks and high tech zones, rather than providing green and recreation areas for urban inhabitants. Most cities want to give the impression of modern, which is associated with high rise buildings, illuminated during the night and with big bill boards describing the latest satellite towns or new business park. Let us analyze this in more detail.

5. URBAN DEVELOPMENT: THE ACTORS

Urban development in Nanjing is a clear example of what is called government-led development, but as such it follows a very sectoral approach and not the integrated approach suggested in my definition of urban management. The different levels of government all play a role in the development of these metropolitan cities. However, although the government is an important actor, its representatives are often less visible than in many western countries, at least for foreigners. There is no governor of Jiangsu Province, appearing in the national

English language newspaper every day. Similarly the mayor of Nanjing is not regularly in the news and the leaders of the districts are not even known to most researchers. However, they often have and share a vision on the development of the province and city and implement this vision rigorously, making available huge amounts of money to achieve the necessary investments. The first three layers (national, provincial and municipal) are clearly hierarchical and work in a coordinated way. At the municipal level coordination is supposed to take place, avoiding duplication at the district level. However, at the level of the district there seems to be more equality and one notes competition between different districts, for example concerning their efforts to attract IT companies. Traditionally the impact tended to be very sectoral as depicted in Tables 11.1 and 11.2.

Provincial and municipal governments showed vision in Nanjing by creating three high tech development zones, two software parks and by upgrading Zhujiang Road to the Zhujiang High tech zone. The respective district authorities were asked to carry out these initiatives. They regularly get targets concerning the number and kind of enterprises to be created in their area. In this case the higher authorities gave the green light and the districts had to create these parks and zones.

In the case of urban management the interaction between different levels of government, in particular the provincial, the municipal and the district authorities is important. The central government wants and does provide support to numerous activities through tax policies, grants and government orders. It is not easy to single out the effects of these incentives, to determine how much they really mean to these industries. However, among the IT entrepreneurs there are a lot of the bigger companies that express their gratitude for the support received from government officials.

The provincial view of Nanjing as the center of a so-called megalopolitan area reflects the ambition to become less dependent on Shanghai. The municipal authorities in 1992 used the increased autonomy to develop stimulating economic policies. Finally, the districts have done the same. The role of local governments goes beyond what one is used to in Europe. They not only provide space and infrastructure, but they help enterprises to gain access to credit and stimulate the presence of accounting firms in the enterprise buildings to assure a good functioning administrative system. We concluded that different districts go as far as competing with each other.

Local governments also determine which company can locate in which enterprise building, or who gets permission to build where. Through 'producer associations' the local governments try to stay in contact with the entrepreneurs, although the enterprises do not always appreciate this close involvement of the authorities.

There are a number of contradictions in the system. Although the different governments plan economic and urban development and implement the policies, the entrepreneurs actually achieve spectacular economic growth figures and they want a certain freedom from bureaucratic interference. The picture becomes even more complicated if one realizes that many entrepreneurs are former government officials, who know their colleagues in the government very well. The two groups help each other if necessary, for example through government orders, favorable loans or grants.

Second, the government has a lot of money to spend and wants to contribute to economic development, but may not always know what is the best way to spend the money. Hence the system has the inherent risk of overinvestment and investment in the wrong things. In particular popular topics like IT and high tech zones and software parks may have a limited absorption capacity. The National People's Congress meetings in 2004 have reflected on this concern and decided that more often choices need to be made where to pursue certain activities, because not every city can have a booming software park.

In the third place, the government wants to and does provide support to numerous activities, but it is mainly familiar with tax cuts and the small starting funds as instruments. It is not so much at ease with creating an innovative milieu (van Dijk, 2006a).

Finally, it is hard to understand that a system that could coordinate easily, because of its centralist character and because there is limited participation to fear from stakeholders, still lacks coordination at the district level. It gives the impression of democracy from below and that is also the level where the authorities have allowed some cities to experiment (Shenzen with elected non-party local government candidates for example).

6. PHYSICAL LOCATION OF IT INDUSTRIES IN NANJING

The dynamics of Nanjing is certainly influenced by the emerging IT sector, which will now be described, to find out what urban managers have contributed to the development of this sector. Nanjing consists of 6 urban districts, 5 suburban districts and 2 rural counties. Nanjing is now an important business center in the eastern part of China. For the IT sector the following five districts are in particular important, because IT activities are concentrated in those districts as shown in Figure 11.3:

- Xuanwu District with an IT cluster (defined as a strong spatial clustering of IT activities) on Zhujiang Road in the center of the city and the location of the Jiangsu Province Software Park (JSP) and Southeast University Technology Park;
- Gulou District with the Nanjing University and Gulou District nationally approved University Science and Technology Park in the western part, extending to the north west until the river;
- Jiangning District in the south, where the Jiangning High-Tech Industry Development Zone is located;

- Xixia District in the north east, where the Nanjing High-Tech development zone is located;
- Pukou, in the north west of Nanjing, where the New High tech development zone is developed, with the so-called Nanjing Software Park (NSP).

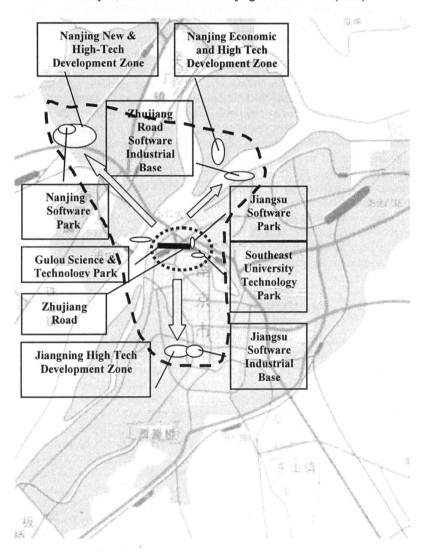

Source: Van Dijk and Wang (2005).

Figure 11.3 Map of Nanjing IT clusters

With so many high tech zones, software parks and science and technology parks it looks like a city-wide IT cluster is emerging, where the inner city is becoming the core of the IT cluster. However, this requires verification and will depend on the definition of such an IT cluster.

In Nanjing the Xuanwu District authorities, in which the Zhujiang Road cluster is located, played an important role in developing the cluster. For example eight business/enterprise buildings were provided by the district authorities and tax incentives were provided to attract IT companies. Paying taxes is a hot issue among the entrepreneurs, although the amounts paid still seem to be relatively low in the IT sector. The accounting services provided in some of Nanjing's business buildings may actually include advice on how to deal with tax issues.

A substantial number of our interviews (ten percent) took place in the Pacific Electronic Commercial Center, one of the biggest enterprise buildings. They were primarily built for IT companies. Common services are offered, such as accountancy, security and cleaning services. The quality of the buildings varies a lot. For the businesses the level of the services offered is important and for the consumers the attractiveness depends largely on the location and access (details in He Jian, 2000).

Local government may help these enterprises to gain access to bank loans and to prepare their tax forms. The Xuanwu District also established the Zhujiang Electronic Road Administrative Office, which collects data on the cluster and has developed plans for its future development.

7. NATIONAL, PROVINCIAL AND MUNICIPAL POLICIES

We will now focus on the role of the external environment and in particular on the importance of local government policies for the development of the IT sector? At the national level several initiatives are taken to develop the IT sector in China. Gu (1999) gives an overview of the science and technology (S&T) system and the role of research and development (R&D) institutes in China. Part two of her book deals with spin-off enterprises. Although her focus is on the machinery industry she clearly describes the efforts to transform R&D institutions to get them focused on the commercial development of manufacturing systems. A similar development is currently taking place in the IT sector where the Gulou District authorities want the universities to supply ideas directly to the IT firms in the cluster.

English language newspapers in China announce new technology projects, usually at the national or provincial level about every other day. Some headings are summarized in Box 11.1. The box gives an impression of the importance attached to the development of the IT sector and the instruments used to achieve its development. Examples of tax incentives in Shanghai are well-known (*China Daily*, 5 August 2000) and there is commitment to channel more overseas funds into high tech industries and the establishment of research and development institutes in Nanjing (*China Daily*, 2 August 2000). In the same articles the municipal government announces efforts to expand the export-oriented economy and to lure more overseas capital for the modernization of the city. A new five-year plan has been drawn up to guide the city's development.

One can conclude that the Chinese authorities expect a lot from the IT sector and are putting a lot of effort into its development. Also they are willing to accept foreign investment in the sector if that could aid its development. Finally the government clearly thinks in terms of public-private cooperation projects to develop the IT sector.

BOX 11.1 SUPPORT FOR IT SECTOR IN THE NATIONAL PRESS

More support for high tech hub (*China Daily*, 5 July 2000)
More investment for IT center (*China Daily*, 21 July 2000)
High-tech industries help economy: zone boosts city's industrial development (in Changsha) (*China Daily*, 27 July 2000)
Capital helps high-tech companies develop at coastal city's universities (*China Daily*, 2 August 2000)
More support for high tech hub (*China Daily*, 5 August 2000)
High tech industries help economy (*China Daily*, 27 July 2000)
Foreign capital highlights high-tech industries (Beijing review 18 January, 2001)
New policies to aid software industry (*China Daily*, 12 February 2001)
High tech sector to get cash injection (*China Daily*, 15 February 2001)
City seeks sustainable economic growth, Government plans to use advanced technology to fuel local development (*China Daily*, 15 February 2001)
The park changes landscape (*China Daily*, 2 August 2000)
Nation plans major IT growth (*China Daily*, 17 February 2001)

---

8. POLICIES AT THE CITY LEVEL

The fact that by now almost every Chinese city is trying to build up an IT center means it may be more interesting for new start-ups to benefit from the incentives provided elsewhere in the country. Some provincial or local governments provide substantial benefits to make investments attractive. For example the national government and the provinces concerned very seriously promote new investments in IT companies in the west of China.

Nanjing at the city-wide level has also undertaken a number of activities to develop the IT sector in the past. The city has, for example, created major industrial estates in the north and the south of the city for technology-intensive firms. In fact almost every city in China is trying to attract high tech industries, for example by giving financial support. In Changsha the municipality provides financial support to attract investment in the sector (*China Daily*, 27 July 2000). One way of doing it is to develop a high tech development zone, covers 18 square kilometers in Changsa counts 515 enterprises. The article mentions that 158 out of the 515 are foreign-funded enterprises and more than 182 are export-oriented high tech projects.

Recently two districts in the center of Nanjing have taken the initiative to develop a Science Park (Gulou district) and a concentration of software companies (Jiangsu Province Software Industry Co. Ltd in the Xuanwu District), two initiatives that will be discussed and compared.

Table 11.3 Public-private cooperation for IT cluster development in Nanjing

Type of activity for cluster promotion
1 Policy-related incentives:
1.1 Fiscal incentives
1.2 Targeted education and training
1.3 Marketing support
1.4 Linking with private or public capital suppliers
1.5 Cluster marketing through advertising
2 Prices and subsidies:
2.1 Land*
2.2 Electricity
2.3 Other services, for example enterprise buildings
3 Innovation promotion through:
3.1 Involving research centers
3.2 Stimulating incubator centers
3.3 Promoting linkages with training and R&D institutions*
4 Physical support, providing:
4.1 Space
4.2 Secondary infrastructure (electronic)
5 Stimulating cooperation through:
5.1 Group formation of enterprises and consultation of these groups
5.2 Promotion of interfirm relations*
6 Other initiatives

Note: * These cases could lead to a public-private partnership.

The most common policy to attract industries is providing tax holidays for two or three years. There is currently a 17 percent turnover tax and a profit tax and a personnel income tax. The big companies in the Jiangzu Province Software Park get an exemption of profit tax (for two years), then they pay for 3 years at only 50 percent.

Table 11.3 provides an overview of all possible forms of support for IT clusters in China. There is certainly a tradition of stimulating the IT sector in general and clusters of enterprises specifically in China. In the *Financial Times* of 19 June 2001 there was for example an advertisement for 'leasing manufacturing or warehousing facilities in the heart of the Panda technological and industrial park in Huizhou, Guangdong Province'. Besides technical features, the advertisement recommends the location because of the excellent transportation network (infrastructure: a 1 hour drive to Hong Kong and 30 minute drive to Shenzen) and the availability of additional land for development (physical support). However, the most striking sentence is that companies are offered 'national preferential policies to foreign investors'.

At the city level usually cooperation between the private and the public sector is required. In Table 11.3 we have put a mark to indicate when there are opportunities for public-private partnerships. The table gives all the possible types of public support for the IT sector. The table will serve as the frame for the analysis below of the policies of different levels of government with respect to IT clusters in Nanjing.

9. LOCAL GOVERNMENT POLICIES FOR IT PROMOTION

9.1 Introduction

The Nanjing city government used its increased autonomy after 1992 to formulate positive economic policies, also with respect to small and medium IT enterprises. A restructuring exercise of Zhujiang Road has been undertaken in 2000 by local government, where companies are only allowed to move in if they are involved in software production and at least 50 percent of their activity is actual production, rather than sales of computers or computer-related products. A lot more has happened in between. Following the framework of Table 11.3, the activities of local government for IT cluster promotion in the case of Nanjing can now be analyzed

9.2 Policy-related incentives

Fiscal incentives
Half of the value-added taxes paid every year by the hi tech enterprises the Jiangsu Software Park will be used for rendering support to the development of the enterprises within five years from the date of going into production. As for

the hi tech projects which have filled in the gap inside the country, within two years starting from the date of going into production, 100 percent of the portion of the value-added taxes reserved by the Park and for the third to the seventh year 50 percent of the portion reserved by the Park shall be used for rendering support to the development of the enterprises.

As for the newly built hi tech enterprises, within two years starting from the date of going into production, 100 percent of the reserved portion and for the period from the third year to the fifth year, 50 percent of the reserved portion shall be used for rendering support to the development of the enterprises.

For the production type projects with the sum of investment exceeding US$ 10 million and the term of operations exceeding 15 years; and for the enterprises with one added sum of investment exceeding 10 million US dollars, within three years starting from the date of going into production, 50 percent of the municipally reserved portion of the value-added taxes paid every year by the enterprises shall be returned.

Targeted education and training
Through involvement of research and training institutions in IT development.

Marketing support
Not observed.

Linking with private or public capital suppliers
Other measures at the city level to develop the IT sector in China include support from a venture capital fund (*China Daily*, 2 August 2000). Various other types of financing services shall be provided to the enterprises entering the Science Park in Gulou. For example the hi tech risk funds owned by Nanjing University Gulou Institutions of Higher Learning Science and Technology Park. Assistance by the Park shall be given to the enterprises for removing obstacles from the financing channels. Help will also be given in the application for the funds related with the support of the scientific and technological development to be given by the State, the Province and the Municipality. Assistance shall be given in the contact with the social investment institutions for the provision of the financing channels.

Cluster marketing through advertising collectively
Provincial and local government are actively promoting the cluster and in particular the two local government initiatives mentioned.

9.3 Prices and Subsidies

Land
The Nanjing city government also offers space and infrastructure in a technology zone at the outskirts of Nanjing, where two technology development areas have been built. In principle that space is meant for factories.

The eight business or enterprise buildings are very important for the development of the sector and were provided by the district authorities. The Xuanwu District also established the Zhujiang Electronic Road Administrative Office, which collects, among other tasks, data on the cluster.

Electricity
No subsidies were observed.

Other services
The Xuanwu District government reinforced the concentration process by reserving a number of buildings as 'enterprise buildings'. They were primarily meant for IT companies. Usually some common services are offered, such as accountancy and cleaning. The quality of the buildings varies a lot. It depends on the location, services offered and attractiveness for consumers (He Jian, 2000).

Preferential charges
For any service type charges which are priced by the governmental authorities, the paid service supplied by any institutions or the intermediary organizations, the expense shall be collected at the rate of two-thirds.

In the Gulou District legal services shall be provided to the enterprises. Also a series of comprehensive associated services shall be given such as the assessment of the intangible assets, unfolding of technical training, technical exchange, demonstration of the products manufactured by the enterprises, transactions of the technical results (net transactions) and so on. Preferential registration is taking place in the Gulou District (see below).

9.4 Innovation Promotion Through

Involving research centers
In the Gulou District case the government conferred with the educational institutions involved.

Stimulating incubator centers in Nanjing
The incubator in the Gulou Science Park is located on Qindao Road and occupies an area of 1500 square meters. It consists of the following five centers, while the objective is to promote linkages between the startups and the training and R&D institutions:

1. University Students Pioneering Center;
2. Teachers Pioneering Center;
3. Alumni Pioneering Center;
4. Overseas Students Pioneering Center;
5. Jiangsu Provincial Post-doctoral Pioneering Center.

Assistance shall be provided in the Gulou science park in handling the high and new technical products, scientific and technological development plans and some other projects as well as the appraisal, registration and so on for the technical achievements.

Assistance shall be provided in doing a good job for the official approval of the high tech and new technical enterprises, the appraisal and assessment of the high and new technical products, the application for the domestic and foreign patents as well as the final appraisal of the products and technical results.

9.5 Physical Support

Space
The space required for office affairs and scientific research shall be provided in the Gulou District to the enterprises at preferential prices; and the rent may be paid in the form of shares. Excellent real-estate management services shall be given. Moreover, the streamlined service in terms of the commercial affairs, communications, accommodation shall be provided to the enterprises. Any enterprise developed and incubated in the University Students Pioneering Center, Teachers Pioneering Center, Alumni Pioneering Center, Overseas Students Pioneering Center and Post-doctoral Pioneering Center shall enjoy zero rental for two years. The Pioneering Center can then pass on the two-year zero rent to the broad masses of the students, teachers, alumni and other eligible candidates as the location for scientific and technological incubation and supply a series of technical and comprehensive services to various scientific research institutions and hi tech enterprises entering the Center.

Secondary infrastructure
In electronics for example China is trying to catch up as far as installing fiberglass cables is concerned.

9.6 Stimulating Cooperation Between Enterprises

Group formation of enterprises and consultation of these groups
Not observed except for the government organized Nanjing Software Industry producers Association, where the government is pulling together different parties.

Promotion of interfirm relations
Not very well developed.

9.7 Other initiatives

The enterprises occupying plots along Zhujiang Road were notified that this street would be reserved for IT companies and that they would have to move if this is not their core business. Alternative locations were offered and empty plots and buildings were allocated to IT firms.

10. CONCLUSIONS

The government does indeed play a very active role in stimulating the development of the IT sector, certainly if compared with Bangalore in India, where we did a similar analysis (van Dijk, 2003c). Different levels of government in Nanjing promoted the IT sector and in particular the Zhujiang Road, its electronic road, since 1989. Zhujiang Road lies in the Xuanwu District; this project and the projects undertaken in the neighboring Xuanwu District turned out to be examples of uncoordinated activities of local government. It shows the absence of coordination of different levels of government, because the implementation of economic policies is left to the lowest level of government, which suggests some de facto decentralization (van Dijk, 2000). This is why we speak about government led development. The authorities will have to make up the balance, whether this is the right way to go for China.

The development of the IT sector in Nanjing shows that active urban management is possible in China. The challenge is to coordinate different levels of government and to be aware that government can do what local government can not do and what local government should not do. It is difficult to say who the real urban manager is in China, but at certain levels leaders manage to bring actors together and succeed to implement a well-defined strategy.

The choice for a big city like Nanjing is to use the networks in which it is functioning properly. The city has the choice between the megalopolitan network, the Nanjing Suzhou Wuxi axis, or the larger PRD region in which Shanghai would be the most important city. Maybe Nanjing is big enough to benefit from all the three networks and can it use them selectively to its own advantage.

NOTES

1. The research concerning the YRD is based on a research project financed by the Netherlands government and carried out by the Sino-Dutch International Business Center (SD-IBC) of the Nanjing University Business School and a consortium of IHS and MSM, the leading partner. See van Dijk and Wang (2005).
2. Metropolitanization is defined in different ways, but always refers to the need to develop a different governance structure for very big cities (see the next chapter).
3. Megalopolitan areas developed in the YRD are centered on Shanghai and Hangzhou.
4. Jianging became a district instead of a rural county only in 2001. The city proper counts 3.3 m. and the five rural counties (including Jianging) 2 m. inhabitants.
5. Dell has been a very successful producer of computers using direct marketing, selling directly to customers (instead of selling through intermediaries). This makes Dell computers relatively cheap.

12. Competition Based on Successful Urban Management: Pearl River Delta Versus the Yangtze River Delta

1. INTRODUCTION

The information revolution and globalization have had enormous effects on the economy of Chinese cities. Urban studies have focused on the evolution of large metropolitan areas within their regional context. We studied in particular the role of the IT sector in the development of Nanjing. This is a city important in the urban hierarchy in Eastern China. With some cities in between Shanghai and Nanjing make up the so-called Yangtze River Delta (YRD, see Figure 12.1) competing with the Pearl River Delta (PRD) with Hong Kong as its center, giving that delta a growth impetus, while Shanghai is the center and engine of the Yangtze River Delta.[1] Around Shanghai a supra regional cluster is developing with the provinces of Jiangsu and Zhejiang as its most important parts, besides the autonomous city of Shanghai. This cluster enjoys a more unified form of governance than the PRD.[2] However, the impact of Shanghai with some 20 million inhabitants and an economic growth rate of 11.8 percent in 2003 can be felt as far as Nanjing almost 300 kilometers land inward! The study of Koppels (2004) of the PRD focused on the agglomeration effects of Hong Kong. The importance of the big cities in these two deltas is remarkable for China's development, if one remembers that only 29 percent of China's population used to live in cities in 1995 (*Economist*, 8 March 1997). The YRD is sometimes described as 'a zone of 15 cities that cluster around the dragon's head' (*Financial Times*, 11 May 2004).

In this chapter we will compare two important regions in China and show how urban governance is embedded in a larger system of regional, provincial, municipal and district level government structures. Van Dijk and Koppels (2004, using Ohmae, 1995) explored what the boundaries of an optimal region state are, comparing the PRD with the YRD. The importance of these 'region states' can be measured by the regional income, the growth of their production and exports, and the foreign direct investment (FDI) attracted. In this chapter the success and governance problems of the PRD will be compared with the success and governance problems of the YRD, where a supra regional cluster is developing around Shanghai, but where Nanjing also has regional aspirations. We want to compare the two regions and try to understand the dynamics and determine the role of urban management in that process. The competitiveness of the PRD will be compared with data on the YRD.

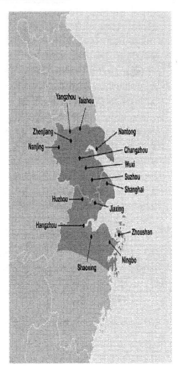

Note: Major and Sub-centers, Shanghai (20 m.) and Nanjiing (6 m.)
Source: http://www.investhk.gov.hk/

Figure 12.1 Map of Yangtze River Delta

2. THE YANGTZE RIVER DELTA

The center of China's economic gravity is moving northward from the delta of the Pearl River to the delta of the Yangtze (*Financial Times*, 11 May 2004). The newspaper adds that in the first quarter of 2004 foreign trade volumes from the YRD surpassed those of the PRD. The YRD's superior record in attracting foreign investments, its booming hinterland and strong transport network allowed it to pull ahead of its southern rival.

Table 12.1 The Pearl River Delta versus the Yangtze River Delta

Variables	Pearl River Delta	Yangtze River Delta
Major city	Hong Kong (6.8 m inhabitants at end of 2002)	Shanghai some 20 m inhabitants
Sub-centers	Guangzhou (9.9 m), Macau (0.5 m), Shenzhen (7 m)	Nanjing (6 m. inhabitants)
Other centers	Six municipalities or prefectures: Dongguan (7 m.) Foshan (5.3 m) Huizhou (3.2 m) Jiangmen (4.0 m) Zhaoqing (3.4 m) Zhongshan (2.4 m)	In Jiangsu Province: Changzou Suzhou Wuxi In Zhejiang Province: Hangzhou, Ningbo, Wengzhan Zhuji
Total population	41 m	80 m
Percentage of migrants	40 (estimate)	Much lower
Foreign investment in 2001	US$14 b	US$ 16 b (*Financial Times* 11 December 2002)
Gross Regional Product	171 b (€ for HK only)	80*2229= US$ 178 b
Rate of economic growth	16.8% (PRD period 1990–2001)	11.8% (Shanghai only in 2003)
Per capita Gross Regional Product	25 103 (US$ for HK only)	2229 (US$ Nanjing only)[3]
Special Administrative Region (SAR)	Hong Kong Macau	Nil
Special Economic Zone (SEZ)	Shenzhen, since 1980 Zhuhai, since 1980 (1.2 m)	Nil
Provincial capitals	Guangzhou of Guangdong Province	Nanjing of Jiangsu and Hangzhou of Zhejiang Province

Note: Sometimes the inland provinces of Jiangxi and Hubei are also considered part of the YRD (Chen, 2000), they are not included in the data in the column on the YRD.

The *Financial Times* goes on to say that the trade figures, which in the first quarter of 2004 for the YRD was worth US$ 83 billion, after export rose with 56.1 percent from the same period a year earlier, while imports rose 60 percent. The PRD recorded total trade of US$ 69.3 billion with exports up 24.3 percent and imports up 22.2 percent. The competitive advantages of the YRD are coming from the booming towns and cities along the Yangtze's navigable middle and upper courses. Table 12.1 compares the information for the two Deltas. Figures 12.1 and 12.2 give maps of the PRD and YRD with major cities and prefectures.

The Yangtze River Delta has not always been considered a natural geographical unit. Sometimes only the two eastern provinces are included, sometimes also the more western provinces of Jiangxi and Hubei. Improved infrastructure and distance shrinking technologies have made it more of a unit, although Nanjing has some hesitations, whether it wants to be in the periphery of Shanghai or be a regional center on its own. Shanghai is one of the original port cities of China.[4] Only in the early 1990s Beijing removed the handcuffs, which had for so long restrained Shanghai's development (*Economist*, 8 March 1997).

Nanjing is an important business center in the eastern part of China. The city has enjoyed strong economic growth since the opening of China to foreign investment in the 1980s. Economic growth between 1991 and 1999 was above 13 percent per year. The city per capita GDP reached US$ 2229 in the year 2000 (*China Daily*, 15-2-2002). According to the *China Daily* (22 February 2001) this is an increase of 135 percent over 1999. This growth is attributed to three factors: technological innovation, investigation of the world market and investment from overseas. The Jiangsu Province has a tradition of producing electronic products. For example it exported 1.25 million TV sets in 2000, worth US$ 115 million. The province is the home of several famous television manufacturers including Nanjing Huafei, Suzhou Philips Electronics and the Panda Electronics Group.

Figure 12.2 Map of Guangdong Province and Pearl River Delta

Recently this YRD has been stealing the limelight. The region has some advantages over the PRD:

1. A more simple governance structure (Table 12.1);
2. The majority of the population are permanent residents with a relatively high purchasing power, meaning the YRD is a tremendous market and labor force reservoir;
3. Shanghai's proximity to Taiwan is another advantage (*Financial Times*, 11 December 2002);
4. Most major cities in this delta are within a distance of three hours traveling time (for Nanjing the 300 kilometers may take four hours, depending on the traffic congestion, but the province is working on an improvement of the highway).

3. THE PEARL RIVER DELTA

The Pearl River Delta is a well-known booming area in China and can be considered one big regional cluster (see Table 12.1).[5] For two decades the region surrounding Hong Kong and Macau have enjoyed 17 percent annual economic growth! They played a privileged role as the testing ground for China's market-oriented reforms. They had access to cheap migrant labor and were closely located to capitalist Hong Kong. However, the region is now facing growing competition for investments from other regions, in particular the YRD industrial complex around Shanghai.

Studwell (2003) describes how after Mao's death in 1978, the beginning of the Chinese economic reform process took place in this region. The PRD is sometimes called a cluster of specialized commercial districts (Hong Kong Trade Development Council, 2003). In the period 1996 to 1999 67.6 percent of the FDI in the PRD region came from Hong Kong and Macau. Subsequently Europe is the biggest investor with a share of 6.3 percent (Enright et al., 2003). According to several authors the level of FDI increases when the cultural distance between the parties concerned is smaller (Grosse and Trevino, 1996; Kogut and Singh, 1998). The big share of Hong Kong and Macau in the FDI in the PRD can be explained partially by the small distance between the parties concerned. Cultural nearness creates the necessary trust for an investment in the People's Republic of China (PRC, Chadee et al., 2003).

According to recent figures the share of Hong Kong and Macau in investments in the PRD region seems to diminish; given the share was 90.8 percent in 1985. One could conclude from these figures that Hong Kong – in investment terms – plays a less important role in the PRD region. However, the official FDI statistics do not capture all the forms of FDI, for example processing and assembly operations are not included.[6] This form of FDI is coming most likely from Hong Kong. Second, the picture is distorted because of the capital coming from 'tax haven economies' such as the Virgin Island (Hong Kong Center for Economic Research, 2003). In 2001 about 55 percent of the registered FDI in Guangdong came from Hong Kong. If the share coming from the 'tax haven economies' and other forms of investment (OFIs) are added to this percentage is becomes about 80 percent (Hong Kong Center for Economic Research, 2003).[7] Hence investments from Hong Kong are still very important for the PRD region, which is largely the Guangdong Province.

'Foreigners' invested a total of € 15.6 billion in the PRD (including investments in the rural areas) in 2001. On top of that about € 1.9 billion was invested in OFIs and other contractual forms (OCFs) in the Guangdong region (Hong Kong Center for Economic Research, 2003).[8] Of the 122 809 companies registered as production or trade companies in Hong Kong in 2001, an estimated 63 000 (estimate based on a representative sample) are active on the mainland of China (Hong Kong Center for Economic Research 2003).[9] A corporation is considered economically active if it has made investments or built up production facilities in mainland China or if it has acquired a share in a production facility on the mainland. Finally a company is considered economically active if it has other contractual obligations with a party on the mainland of China (OCFs).

In the analysis we can separate 'official' FDI from OFIs and OCFs, because the figures are available separately. Of the 122 809 registered companies in Hong Kong about 53 300 have financed production facilities in Guangdong (FDI). Of these production facilities, 21 300 are under the group of foreign investment enterprises (FIE) and 32 000 belong to OFIs and other contractual forms (Hong Kong Center for Economic Research, 2003).[10] Hong Kong invests most in production facilities in the eastern part of the PRD region, Shenzhen, Dongguan, Huizhou and Guangzhou.[11] The western prefectures in the PRD are: Zhongshan, Foshan, Jiangmen and Zhaoqing. If agglomeration effects radiating from Hong Kong are being experienced one would expect that the prefectures in the PRD that are easily accessible from Hong Kong by car are the preferred investment location (Tuan and Ng, 2001). If there would be no agglomeration effects investors would choose on lower labor cost for a prefecture at the edge of the PRD region or even beyond it.

Of the total number of factories in which Hong Kong invested in Guangdong 78 percent can be found the eastern part of the PRD region. Based on the official FDI statistics 70 percent of the FDI in the PRD is concentrated in the eastern prefectures. In Dongguan and Shenzhen about 70 percent of all industrial enterprises are funded with capital from Hong Kong and Macau (National Bureau of Statistics of China, 2002). In the eastern prefectures of the PRD Hong Kong and Macau funded enterprises play a major role in the prefectures economy. Guangzhou is a bit of an exception, because state and collective-owned enterprises have a major share in the total registered industrial enterprises in Guangzhou. The eastern PRD prefectures are more easily accessible by car from

Hong Kong than the western prefectures. The degree of accessibility of a PRD prefecture by car from Hong Kong could explain the distribution of FDI in the PRD.

Source: Enright et al. (2003).

Figure 12.3 Map of Pearl River Delta

Koppels (2004) tests the hypothesis that agglomeration effects in the region are linearly related to the distance between the concerned prefecture and Hong Kong. A linear regression analysis was applied to the official FDI figures per PRD prefecture. Traveling time per car to Hong Kong, GDP, growth of GDP, GDP per capita, retail sales to consumers, labor productivity, labor cost unschooled, innovation investments and R&D funds are used as the explanatory variables.

The only significant variables are traveling time by car to Hong Kong and the GDP of the prefecture. This simple model explains 91 percent of the variance in FDI and the explanatory variables are highly significant (GDP: significance = 0.005 and DIS HK: significance = 0.036).

The model used is:

FDI = 2.377 + 7.052 * 10^{-12} * GDP − 0.009 * (DIS HK) + ε
FDI = Foreign direct investment (in billions of euros)
GDP = Gross domestic product of prefecture (in billions of euros)
DIS HK = Traveling time per car to Hong Kong (in hours)
ε = disturbance term

According to the used model an increase of traveling by one hour means a decrease of € 0.54 billion in FDI in the prefecture. Foreign partners also indicated in interviews that they considered three hours the maximum traveling time they wanted to cope with for visiting production facilities in the PRD. The people interviewed indicated also that they want to be able to visit production facilities within three hours from Hong Kong without depending on a ferry (Enright et al., 2003).

Which prefectures in the PRD region are within this magic threshold of three hours traveling time? This turns out to be in particular the eastern prefectures: Shenzhen, Dongguan and Guangzhou. Huizhou is just a little bit too far (3.5 hours). Zhongshan is the only western prefecture at three hours from Hong Kong. Seventy-seven percent of the factories partially or wholly owned by Hong Kong investors (including OFIs) in PRD prefectures, are accessible within three hours. The construction of a bridge between Hong Kong and Macau and Zhuhai will increase the accessibility of the western prefectures substantially and will hence bring other western prefectures under the region state Hong Kong.[12]

Traveling time per car to Hong Kong turns out to be a good explanatory variable for the level of FDI in the PRD region. These findings confirm the theory that agglomeration economies around Hong Kong are limited to a three hour zone. This suggests there is a limit to the region state suggested by Ohmae (1995). To test the validity of the results, the same analytical model will also be used for the Chinese counterpart of Hong Kong, Guangzhou.

The bridge over the mouth of the Pearl River linking Hong Kong and Macau and Zhuhai will result in a more equal distribution of the FDI in the PRD region. However, the western prefectures will have to satisfy a number of basic conditions, such as proper economic policies, to really benefit from this new opportunity to gain more from the agglomeration economies of the Hong Kong area.

4. ROLE OF THE PROVINCIAL CAPITAL GUANGZHOU

Tian (1996) examines the role of Shanghai in China's economic development between 1949 and 1995, comparing it with Guangzhou. Guangzhou received the lion's share of foreign investment since the reforms in 1978 and its growth of exports has outstripped that of Shanghai. Was this due to the Guangdong Province's natural advantages (its comparative advantage in cheap labor combined with a cultural affinity and geographical location close to Hong Kong), or to the fact that economic reforms and special policies were carried out there first while Shanghai remained under tight central control?

The service sector has a relative high share in the GDP of Guangzhou (54.5%) (National Bureau of Statistics of China, 2002). We investigated whether the concentration of service activities in Guangzhou generate agglomeration effects for the surrounding prefectures? From the available data on FDI it cannot be concluded that Guangzhou is partially an autonomous economic center with its own agglomeration effects, like Hong Kong. Given the difference in size of the economies of Hong Kong and Guangzhou it seems that the zone of polarization of Guangzhou (if there is one) would be much smaller than the one of Hong Kong.

To test if there are any agglomeration effects radiating from Guangzhou a similar linear regression analysis was applied to the official FDI figures per PRD prefecture. Prefectures that are included are: Zhaoqing, Foshan, Dongguan, Huizhou from the PRD region and the prefectures Heyuan and Qingyuan just outside the PRD region. Traveling time per car to Guangzhou and GDP are used as explanatory variables. The model used is specified in the same way as for the Hong Kong area, but should now explain FDI in the Guangzhou area. It gives a poor explanation for the distribution of FDI and it is not even significant ($R^2 = 0.104$ and a significance of 0.848). In the case of Guangzhou there are no agglomeration economies perceived by foreign investors. The fact that the business support services sector is considered not yet to be fully developed may have contributed to the current situation.

5. ECONOMIC INTERACTION AND LOCATION FACTORS

The economic interaction between Hong Kong and the PRD is changing. The PRD used to be considered as a cheap workshop where labor intensive production could be performed. Now-a-days more and more Hong Kong based companies consider the PRD as an attractive consumer market and also more high value activities are relocated to the PRD.

The location selected by multinational corporations (MNCs) can differ from the investment locations selected by regional enterprises. Location nearby urban agglomerations, harbors and in sub-national cluster are generally preferred by MNCs (Yannopoulus and Dunning, 1976). The reasons why international companies invest in the PRD region only partially confirm the arguments used by regional operators. Sixty percent of the European entrepreneurs interviewed in the PRD indicate that the most important reason to be there is entering the regional PRD market (Leung et al., 2003). Twenty-four percent indicates that the good infrastructure, the lower production cost and the proximity to Hong Kong are the important factors to settle in the PRD.

Japanese entrepreneurs said that they had selected the PRD region (40.4 percent) because of the proximity to Hong Kong and the low production cost

(36.6 percent). Also the large PRD market is a reason for 30.9 percent of them (Leung et al., 2002). The most important reasons to move production facilities from Hong Kong to Guangdong are: lower wages, lower rent and lower cost of land. Finally, economies of scale, being closer to consumers and to business partners are mentioned, just like serving the local market (Hong Kong Center for Economic Research, 2003).

For European and international operators the most important factors to invest in the PRD are: the local market, the proximity of Hong Kong and somewhat less the lower cost. For operators from Hong Kong lower wages are the most important reason to invest in PRD region. Enright et al. (2003) estimate that between 10 and 11 million jobs have been created in the PRD by foreign investments. Yulong and Hamnett (2002) claim that at least 7 million jobs have been created by investments in China from Hong Kong, of which 50 percent are in the PRD.

Regional investors consider the big bottlenecks for investments in the PRD: the import and export regulations, custom procedures, taxes to be paid to local authorities, labor regulation and regulation with respect to foreign exchange (Hong Kong Center for Economic Research, 2003). International parties mention almost the same bottlenecks, except that the limited convertibility of the Chinese currency (the renminbi or yuan) is not considered a problem. For foreign entrepreneurs wanting to repatriate their earnings there exists a special system. This system is considered far too complicated and foreign investors consider the procedure as unnecessarily time consuming. Foreign banks cannot provide loans in renminbi, but they can do it indirectly by providing a guarantee to a local bank, which subsequently provides the loan in renminbi. However, again this involves a lot of paper work.

6. THE REGION STATE: THE PRD VERSUS THE YRD

A comparison between the PRD and the YRD shows big similarities, with one city being the clear leader in both cases, although this is not without problems. For Hong Kong serious challenges come from Guangzhou and Shenzhen, while for Shanghai, Hangzhou and Nanjing are competing, but also the famous cities Wuxi and Suzhou in between Nanjing and Shanghai are important competitors. However, Nanjing also wants to be an independent regional capital, while at the same time Nanjing is becoming more and more part of the YRD and faces competition and complementarity with Shanghai and the cities emerging between Nanjing and Shanghai. The evidence is not totally clear, which option will be pursued. It does show, however, that Nanjing takes the relations with its hinterland seriously.

In the YRD a supra regional cluster is developing around Shanghai, a kind of region state in Ohmae's terms. However, according to the Jiangsu Provincial authorities Nanjing is considered the center of a so-called megalopolitan area.

This is an area around the city including six cities in East China's Jiangsu and Anhui Provinces. It reflects the ambition not to become totally dependent on Shanghai, which is only about 300 kilometers from Nanjing.

The development of a megalopolitan area around the city of Nanjing has been given great importance by both government officials and experts since it was first planned in March 2002. The megalopolitan circle around Nanjing contains Zhenjiang and Yangzhou in Jiangsu Province and Wuhu, Ma'anshan and Chuzhou and part of Chaohu in Anhui Province as well as the southern part of Huai'an in Jiangsu Province (*China Business Weekly*, 9 September 2003). It is important for Nanjing since Nanjing plays the role of center of this urban hierarchy and as such it is an important market place for more advanced products such as computers and software. If this is considered the future role of Nanjing, it is doubtful whether efforts will be made to integrate more in the YRD. A conference of concerned mayors decided that cooperation in economic development is the key point in building the Nanjing megalopolitan circle.[13] All cities and districts in this area intend to make joint plans for their different industries and environmental protection. They also intend to build coordination mechanisms among governments, agencies and experts from all the cities. It is difficult to find whether they really are achieving this coordination.

Furthermore, the YRD consists mainly of two provinces, which are competing and one autonomous and important city, Shanghai, which is not part of Jiangsu or Zhejiang Provinces. Shanghai's neighboring province of Zhejiang may have played its cards much better than the Jiangsu Province, as shown by its star appearance in the 2004 World Competitiveness Yearbook, where it has stepped up 19 places to the 19th place![14] It is one of the four Chinese cities/regions figuring on the list besides Mainland China (on the list also figures Taiwan, Hong Kong, Singapore). Only Hong Kong with the sixth place is better placed than Zhejiang, which is taken here as an indicator of the increasing attractiveness of the YRD.

In the YRD, just like in the PRD there is little coordination between the different governments and levels of government. It is hard to understand that a system that could coordinate easily, because of its centralist character and because there is currently limited participation to fear from stakeholders, still lacks coordination at the highest and the lowest level of government. Van Dijk (2003b) illustrates how districts in Nanjing undercut each other to attract foreign investors. It almost gives the impression that democracy from below is possible and happening. Interestingly enough, it is indeed also at this level that the central authorities have allowed some cities to experiment (Shenzen with elected multi-party local government for example).

Contrary to the point of view of the Jiangsu Provincial authorities Nanjing may have an interest in looking at the potential of being full part of the larger YRD, instead of trying to become its own center of regional development. In that sense its position is somewhat similar to Guangzhou in the PRD that may have to accept a secondary position to a neighboring city. Finally there is the option to go for the development of IT industries on the Nanjing Changzhou Wuxi Suzhou axis. On this 250 kilometer stretch one finds major computer, software and computer related industries. Together they may be able to face the competition of better-known computer-related industry concentrations around Beijing and Hong Kong.

7. CONCLUSIONS CONCERNING PEARL RIVER DELTA

The PRD has a complex governance structure, consisting of different forms of governments. There are two special administrative regions (Hong Kong and Macau), two SEZ, one provincial capital and six city level prefectures. Ohmae (1995) argues that a region state should be capable of raising its own capital, develop and realize infrastructure projects and should be able to attract foreign investors.

For the realization of large infrastructure projects (for example the bridge between Hong Kong, Macau and Zhuhai) in the PRD permission is necessary from the national government of PRC. In the PRD region there is also a lack of coordination between the different governance forms, this is shown by the large number of international airports in the direct radius of Hong Kong and increases the risk of destructive competition between different prefectures. The *Financial Times* (11 December 2002) calls this the threat from within: over-competition.

The local production networks in the PRD region are currently focused on Hong Kong. Hong Kong fits Ohmae's (1995) definition of a region state. His thesis is that these region states tend to grow faster than nation states and may be the unit of analysis for economic development. This has certainly happened in the 20th century, but Hong Kong has gone through a crisis (from lavish parties to pessimism; *Financial Times*, 1 July 2002) and growth may be more dispersed in the PRD region at the moment. The city and its hinterland will still need each other, however. The analysis has shown that the traveling distance to Hong Kong is still an important measure for the degree of agglomeration economies that mainland prefectures enjoy, if measured by the resulting foreign investments.

This implies that the bridge to be built between Macao and Hong Kong will alter the picture drastically for the concerned prefectures, enlarging the efficient region state. The current problem is to achieve a more coordinated governance structure, which could be used to maximize the existing complementarities between Hong Kong and the relevant mainland districts.

In the current situation the different governments take their decisions in an uncoordinated way. More coordination could have avoided spoilage of investments and could have allowed more investments in roads and bridges, infrastructure that is really necessary to reduce traveling time in the region and to maximize the complementarities between the different cities and prefectures.

8. CONCLUSIONS CONCERNING YANGTZE RIVER DELTA

In China, provincial authorities are also very active in the field of economic and IT development. The latter can be shown by the example of the Jiangsu Province Software Park in Nanjing and a number of policy initiatives stemming from the provincial authorities to develop this city and the adjacent region. The authorities want to use science and technology to propel economic development and to build Nanjing into a large modern city with an international reputation (*China Daily*, 15 February 2002).

At the municipal level it is noted that a new Nanjing Software Park was launched and a Municipal Bureau has been created to attract foreign investments for Nanjing. For the city the municipal authorities are important because they are promoting the city as a center of IT activities and provide the necessary infrastructure, such as the subway system, the new bridge and the optic fiberglass wires. Second, they coordinate the activities with higher levels of government and allow competition between the districts in the city, the lowest level of government in China. Finally, the municipal authorities have clearly chosen to expand the export-oriented economy and to lure more overseas capital for the modernization of the city (*China Daily*, 15 February 2002).

At the district level the competition is fierce and the officials in different districts of Nanjing admitted that in the end they are competing for the same potential customers. Each one seems to be willing to provide even more incentives to attract potential investors to their district. According to the *Beijing review* (18 January 2001) foreign capital is very much interested in investing in China's high tech industries. In fact 86 multinationals that have investments in China provided the major portion of foreign investment in China's high tech industries. However, most of them do not select Nanjing for a number of reasons, which we summarized as 'limited competitiveness' of Nanjing compared to Beijing and Shanghai (van Dijk, 2003b).

Nanjing is an example of government led development, with an important role for information society technologies and using the locally developing innovative milieu. In this process the companies are becoming more and more part of international value chains. The city has specific advantages and disadvantages, but it has always been able to use the advantages successfully.

9. GENERAL CONCLUSIONS

Regional structures have a governance structure and a large number of stakeholders. In the PRD different government structures work in parallel and sometimes against each other. Hong Kong is a Special Administrative Region (SAR), Shenzhen a SEZ and Guangzhou a provincial capital. The other prefectures have less authority to develop and implement their own financial, economic and social policies. This situation hinders a coordinated development of the region. Although the YRD is administratively in a better position to function as a region state, Nanjing seems somewhat ambiguous whether it wants to be complementary to Shanghai, to compete with it through the development of IT industries on the Nanjing Changzhou Wuxi Suzhou axis, or whether it wants to opt for becoming a center of its own in the described megalopitan area.

High tech industry development zones have become important and overseas funds invested in these zones accounted for 65.8 percent of the Jiangsu Province's total contracted overseas funding (*China Daily*, 16 May 2001). However, the conviction is growing that the market and not the government should develop technology parks (*China Daily*, 27 March 2002). Government's support, especially favorable land transferring policies is considered essential: 'only the market can test and improve their operations'. It has been argued that in a first effort to promote IT in Nanjing a cluster of hardware and software selling shops and workshops developed in the inner city. However, in a second wave a number of software producing companies located in different central and peri-urban clusters grew rapidly under favorable local, national and international conditions. An international value chain is developing in the case of the software sector of Nanjing and the city has interest to maximize the favorable effects of that process.

The PRD and YRD depict characteristics of region states, this does not mean that there is less competition in the global market where they also operate. Ohmae (1995) suggested as criteria that region states should have the authority to attract capital themselves. This is the case in both regions. Second, it should be possible to achieve big infrastructural projects independently, which has been done and has even led to doubling ports, airports and mass transport systems. Finally, the region state should be able to attract foreign investments and here they are both successful, although again competing with each other and the cities within each delta. However, gradually the YRD has received more FDI (Table 12.1), although the PRD has almost half the number of inhabitants, so in per capita terms the picture would be different again.

The empirical findings for Hong Kong suggest that there is a natural limit to the region state. There are also administrative, bureaucratic and political barriers to more cooperation and much depends on the willingness of the parties to cooperate and achieve the benefits of cooperation and reaching a certain scale. In the PRD the current situation seems to lead to a lot of over investment and unnecessary expenditure. In the YRD the focus is on regional development or provincial protection, which in an increasing global economy may not be the right objective to pursue. The role of cities and good urban management in these cities is striking and stresses the importance of training good urban managers!

NOTES

1. Prior to 1978 Shanghai was able to maintain its premier position in the Chinese economy while shouldering a high tax commitment. Tian (1996) assessed to what extent Shanghai would be able to reestablish its prewar role as a leading financial and commercial center in East Asia after 1978. It certainly is a leading financial center and an increasingly important commercial city for a large hinterland.
2. Research considering the PRD has been undertaken with Philip W. Koppels (Koppels, 2004) and van Dijk and Koppels (2004).
3. To be compared with US$ 100.50 as the cash income of rural residents in China (*Business Weekly*, 3 May 2004).
4. The other four original ports (during the period 1842–44) are Fuzhou, Xiamen, Guangzhou and Ningha.
5. Van Dijk (2006a) suggests a classification of clusters according to the geographical level, ranging from a national to a suburban cluster. The levels distinguished are national, regional, city-wide, inner city and suburban clusters.
6. OFIs and OCF are FDI forms that are not included in the official FDI statistics.
7. It is impossible to determine exactly which part of the FDI comes from the 'tax heaven economies' and has its origin in Hong Kong.
8. Under this category the foreign investments coming from Hong Kong are included. For EVA investments (export processing or assembling) there are no separate PRD figures.
9. In Hong Kong a total of 120 809 companies are registered as production or import and export companies. All these companies have received a questionnaire and 2597 useful answers were received, suggesting a reasonable representative sample with just over 2 percent of the population.
10. The three forms are assembling, processing for export and compensatory trade.
11. Shenzen and Zhuhai are Special economic zones near Hong Kong, while Shantou and Xiamen are two special economic zones near Taiwan. Finally Hainan also has this status.
12. The *Financial Times* reported on the bridge under the heading: HK aims to bolster economy by bridging the regional divide (20 February 2003).
13. Other megalopolitan areas being developed in the Yangtze River Delta are centered on Shanghai and Hangzhou, capital of East China's Zhejiang Province.
14. Zhejiang Province is one of the most prosperous in China because of the large concentration of township enterprises and an urbanization rate of 39 percent. For details of its economic development see Studwell (2003).

PART FIVE

New challenges and emerging themes in urban management

13. Conclusions

1. INTRODUCTION

My preferred definition of urban management is that an urban manager puts urban plans into practice, but I gave a more elaborate definition in my inaugural address in Rotterdam and in Chapter 4 of this book. The definition implies:

1. Urban issues are often related, requiring an integrated problem analysis;
2. The urban manager has to come up with integrated solutions;
3. She/he/they are the linchpin in linking the integrated problem analysis and the integrated solutions.

The good news is that decentralization provides opportunities to urban managers to do these things. Also the urban managers can use theories, methods and tools developed for that purpose. However, the urgency of the problems differs from place to place and there are no standard solutions. The book shows that we can learn from experiences elsewhere and that it is important to be informed about new trends and developments. For that reason we will first deal with the challenge of globalization. Then some of the remaining research issues will be formulated in this chapter. Finally the future themes will be discussed, namely the need to:

1. Create metropolitan governance structures in big cities;
2. Provide proper urban services in most cities, in particular to the poor;
3. Involve the private sector more in urban development and regeneration;
4. Increase the efficiency of government services by applying the principles of the NPM;
5. Do these things through a multi-stakeholder approach.

2. GLOBAL CITIES AND PERIPHERAL NODES

Institutional structures for urban development have rapidly changed in the 1990s. New decentralization policies are widely implemented, enhancing local governments' role. Nowadays, local government having adopted an enabling approach can be seen as entrepreneurial, encouraging multi-actor involvement in urban development. However, we have stressed that cities are competing and globalization and the neo-liberal economic development paradigm are increasing this process. According to Sassen (1991) globalization exposes cities to ideas, goods and services from elsewhere, which challenges the local production of industrial goods and of services. The old model of global integration was based on increased exports of goods and services. Developing countries were considered the periphery of a dominant capitalist system residing in Europe, North America or Japan. The dominant metropolitan core controlled the process from within. The original meaning of metropolitan zone of influence meant forming part of the motherland as distinct from its colonies. The term is now used for an ever expanding urban area with some supra regional government playing a role in trade or providing goods and services to a larger area. Cosmopolitan refers to the life style that tends to come with such metropolitan areas.

BOX 13.1 GLOBAL CITIES ACCORDING TO SASSEN

Global cities like New York, London and Tokyo are the production sites of global control over lengthening production chains of which even the industrial home workers in remote rural areas are now part (Sassen, 1991: 4–5):

1. Globalization is not just about networks and resulting flows, it is also about places.
2. This concentration is the result of globalization and can be explained by:

   a. Financial service providers concentrating around important financial centers.
   b. The need to have an innovative milieu requires networking among specialized business services to produce new managerial technological solutions.
   c. A high tech infrastructure is required to assure permanent connectivity.
   d. A specific logistical infrastructure based on the previously mentioned functions.

3. Professional business services are the managers of the decentralization and globalization process.

The importance of the global cities concept is that the impact of these cities goes beyond a region or metropolitan area. Sassen (1991) points to the role of knowledge, information and business services play in the longer existing process of concentration of global production chains in the global cities or metropolitan areas. The characteristics of the global city are summarized in Box 13.1. In her definition the emphasis is on global control over lengthening production chains.

A critique of Sassen's definition of global cities could be that she focuses on one particular type of city, namely the global service center. At a second level there are lots of cities in for example China and India that are centers of manufacturing activities and export an important part of their production to other countries, being part of all kinds of global value chains.

The governance structure of such value chains tend to be concentrated in such global manufacturing or services cities. These cities can compete with other aspiring global cities if it is fed by knowledge activities such as research and development, finance, marketing and design activities. However, the dynamics of the current world economic system is that other cities than the traditional metropoles are trying to take over the role of leader of production chains and try to become centers of knowledge and innovation. This process of competition offers chances to cities as far apart as Bangalore as a services city (van Dijk, 2003c), Shanghai as a manufacturing city (van Dijk, 2006a). If they do not succeed in becoming global cities, these cities may still be important as peripheral nodes in the world capitalist system. This seems to be the case of Dar es Salaam, the capital of Tanzania (van Dijk, 2006b). A city which can serve a large hinterland and even obtain a regional function in East Africa. The urban manager plays an important role in these processes. He or she can make the difference!

Further involvement of the private sector, non-governmental organizations and community groups in urban development processes requires new forms of urban management. Access to urban management processes has as well benefitted from technological developments as from liberalization of the information technology and communication market. The whole cycle from formulation of a strategy to implementation of an urban development project becomes more and more a continuous process rather than an isolated project or program, involving different actors in each stage. The different cases showed diversity and the practice of multi-actor approaches that have appeared over the years.

3. REMAINING URBAN MANAGEMENT RESEARCH ISSUES

3.1 The Effects of Decentralization

To find out how the decentralization process is working out, exact monitoring and independent research is necessary. We should check which responsibilities were transferred to cities in India, Indonesia and Thailand, to be able to answer the question: is it enough? Is this enough to allow active urban managers to be successful? Different levels of urban management (national, regional, metropolitan, municipal and district or neighborhood levels), with an extensive role for the local government, and a tendency towards more transparency in decision making increases the number of actors participating in the urban development processes.

Research has shown that local governments indeed get more responsibilities in the framework of decentralization and it is expected that these local governments will be held accountable in the end. Comparative research, comparing how European cities and important cities in Asia deal with the new opportunities provided in the framework of the decentralization policy is rare. The effects of decentralization are manifold and rarely quantified, but can be measured through the following indicators:

- The responsibilities, or possibilities urban managers have to strengthen the local economy and their results;
- The presence of good governance: how can decentralization increase transparency and accountability?
- The quantity and the quality of the houses built;
- Improved management of the cultural heritage of cities;
- The generation of more local revenues;
- Improvement of urban management in general; and
- Closer cooperation between local and metropolitan government.

The real issue is that decentralization may fail if no attention is paid to the conditions determining its success, such as a healthy financial basis and better cooperation between different levels of government, which role each level should play, the role assigned to them and the extent to which they do not try to do the work of other levels of government.

To judge the effects of decentralization cities can be ranked on the basis of indicators such as the growth of their revenues, their capacity to attract investments and other performance indicators for government departments and organizations.

3.2 How to Promote the Economic Dynamics of Clusters

What explains the dynamics of cities and their competitiveness? A lot of my research until now concerned the competitiveness of small enterprises and clusters of these enterprises. There is indeed a need for more comparative studies of the urban dynamics in emerging economies. We developed a questionnaire to determine competitiveness at different geographical levels. It has been used in Egypt and in China (van Dijk, 2004c). This research confirms that clusters can contribute to the dynamic development of urban centers. The question is each time to what extent the government can promote the clustering process and to what extent it is largely a spontaneous process (Castells and Hall, 1994).

3. 3 How to Mobilize the Necessary Finance

How can urban managers achieve more private financing of urban infrastructure: which instruments are successful and which legal forms are to be recommended? In Chapter 8 we showed that more sources of finance are available, that different legal forms can be tried and that the private sector may be willing to contribute to urban development. This requires economically and financially feasible projects and sometimes an intermediary organization, because not every small municipality may be able to gain access to the capital market. Learning from experiences elsewhere remains very important.

3.4 How to Use ICT Better for Urban Management

What are possibilities to use IT more in urban management and in our teaching about urban management? The use of IT in urban management will become more and more important and it is important to study the possibilities to link urban data sets to geographical information systems for urban management purposes. New technologies and means of communication have become available for urban managers in developed and developing countries as described in Chapter 9. This changes the functioning of the urban economy, of cities and of urban management. This also affects the way people communicate with authorities and the way officials and inhabitants can be trained and organized. The use of computers and information systems can certainly help to improve urban management. Access to data allows more transparency and more participatory decision making in urban affairs by inhabitants and other urban actors. Computers also facilitate the provision of training and information to urban managers and the population at large. It is important to learn from experiences elsewhere.

4. FUTURE CHALLENGES

4.1 Developing Metropolitan Governance

The question of cooperation on a larger scale level, or the installation of some kind of metropolitan government is not just an issue for huge Chinese or Indian cities, but also an important issue in Indonesia and many African and Latin American countries. It is one of the issues that Erasmus University has worked on for a long time (van den Berg et al., 1993). Different solutions have also been tried in the Netherlands to achieve cooperation and coordination between the large numbers of municipalities involved in important decisions concerning for example the harbor of Rotterdam.

An effort to create a city-province for Rotterdam has failed. Elsewhere single metropolitan authorities have been created in the 1990s and attempts have been made to put in place the policies and institutions to become effective (Roberts et al., 1993). It would be extremely interesting to compare these experiences in Europe with what is actually happening for example in Indonesia, where the need for a metropolitan authority is recognized, but no uniform provisions have been taken. Only Jakarta benefits from the provincial status with its own governor, to allow smooth cooperation between the different local governments in that city.

4.2 Proper Service Delivery for the Poor

World Bank (2004) summarizes the experience with proper urban service delivery and draws a number of relevant conclusions. The problem is often how to organize service delivery for the urban poor, who can only pay minimal amounts for such services. The reform of organizational structures touches the receivers of urban development, the inhabitants and their community. Participation of low-income groups might fail in the first instance because of exclusion in the identification and formulation phase of urban projects. Or it fails due to financial constraints on the side of the community itself. Attention should be paid to financial support systems in urban development programs to include, rather than exclude the urban poor.

Several alternative financing systems were mentioned, partially with a focus of including low-income groups. Rotating Savings and Credit Associations (ROSCAs), were discussed for example by Smets (2002). They exist among community members in India but similar institutions can be found worldwide. Citizens deposit regular savings into a common fund. In turn the amount collected is allotted in part or in total to each participant. Citizens are given the chance to save and allot the money when they need it the most. Unfortunately the poorest inhabitants often do not get access to the ROSCA since they cannot save even such small amounts.

The same problem of exclusion exists in Ethiopia as described in Chapter 6 and also by Beeker (2002). In those cases the poorest are excluded from drinking water and housing projects. The minimum payment fixed is often too high for this group. They cannot claim to be creditworthy. Hence the urban poor often end up in spontaneous settlements or slums, unless appropriate financial institutions can be developed to cater for these groups. Micro finance institutions would be one possible solution.

Slum upgrading may also be a solution, because it helps the poor directly. Good examples of successful upgrading of spontaneous settlements are rare, compared with the large number of forced evictions of squatters, which are described in many publications. Inclusion of the very urban poor in urban development processes is necessary for improving the living circumstances of low-income groups. The cases in the previous chapters show the difficulty of serving this particular group of people. Present urban development models do not seem sufficient or adequate to serve the whole city. A continuous challenge in the urban sector is the finding of optimal institutional structures serving as many inhabitants as possible, not leaving aside the very poor.

4.3 Involving the Private Sector

Finance is the oil of urban development, hence the importance of financial aspects of developing cities and of involving the private sector. For urban managers it is always necessary to search for opportunities to involve the private sector and to find out which instruments and legal forms are most appropriate for this purpose. Which possibilities exist to identify risks, to allocate them between the different partners and eventually to cover the risks involved through for example insurance.

4.4 Increase Efficiency by Applying the Principles of the NPM

The most important assumption behind the NPM theory is that by mimicking the practices of 'private sector' organizations, public sector organizations would accrue the benefits of efficiency, flexibility and consumer-orientation that are often associated with private sector organizations. Finally more market-orientation would force them to become more efficient by subcontracting those activities that other organizations can do at lower unit cost. This theory is highly relevant for managing urban development as well, but also requires a critical assessment because the pre-conditions may not always be in place and the effects are not always what is expected (see Chapter 6).

4.5 A Multi-stakeholder Approach

Housing delivery systems developed from provision by the government, towards the site and services approach, presently including communities' role. Policies initiated by major research and development institutes and donor agencies follow a similar pattern. A clear distinction between these approaches was found by Aliaj (2002) in the case of Tirana, Albania. The initial sites and services approach is mainly seen as a joint effort between the public and the private sector, whereas a latter development shows real involvement of CBOs and NGOs.

A long-term commitment from all the stakeholders is required in order to increase the effects of an urban development project. In this regard capacity building including training can benefit urban managers dealing with urban development processes. Participatory planning techniques and multi-actor approaches towards urban management require new techniques and skills, serving the new institutional forms established.

The main actors in the development process are the people affected by the new program. In the case of Vitebsk, twenty representatives under which the private sector, local media, NGOs, the concerned public office and the community attended a grass-root meeting and exchanged ideas. A multi-actor approach has also been used in Burkina Faso in the promotion of slum improvement without destroying the existing houses. Despite the responsible Department of Town Planning, municipal housing offices, National Water Office and the National Fund for Land Reclamation and Maintenance being involved in the project, the involvement of the population on a systematic base was regarded too costly. Unrest among the citizens in the project area, due to a lack of community involvement, affected the progress of the project negatively. Inclusion of all actors affected in the identification phase of an urban development process is recommended, reducing the influence of counter forces and increasing the feeling of ownership.

5. CONCLUSIONS

The development in urban management from a single actor approach towards a multi-actor approach in urban development processes is believed to synergize the actions of the parties involved. As can be seen in the cases discussed in the previous chapters, other factors highly influence success of this so-called stakeholder approach.

An important prerequisite mentioned several times is commitment and involvement of all actors. Each party has it's own 'stake' in the partnership. A lack of transparency, distrust and corruption appear to reduce the possibilities for a successful joint approach of urban management as can be seen in the case of Indonesia described by Suselo and van der Hoff (2002). Also the Slum Redevelopment Scheme in India (de Wit, 1996 and Desai, 2002) proved to be a failure because of its isolated approach. The combined strength of the private sector, the public sector and the community (public-private-community partnerships or PPcP) can bring together financial means, awareness of local needs and institutional back up, if full commitment of all parties can be reached.

The challenge for urban managers is to promote an integrated strategy to deal with the major issues of their cities. They serve the public cause they help the inhabitants, in particular the poorest, for the people, but also with these people, to develop a truly sustainable city.

References

Several websites and newspapers were used, such as the *India Today, China Daily* (CD), *China Business Weekly,* the *Shanghai Star* (China), the *Jakarta Pos* (Indonesia), the *Financial Times* (FT), *NRC* (the Netherlands), the *International Herald Tribune* (IHT) and the *Wall Street Journal* (WSJ).

ADB (1994): Asian Development Outlook 1994. New York: Oxford.

Alisjahbana (1995): Institutional body for development cooperation between local governments within the metropolitan region: a case study of the Surabaya Metropolitan region. Rotterdam: UMC MA thesis.

Aliaj, B. (2002): NGOs/CBOs and housing for low-income people in Albania. In: van Dijk et al. (2002).

APUSP (1998): Draft final report. Hyderabad: DHV-IHS.

Baharoglu, D. and C. Lepelaars (2002): A bottom-up approach within the top-down tradition of Belarus, Action planning behind the former iron curtain. In: van Dijk et al. (2002).

Bamberger, M. and E. Hewitt (1990): Monitoring and evaluating urban development programs. Washington: World Bank.

Baross, P. (1991): Action planning. Rotterdam: IHS Working paper No. 2.

Bartone, C., J. Bernstein, J. Leitmann and J. Eigen (1994): Toward environmental strategies for cities. Washington: UMP.

Barzelay, M. (1992): Breaking through bureaucracy: a new vision for managing in government. University of California Press: Berkeley.

Beeker, M.C. (2002): Access to the urban field in Ethiopia. In: van Dijk et al. (2002).

Berg, L. van den (1987): Urban systems in a dynamic society. Aldershot: Ashgate.

Berg, L. van den, H.A. van Klink and J. van der Meer (1993): Governing metropolitan regions. Aldershot: Ashgate.

Berg, L. van den and W. van Winden (2000): ICT as potential catalyst for sustainable urban development, experiences in the cities of Eindhoven, Helsinki, Manchester, Marseilles and The Hague. Rotterdam: EURICUR.

Berg, L. van den, E. Braun and W. van Winden (2001): Growth clusters in European metropolitan cities. Aldershot: Ashgate.

Berg, L. van den, E. Braun and A. Otgaar (2002): Sports and city marketing in European cities. Aldershot: Ashgate.
Berg, L. van den, P. Pol, W.van Winden and P. Woets (2005): European cities in an the knowledge economy. Aldershot: Ashgate
Best, M.H. (1990): The new competition, institutions of industrial restructuring. Cambridge: Harvard.
BNG (1999): Bank of the public sector. The Hague: Bank of the Dutch Municipalities.
BNG (2003): Annual report. The Hague: Bank of the Dutch Municipalities.
Bohle, L.M. (1992): Financial institutions and markets. New Delhi: Tata-McGrawhill.
Bramezza, I. (1996): The competitiveness of the European city and the role of urban management in improving the city's performance. Rotterdam: Tinbergen Institute, No. 109.
Brealey, R.A. and S.C. Myers (1996): Principles of corporate finance. New York: McGraw-Hill.
Bruijn, C.A. de (1987): Monitoring a large squatter area in Dar es Salaam with sequential aerial photography. In: *ITC Journal*, 3, pp. 233–38.
Buechler, H. and J.-M. Buechler (2005): They were promised a rose garden: Reunification and globalization in small and medium-size firms in Eastern Germany. In: Smart and Smart (2005).
Burki, S. and G. Perry (1998): Beyond the Washington Consensus: institutions Matter, World Bank Latin American and Caribbean Studies, Washington: World Bank.
Capel-Tatjer, L. (1999): Urban regeneration and the social dimension, the case of waterfront redevelopment in Rotterdam and Barcelona. Rotterdam: MA Thesis.
Casley, D.J. and K. Kumar (1988): Project monitoring and evaluation in agriculture. Baltimore: Johns Hopkins.
Castells, M. and P. Hall (1994): Technopoles of the world, The making of 21st century industrial complexes. London: Routledge.
Chadee, D.D., F. Qiu., E.L. Rose (2003): FDI location at the sub national level: a study of EJVs in China. In: *Journal of Business Research* 56: 835–45.
Chang, G.G. (2002): The coming collapse of China. London: Arrow Books.
Cheema, G.S. (ed., 1993): Urban management, policies and innovations in developing countries. Westport: Praeger.
Chen, H. (2000): The institutional transition of Chinas township and village enterprises. Aldershot: Ashgate.
Chen, H. (2001): Inside Chinese business, a guide for managers worldwide. Boston: Harvard Business School.
Clissold, T. (2004): Mr. China. London: Robinson.
Coase, R.H. (1960): The problem of social cost. In: *Journal of Law and Economics*, 3, October.

Cohen, M.A., B.A. Ruble, J.S. Tulchin and A.M. Garland (1996): Preparing for the urban future. Baltimore: John Hopkins University Press.
Correa de Olievera, M.T. (2002): Towards more cooperative cities. In: van Dijk et al. (2002).
Correa de Olievera, M.T. (2003): Multi-sectoral partnerships for low-income land development in Brazil. Utrecht: University, Ph.D.
Davidson, F. (1999): Strategic and action planning. Rotterdam: IHS, Course material.
Davidson, F. and P. Nientied (1991): Introduction to a special issue on urban management in the Third World. In: *Cities*, 8, 2, May.
Delvecchio, D. (1999): Amsterdam: the hook-up city. In: *Urban age*, 7, 2, Fall.
Desai, P. (2002): Slum development scheme in Mumbai: Building castles in the air? In: van Dijk et al. (2002).
Desai, P. (2003): Slum development scheme in Mumbai. Utrecht: University of Utrecht.
Desta, M. Kifle (2003): Assessment of the water sector reform for AAWSA in Ethiopia. Delft: UNESCO-IHE.
Devas, N. and C. Radkodi (eds, 1993): Managing fast growing cities, new approaches to urban planning and management in the developing world. Essex: Longman.
Dijk, M.P. van (1992): Socio economic development funds to mitigate the social cost of adjustment. Experiences in three countries. In: *Journal of Development Research*, 4, 1, June, pp. 97–112.
Dijk, M.P. van (1993): Industrial districts and urban economic development. In: *Third World Planning Review*, 15, 2, pp. 175–87.
Dijk, M.P. van (1997): The economic activities of the poor in Accra, Ghana. In: D. Bryceson and V. Jamal (eds, 1997): Farewell to farms, de-agrarianization and employment in Africa, Hampshire: Ashgate Publishing, pp. 101–17.
Dijk, M.P. van (1998): Reforming the state-owned industrial enterprises in China. In: *MSM Research Papers,*. XVII, 1 & 2, June–December.
Dijk, M.P. van (1999a): Globalization and economic restructuring: Competitiveness at the regional, country, city and enterprise level. In: M.S.S. El-Namaki (ed., 1999): Strategic issues at the dawn of a new millennium. Leiderdorp: Lansa.
Dijk, M.P. van (1999b): Municipalities access to (inter-)national capital markets for financing urban infrastructure. In: K. Singh and B. Thai (1999): Financing and pricing of urban infrastructure. New Delhi: New Age International, pp. 157–79.
Dijk, M.P. van (2000): Summer in the city, decentralization provides new opportunities for urban management in emerging economies. Inaugural address, 15 June. Rotterdam: IHS (English version), pp. 1–36.
Dijk, M.P. van (2002b): Local government policies with respect to a concentration of IT companies in Nanjing, China. In: Urban Forum, Issue 1, Summer 2002, pp. 93–105.

Dijk, M.P. van (2003a): Liberalization in the drinking water sector. Delft: Unesco-IHE. Inaugural address.

Dijk, M.P. van (2003b): Is Nanjing's concentration of IT companies an innovative cluster? In: D. Fornahl and T. Brenner (eds, 2003): Cooperation, networks and institutions in regional innovation systems. Cheltenham: Edward Elgar, pp. 173–94.

Dijk, M.P. van (2003c): Government policies with respect to an information technology cluster in Bangalore India. In: *European Journal of Development Research*, 15, 2, pp. 93–109.

Dijk, M.P. van (2004a): The role of financial institutions and markets in urban development in India, with examples from Karnataka and Gujarat. In: Gupta (ed., 2004).

Dijk, M.P. van (2004b): Research methods and tools for an MBA course in Nanjing, Delft: UNESCO-IHE Institute for Water education, 69 pages.

Dijk, M.P. van (2004c): A comparative study of competitiveness in the ICT sector in China and India, in Chinese, in: *Nanjing Business Review*. 3, pp. 143–58.

Dijk, M.P. van (2005a). Nanjing, promoting the ICT sector. In: Nas (ed., 2005).

Dijk, M.P. van (2005b): India-China, a battle of two new ICT giants. In: Saith and Vijayabaskar (eds, 2005), pp. 440-460.

Dijk, M.P. van (2006a): Can China remain competitive? The role of innovation systems for an emerging IT cluster, Rotterdam: EUR, book, forthcoming.

Dijk, M.P. van (2006b): Flows of people, goods and money, the role of the informal sector to spread development beyond Dar es Salaam. Leiden: NVAS conference, 16 pages. Leiden: ASC (forthcoming)

Dijk, M.P. van and N.G. Schulte Nordholt (1994): Privatization experiences in Africa and Asia. Amsterdam: SISWO.

Dijk, M.P. and S. Sideri (eds, 1996): Multilaterism versus regionalism: Trade issues after the Uruguay Round. London: F. Cass.

Dijk, M.P. van and R. Rabellotti (eds, 1997): Enterprise clusters and networks in developing countries. London: F. Cass.

Dijk M.P. van and S. Shivanand (1999): Draft final report on a SAIL Research project. Rotterdam: IHS.

Dijk, M.P. van, M. Noordhoek and E. Wegelin (eds, 2002): Governing cities, new institutional forms in developing countries and transitional economies. London: ITDG.

Dijk, M.P. van and P. Koppels (2004): Governance structures and the optimum region state according to a gravitation model in the Pearl River Delta in China. Paper for the conference Business Management in the New Economy in Macao, 2-5 May.

Dijk, M.P. van and Q. Wang (2005): Cluster governance in an emerging city-wide ICT cluster in Nanjing. In: Guiliani et al. (eds, 2005).

Dijk, M.P. van and M. Zhang (2005): Sustainability indices as a tool for urban management. In: *Environmental impact assessment review*. 25, pp. 667–89.

Dillinger, W. and M. Fay (1999): From centralized to decentralized governance. In: *Finance and Development*, December, pp. 19–22.
Enright, M. J., Ka-Mun Chang, E.E. Scott and Wenhui Zhu (2003): Hong Kong and the Pearl River Delta: The economic interaction. Hong Kong: The 2022 Foundation.
England, J.R., K.I. Hudson, R.J. Masters, K.S. Powell and J.D. Shortridge (1985): Information systems for policy planning in local government. Longman: Essex.
Expert group on commercialization of infrastructure projects (1996): The India infrastructure report: policy imperatives for growth and welfare (three volumes). New Delhi: GOI.
Fainstain, S.S., I. Gordon and M. Harloe (eds, 1992): Divided cities, New York and London in the contemporary world. Oxford: Blackwell.
FIRE (1996): Municipal bond market for urban infrastructure. New Delhi: FIRE project, pp. 1-23.
Florida, R. (2004): The rise of the creative class. New York: Basic Books.
Frank, A.G. (1990): A theoretical introduction to 5000 years of world system history. *Review*. XIII, 2, Spring.
Freire, M. and R. Stren (eds, 2001): The challenge of urban government, policies and practice. Washington: World Bank Institute Development studies.
Gates, H. (2005): Petty production: the enduring alternative. In: Smart and Smart (2005).
Gorter, P. (1998): Industrial pollution in Vapi (India). Amsterdam: CASA, Ph.D.
Grosse, R. and L.J. Trevino (1996): Foreign direct investment in the United States; an analysis by country of origin. In: *Journal of International Business Studies*,. 27, 1, pp. 135–55.
Gu, Shulin (1999): China's industrial technology, market reform and organisational change. London: Routledge/Maastricht: UNU/Intech.
Guiliani, E., R Rabellotti and M.P. van Dijk (eds, 2005): Clusters facing competition: The importance of external linkages. Aldershot: Ashgate.
Gujarat (2000): Infrastructure development in Gujarat. Ahmedabad: State Government, a CD rom.
Gupta, K.R. (ed., 2004): Urban development in the new millennium. New Delhi: Atlantic.
He Jian (2000): Relevance of enterprise clusters for local economic development in Nanjing. Rotterdam: Urban Management Center, MA thesis.
Helmsing, A.H.J. (2000): Decentralization and enablement. Utrecht: University, Inaugural address.
Hong Kong Trade Development Council (2003): The link age, connecting the Greater Pearl River Delta, January.
Hong Kong Center for Economic Research (2003): Made in PRD; the changing face of HK manufacturers. Hong Kong: Federation of Industries.
Jacobs, J. (1970): The economy of cities. New York: Vintage.

Janssens, J. and A. Baietti (2002): Internal World Bank publication. Washington: IBRD.
Juppenplatz, M. (1991): Urban environmental surveys. In: *Cities*, February, pp. 2-9.
Kettl, D. (2000): The global public management revolution: a report on the transformation of governance. Washington: The Brookings Institute.
Klaassen, L., J. Paelink and S. Wagenaar (1979): Spatial systems. London: Saxon House.
Klink, A. van and I. Bramezza (1995): Besturen van gebieden met nieuw elan In: *City Management & Marketing*, 33, 1, pp. 33–42.
Kogut, B. and H. Singh (1998): The effects of national culture on the choice of entry mode. In: *Journal of International Business Studies*, 19, 3, pp. 32–41.
Koppels, P.E. (2004). The optimal size of a region state, Hong Kong, Macau and the PRD (in dutch). Rotterdam: Erasmus University, MA Thesis.
Kresl, P.K. and G. Gappert (1996): North American cities and the global economy: challenges and opportunities. In: *Urban Affairs Annual Review*, 44, pp. 1–17.
Lardy, N. (2002): Integrating China in the global economy. Washington: Brookings Institutions Press.
Leung, E. et al. (2002): Why Hong Kong? A Survey of Japanese firms in the Pearl River Delta. Hong Kong: Hong Kong Trade Development Council.
Leung, E. et al. (2003): Why Choose Hong Kong as a service platform? A Survey of EU Companies in the Pearl River Delta. Hong Kong: Hong Kong Trade Development Council.
Liang, G. (2004): New competition, foreign direct investment and industrial development in China. Rotterdam: Erasmus University.
Lindfield, M. (1998): Preparing markets for private financing of urban infrastructure. Rotterdam: Erasmus University, Ph.D.
Lindsey, M. (1998): Urban management. Bali: Conference UNCHS.
Lee, K.S. and R. Gilbert (1999): Developing towns and cities: lessons from Brazil and the Philippines. Washington: World Bank.
Loon, F.D. van and M.P. van Dijk (1995): The financial flows to and capital markets in Asia. In: K. Fukasaku (ed.): Regional co-operation and integration in Asia. Paris: OECD, pp. 175–93.
Luyn, F.J. van (2004): Een stad van boeren. Amsterdam: Promotheus.
Lynn, L. (1996). The new public management as an international phenomenon: a skeptical view. Paper presented at the conference on the new public management in international perspective, 11–13 July, St. Gallen, Switzerland.
Marshall, A. (1920): Principles of economics. London: MacMillan.
McAuslan, P. (1997): The making of the urban management program. In: *Urban Studies*, 34, 10, pp. 1705–27.
McGuigan, J.R., R.C. Moyer and F.H. De B. Harris (1999): Managerial economics: applications, strategy and tactics. Cincinnati: South-Western College Publishing.

Mintzberg, H. (1994): The rise and fall of strategic planning. New York: Free Press.
Mishan, E.J. (1988): Cost-benefit analysis. London: Unwin Hyman.
Mukundan, C. (1998): Performance criteria municipalities. Madras: Karloskar.
Nas, P. (ed., 2005): Directors of urban change in Asia. London: Routledge.
National Bureau of Statistics of China (2002). Guangdong Statistical Yearbook 2002. Beijing: China Statistics Press.
Ndimo, D.N. (1998): The potential for private provision in urban water supply and solid waste in Mbarara Municipality in Uganda. Rotterdam: UMC Thesis.
NMP (1988): National Environmental Policy Plan (NEPP). The Hague: Ministry of Housing, Physical Planning and the Environment.
NMP-Plus (1990): National Environmental Policy Plan Plus. The Hague: Ministry Housing, Physical Planning and the Environment.
NMP Two (1993): National Environmental Policy Plan Two. The Hague: Ministry of Housing, Physical Planning and the Environment.
North, D.C. (1993): Institutions, institutional change and economic performance. Cambridge: University Press.
Nunn, S. and J.B. Rubleske (1997): 'Webbed' cities and development of the national information highway: the creation of world web sites by US city governments. In: *Journal of Urban Technology*, 4, 1, pp. 53–79, April.
OECD (1999): Voluntary approaches for environmental policy. Paris: Organization for Economic Cooperation and Development.
Ohmae, K. (1995): The end of the nation state, the rise of regional economies, London: Harper Collins.
Osborne, D. and T. Gaebler (1992): Reinventing government: how the entrepreneurial spirit is transforming the public sector. Reading: Addison-Wesley.
Paulsson, B. (1992): Urban applications of satellite remote sensing and GIS analysis, Washington: World Bank, Urban Management Programme.
Pelt, M. van (1993): Sustainability oriented project appraisal for developing countries. Wageningen: Agricultural University.
Petersen, J. (1999): A primer on State bond banks in the US. Santander: World Bank conference.
Piore, M. and C.F. Sable (1984): The second industrial divide, possibilities for Prosperity. New York: Basic Books.
Porter, M.P. (1990): The competitiveness of Nations. London: MacMillan.
Post, J. (1996): Space for small enterprise, reflections on urban livelihood and urban planning in the Sudan. Amsterdam: Thesis Publishers, Ph.D.
Rabinovitsch, J. (1999): From urban management to urban governance: towards a strategy for the new millennium. In: *City development*, pp. 23–26.
Rees, W.E. (1992): Ecological footprint and appropriated carrying capacity: what urban economics leaves out. In: *Environment and Urbanization*, 4, 2, pp. 121–31.
Richardson, H.W. (1976): Urban economics. Middlesex: Penguin.

Roberts, P., T. Struthers and J. Sacks (eds, 1993): Managing the metropolis, metropolitan renaissance, new life for the old city regions. Aldershot: Avebury.
Rondinelli, D.A. and K. Ruddle (1978): Urbanization and rural development, A spatial policy for equitable growth. New York: Praeger.
Roth, G. (1989): The private provision of public services in developing countries. Washington: World Bank.
Rukmana, N., F. Steinberg and R. van der Hoff (1993): Managemen pembangunan prasaran perkataan. Jakarta: LPES.
Saith, A. and M. Vijayabaskar (eds, 2005): ICTS and Indian economic development. New Delhi: Sage Publications.
Samuelson, P. and W.D. Nordhaus (different editions): Economics, a text book.
Sassen, S. (1991): The global city. New York, London, Tokyo. Princeton: University Press.
Saunders, M., P. Lewis and A. Thornhill (2003): Research methods for business students. London: Prentice Hall.
Satyanarayana, V. (2006): Sustainable urban services and private sector participation an Indian experience. In: Sijbesma and van Dijk (2006).
Schotten, C.G.J. et al. (1997): De ruimtescanner, geïntegreerd ruimtelijk informatiesysteem voor de simulatie van toekomstig ruimtegebruik. Bilthoven: RIVM.
Schwartz, K. and M.P. van Dijk (2003): A series of case studies of well performing drinking water companies. Delft: UNESCO-IHE, 17 pages.
Schwartz, K. and M.P. van Dijk (2004): Modes of engagements. Delft: UNESCO-IHE.
Scott, J.T. (2005): The concise handbook of management. New York: Best Business Books.
Sen, A. K. (1999): Development as freedom. Oxford: Oxford University Press.
Senter, H. (1997): Considerations for the development and use of a GIS within the HCMC Urban Planning Institute. Saigon: UPI.
Serageldin, I., R. Barrett and J. Martin-Brown (eds, 1994): The business of sustainable cities, public private partnerships for creative technical and institutional solutions. Washington: World Bank.
Sijbesma, C. and M.P. van Dijk (eds, 2006): Water and sanitation, Institutional challenges in India. New Delhi: Manohar.
Smart, A. and J. Smart (eds, 2005): Petty capitalists and globalization, flexibility entrepreneurship, and economic development. New York State University.
Smets, P. (2002): ROSCAs and housing finance in Hyderabad, India: their potential for development. In: van Dijk et al. (2002).
Snrech, S. (1994): Preparing for the future, a vision of West Africa in the year 2020. Paris: Club du Sahel (OECD).
Sparreboom, T. (1999): Improving labor market information in Southern Africa. Harare: ILO SAMAT Policy Paper, No. 10.
Spencer, J.D. (1990): The search for modern China. New York: Norton.

Stiglitz, J. (1988): Economics of the public sector. New York: Prentice Hall.
Storper, M. (1990): Industrialization and the regional question in the Third World: lessons from postimperialism; prospects of post-Fordims. In: *International Journal of Urban and Regional Research*, 14, 3.
Stren, R. (1993): Urban management in development assistance, An elusive concept. In: *Cities*, May, pp. 125–38.
Studwell, J. (2003). The China Dream. New York: Grove Press.
Suselo, H., E.A. Wegelin and J.L. Taylor (1995): Indonesia's urban infrastructure development experience. Nairobi: UNCHS.
Suselo, H. and R. van der Hoff (2002): Emerging institutional forms for urban management. In: van Dijk et al. (2002).
TCS-IHS (2000): Final report in the framework of the ADB project strengthening urban infrastructure. New Delhi: Tata Consultancy Services.
Thynne, I. (1994): Government companies as instruments of state action. In: *Public administration and development*, 18, pp. 217–28.
Tian, G. (1996): Shanghai's role in the economic development of China, reform of foreign trade and investment. London: Praeger.
Tribillon, J.-F. (1985): La gestion urbaine africaine: de la gestion de l'urbanisme à celle de l'urbain. In: *Journées d'études*, January.
Tuan, C. and L.F.Y. Ng (2001): Regional division of labor from agglomeration economies perspective: some evidence. In: *Journal of Asian Economics*, 12, pp. 65–85.
Turkstra, J. (1998): Urban development and geographical information, spatial and temporal patterns of urban development and land values using integrated geo-data, Villavicencio, Colombia. Enschede: ITC Publications.
Turner, J.F.C. (1986): Housing by people, towards autonomy in building environment. New York: Pantheon Books.
UNCHS Bulletin (1999): Urban governance, 5, 4.
UNCHS (2004): The state of the world's cities. Nairobi: UN Habitat.
UNFPA (1998): World population report 1999. New York: United Nations Population Fund.
UN (1994): Workshop on waste treatment in industrial parks. Geneva: Economic and Social Council, Economic Commission for Europe.
UNITAR (1998): Proceedings of the international sharing workshop on urban information systems, UNITAR Geneva.
USAID (1994): National environmental action plan for Uganda. Kampala. Washington: USAID.
USAID (1996): Using the bond market for urban development. New Delhi: FIRE Program.
VEWIN (2001): Reflections on performance 2000. Benchmarking in the Dutch Drinking water industry. Rijswijk: VEWIN. http://www.vewin.nl.
Viscusi, W.K., J.M. Vernon and J. Harrington (2000): Economics of regulation and antitrust. Cambridge: MIT Press.

Visser, E.J. (1996): Local sources of competitiveness, spatial clustering and organizational dynamics in small-scale clothing in Lima, Amsterdam: Ph.D.

Vliet, J. van and J. Frijns (1997): Pollution control in Nairobi. Wageningen: University.

Wahyu Kusumosusanto, J. (1998): Improving metropolitan performance through inter-municipal co-operation, the case of Bandung Metropolitan area, Indonesia. Rotterdam: UMC, MA thesis.

Wallis, J. and B. Dollery (2001): Government failure, social capital and the appropriateness of the New Zealand model for public sector reform in developing countries. In: *World Development,* 29, 2, pp 245–63.

Wegelin, E., K. Wekwete and F. Vanderschueren (1995): Options for municipal actions in poverty reduction. Washington: Urban Management Program.

Williamson O.E. (1998): Transaction cost economy: how it works and where it is headed. In: *De Economist*, 146, pp. 23–58.

Widner, R.R. (ed., 1992): Divided cities in a global economy. Report on the European-North American 'State-of-the-cities'.

Wiemann, J. (1996): Green protectionism, a threat to Third World exports? In: van Dijk and Sideri (eds, 1996).

Wit, M.J. de (1992): Geographical information systems, remote sensing and slums in Indian Cities; the case of Bangalore, The Hague: NUFFIC IDPAD.

Wit, J.W. de (1996): Poverty, policy and politics in Madras slums: dynamics of survival, gender and leadership. New Delhi: Sage.

Wit, J.W. de (2002): Cooperation between governmental, non-governmental and community-based organizations: the Bangalore Urban Poverty Alleviation Programme. In: van Dijk et al. (2002).

World Bank (1993): The East Asian miracle. New York: Oxford.

World Bank (1994): World development report on Infrastructure. New York: Oxford.

World Bank (2000): Attacking poverty, World development report. New York: Oxford.

World Bank (2004): Making services work for the poor, World Development Report. New York: Oxford. (also as CD rom).

Water and Sanitation Program (WSP) (2002): New designs for water and sanitation transactions. Washington, Water and Sanitation Program.

Yannopoulus, G.N. and J.H. Dunning (1976): MNEs and regional development: an exploratory paper. In: *Regional Studies,* 10, 5, pp. 389–401.

Yiwen Fei (2004): The institutional change in China after its reform in 1979. Rotterdam: Erasmus University, Ph.D.

Yulong, S. and C. Hamnett (2002): The potential and prospect for global cities in China: in the context of the World System. In: *Geoforum,* 33, pp. 121–35.

Zhang, Y. (1989): Economic system reform in China. Helsinki: UNU WIDER., Working paper 55.

Zhang, M. (2002): Measuring urban sustainability in China. Rotterdam: Erasmus University, Ph.D.

Index

AAWSA 86–7
accountability 45–6, 48–9, 81, 93
action planning 6, 23–4, 55–7, 65–6
action research 69–70
ADB 104–5, 108, 112, 118, 199, 207
Addis Ababa 19, 23, 48, 75–86
agglomeration 99,174,179, 181–2, 185
Ahmedabad 26, 51–3, 114, 117, 122
AMC 51, 117
APUSP 39,110,114
asset management 60, 66, 68–9, 86
AUDA 51
autonomy 18, 35, 37, 45–6, 78, 81–3, 87–8, 90–3, 116, 140–1, 158, 163

Bangalore 16, 21–3, 42, 44, 66, 71, 117–20, 127, 173, 193
BDA 119
BIS 69
BNG 115–6
BOD 87
Bond Bank 109, 114–6
BOO 77
BOT 83, 110, 117–8
BUPP 21
BWSSB 117–9

Cairo 26
case study 70
CBA 62, 86
CBOs 17, 19, 21–2, 54, 117–8, 197
CCF 114, 121–2
CD 146–7, 203, 208
city development strategy 95, 161
city marketing 49, 57, 59, 65–6, 133
civil society 16–7, 21, 51, 68, 72, 120

cluster 39–43, 49, 52, 56, 98–100, 106–8, 143, 156–7, 164–6, 168–71, 174–5, 178, 182–3, 187–8, 194–5
collective efficiency 108
communication 16–7, 21, 25, 59–61, 63, 67–8, 71–2, 76, 121, 123–4, 129, 146, 172, 193, 195
comparative advantage 39–40, 105, 143, 181
competition 9,12, 44, 47–8, 61, 66, 88, 92, 99, 121, 140, 143, 152–3, 163, 174, 178, 183, 185–7, 193
competitive advantage 40, 55, 65, 177
contract 45, 47–8, 50, 76, 78, 80, 82–3, 88, 92–3, 108, 113, 116, 119, 140, 141–2, 150
cost benefit analysis 57, 62, 86
cost recovery 39, 55, 62, 93, 111, 113, 120–1
crash program 87, 89
customer orientation 45, 47, 78, 80, 86, 88, 91–3

Dakar 127, 131–2, 134
Dar es Salaam 198
DCA 119
decentralization 4–5, 9, 12–6, 20–1, 25, 27, 31–9, 49–51, 53, 57–8, 75, 83–4, 86, 88, 90, 109–10, 115, 139–40, 173, 191–4
devolution 35
DFBO 110
DFID 8, 108
Dhaka 3, 5, 104
distant learning 17, 123–4
divided city 48

DL 123
DVD 146–7, 149

ECAP 39
economics 7, 9, 11, 24, 31, 43, 49, 60–1, 121
ECSC 96
environment 8, 10, 20, 22, 26–7, 35, 51, 53–5, 57, 60, 63, 66, 72, 97–108, 126, 146, 157, 160–1, 184
environmental issues
  analysis 59
  impact 4, 104
Erasmus university 9–10, 11–2, 14, 27, 49, 53, 77, 123, 195
ethnography 69–70
EURICUR 27, 129
evaluation 57, 59–60, 62–3, 68–9, 71, 86–7, 111
evolution 61, 139, 156, 174
exclusion 48, 129, 196

FDI 175, 178–82, 187–8, 200
FIE 179
FIRE 115, 117, 119, 140, 203, 207
flexible specialization 41, 48, 99, 108
foreign direct investment 175, 178–82, 188
financial
  analysis 57, 59, 62
  autonomy 93
  instruments 59, 111–23
  markets 4, 10, 26, 51–2, 55,
  private 85, 195
  support 168, 192

GDP 86, 153, 158, 177, 180–2
gender 12, 208
geographical level 17, 156, 188, 194
GIDB 116
GIS 123, 126–7, 129–32, 205
global city 156, 192–3
global value chains 193
globalization 4, 27, 138, 152, 156, 174, 191–2, 200
governance 10, 11, 13–4, 34, 38, 49, 122, 173, 175, 178, 185–6, 191, 193–5

good governance 10, 11, 22–3, 32, 44, 112, 194
urban governance 17, 43–4, 174
grounded theory 69–70

hierarchy 156–7, 184
Hong Kong 142–3, 145, 150, 169, 174, 176, 178–88
housing 10, 12, 17–20, 22–3, 31, 50, 53–6, 58, 60, 71, 104, 115, 125, 127, 129–30, 133, 148–50, 160–2, 194, 196–8
HRD 91
HUDCO 112, 115
Hyderabad 8, 42, 44, 51
hypothesis 48, 70, 79, 180

ICAI 118
ICT 124, 195
IHE 123, 201–2, 206
IHS 10, 12, 24, 49, 53, 55, 112, 118, 122, 132, 173
ILO 206
IMF 41, 69
indicator 38, 40, 42, 47, 59, 62–3, 78, 82, 87, 92, 94, 104, 111, 129, 184, 194
industrial district 48, 98–9, 106
inequality 3–4
information technology (IT) 13, 39, 56, 58, 64, 125–36, 159, 193
informal sector 53, 58, 138, 144–8, 151–4
infrastructure 4, 8, 10, 14, 18–9, 21, 31, 42–3, 50, 54–5, 61, 67, 75–6, 85–6, 106, 109–11, 113–7
innovation 26, 33, 40–1, 43, 46, 48–9, 99, 108, 123, 142, 158, 168, 171, 180, 193
institution 10, 12–3, 15–22, 24, 27, 31, 38, 40, 42, 46, 49, 51–2, 54–5, 57, 60–1, 69, 71, 81, 84–7, 93, 101, 103, 105, 108–10, 113–7, 119–20, 123, 131–2, 139, 141–2, 151, 156, 166, 168, 170–2, 192, 196–8
integrated approach 10–11, 16–7, 32, 50–1, 57, 133, 161–2
internet 17, 44, 124, 126, 129–32
IUIDP 21

Index 211

Jakarta 35, 98, 196
joint venture 9, 140, 142–3, 146

KUIDFC 109, 116

labor 40, 49, 99, 198, 128–30, 139, 142–4, 146–7, 150–3, 155–6, 161, 178–83, 191
lease 80
liberalization 53, 61, 138–9, 143, 152, 193
linkages 168, 171
local government 5, 6, 10, 13, 15–21, 23, 32–3, 35–9, 43, 45–50, 52, 79, 81, 86, 90, 109, 111–6, 118, 120–1, 124, 125, 129, 132, 139, 148, 159, 163–4, 166–7, 169–70, 173, 184, 192, 194, 196
London 5, 192

MAPP 111
market orientation 45, 47–8, 78, 80, 88
master plan 54–5, 119
methods 6, 12, 14, 32, 56–7, 59–70, 103, 112, 118, 191
metropolitan 11, 38, 51–2, 67, 117, 119, 152, 156, 158–9, 162, 173–4, 191–6
microfinance 196
MC 51, 117
MDG 95
MNC 182
monitoring 39, 57, 59–60, 62–63, 68, 78, 94–5, 103, 111, 123, 125–9, 193
MSM 173, 201
Mumbai 3, 15, 20, 23, 42, 44

neo classical 31, 60
NEPP 100–1, 205
network 23, 25, 41, 54, 61, 67–9, 108, 117, 121–2, 141, 143, 161, 169, 173, 176, 185, 192
New Delhi 3, 8, 98, 104
new public management 14, 43–5, 47–8, 58–9, 64, 75, 77–9, 87, 94–5, 191, 197
New York 23, 192
NGOs 13, 16–7, 19, 21–2, 46, 54, 76, 81, 94, 105, 117–8, 120, 197–8
NMP 97, 99–100, 205

OCF 179, 188
OECD 25, 108, 204–6
OFI 179, 181, 188
operations and maintenance 69, 88, 93
operationalization 70
organization 4, 8, 10, 13–4, 19, 22–3, 27, 32–3, 40, 45, 47, 54, 61–3, 66–9, 83–4, 87, 91, 100–3, 105–9, 112–6, 123, 130, 140, 160, 171, 193–7
organizing capacity 60, 66–8
Ouagadougou 25, 41
outsourcing 47–8, 76, 82–3, 120
O&M 69, 88, 93

parks
  business 98, 115, 162
  industrial 98, 107
  science 157, 168, 170–1
  software 157, 163–4, 169
participation 7, 10, 18–21, 23–5, 41, 47, 50, 56–7, 60, 64, 71–2, 76, 78, 89, 95, 101–2, 107, 111, 116–8, 124, 126, 130–4, 146–7, 149, 153, 164, 184, 194–7
PDCOR 113, 116
policy impact analysis 60, 69
positivism 70
POWER project 123
PPcP 51, 198
PPP 19, 21, 51, 54
PRD 142–3, 145, 155, 173–188, 204
Pricing 142, 201
PRISMA 103
private sector 4, 8, 10–11, 13, 19–21, 36, 44, 47, 52, 54–6, 58, 62, 64, 68, 76–8, 80, 83, 85, 93, 99, 110, 113–4, 116–21, 146, 153, 191, 193, 195, 197–8
privatization 25, 44, 54, 76, 80, 113
productivity 40, 105, 154, 156, 180
proposition 70
PSI 83
PSP

quality 4, 10, 63, 71, 75–6, 78, 86, 92, 94, 98, 100–1, 104–5, 119–20, 171, 194
questionnaire 53, 70, 188, 194

reform 9, 13–4, 21–2, 26, 36, 39, 41, 57, 61, 71, 75–6, 78–95, 109–17, 119, 122, 138–44, 151, 178, 181–2, 196
research method 12, 57, 60, 69–70
research objective 70
research process 70
research question 69–70
Rio de Janeiro 104, 107–8
Rotterdam 9, 14, 26–7, 96, 102, 191, 196
rural urban linkage 25, 55
R&D 150, 166, 168, 171, 180

sanitation 33, 67–9, 75, 77, 85–6, 90, 95, 104, 109, 114–5
scenario 60, 72, 119, 127
Shanghai 23, 143, 145, 149–51, 154, 156–7, 159, 162–3, 166, 173–8, 181–4, 186–8, 193
Singapore 80, 83, 184
social issues 4, 6, 9, 18–9, 33–5, 38, 48, 51, 57–8, 60–61, 63, 68–71, 84, 104, 106, 126, 128, 137–9, 143–4, 149, 160–1, 170, 187
software 44, 126, 147, 156–7, 159, 163–4, 166–9, 184–7
specificity 75, 76
stakeholder 12, 13, 15, 18–20, 24, 26–7, 50, 57, 60, 64, 71, 89, 92, 95, 120, 164, 1846, 191, 197–8
state owned enterprise 139–40, 142, 145, 151
strategic plan 6, 21, 24–5, 32, 41, 54–7, 64–5, 130–1
subcontracting 41, 108, 197
subsidiarity 36
sustainability 12, 63, 84, 87, 104, 108
SWOT 60, 66, 69

technology 26, 41, 61, 64, 100–1, 117–8, 129, 142, 154, 159, 164, 166–7, 170, 186–7, 193
Tokyo 192
tools 6, 24, 32, 56–7, 59–60, 62, 64, 66–9, 71–2, 78, 83, 86–7, 94, 123, 125–6, 191

UDA 51

UIS 123–5, 128–9, 131–4
UMC 9, 49, 96, 199, 205, 208
UMP 8, 199
UNCED 104, 108
UNCHS 3–5, 10, 18, 55, 58, 204, 207
UNDP 8
UNESCO 123, 131, 201–2, 208
UNFPA 5–6, 207
upgrading 71, 142, 163, 196
urbanization 4–5, 8, 114, 188
USAID 102, 115, 118–9, 207
utility 45–8, 60–1, 76, 78–95

value chain 145, 156, 186–7, 193
Vitebsk 24, 71, 198

water 6, 8, 17, 19, 26, 33, 48, 51, 53, 63, 67–9, 75–91, 94–5, 97–8, 104–5, 109–10, 114–5, 117–23, 126–7, 132, 160–1, 196, 198
WBI 9–12, 21
World Trade Organization, WTO, 107, 140
WSJE 102–3
WSP 86, 208

YRD 143, 157, 173–8, 183–4, 187